OUTLAW

OUTLAW

THE LIVES AND CAREERS OF

JOHN RECHY

BY CHARLES CASILLO

Advocate
BOOKS

Manufactured in the United States of America.

This trade paperback original is published by Advocate Books,
an imprint of Alyson Publications,
P.O. Box 4371, Los Angeles, California 90078-4371.
Distribution in the United Kingdom by Turnaround Publisher Services Ltd.,
Unit 3, Olympia Trading Estate, Coburg Road, Wood Green,
London N22 6TZ England.

First edition: December 2002

03 04 05 06 ✳ 10 9 8 7 6 5 4 3 2

ISBN 1-55583-734-4

Library of Congress Cataloging-in-Publication Data
Casillo, Charles.
  Outlaw : the lives and careers of John Rechy / Charles Casillo.—1st ed.
  Includes bibliographical references and index.
  ISBN 1-55583-734-4
  1. Rechy, John. 2. Novelists, American—20th century—Biography. I. Title.
PS3568.E28 Z623 2002
813'.54—DC21
[B]   2002028188

Credits
All cover and interior photographs courtesy of John Rechy. unless otherwise
  indicated.
Cover design by Matt Sams.

For My Parents,
Gloria and Ralph

THE SOUL OF A MAN IS A FAR COUNTRY,
WHICH CANNOT BE APPROACHED OR EXPLORED.

—D.M. THOMAS, *THE WHITE HOTEL*

In his literature and film lectures, John Rechy likes to talk about the three ranks in the hierarchy of literary liars. At the top of this list he places the autobiographer, for daring to say, "This is exactly how it happened." Rechy argues that events are censored and transformed by time and can never be re-created from memory exactly as they occurred. Second in his rank of liars is (dare I say it) the biographer. Rechy takes issue with a writer claiming, "I am capable of knowing another's life," feeling instead that one can only hope to capture a "shadow of a life. A shade of it. A reflection." The least dishonest type of literary liar is the fiction writer, according to Rechy. In fiction, he maintains, the writer frankly declares, "This is a lie, a fiction, but I'm going to try like hell to make you believe it's true."

I have entered the company of literary liars with the most honest of intentions. What you hold in your hands is my attempt to discover the true man behind the many selves that make up John Rechy. My primary resource was Rechy himself, whose recollections during my interviews with him form the backbone of the book. I have also included details of Rechy's life, gathered through archival research and from interviews with friends and colleagues who shared their insights into Rechy's famously tangled personal history. And I have closely read Rechy's body of work, where his brilliant writer's mind transformed his extraordinary experiences into some of the most controversial fiction published during the second half of the 20th century. By combining elements of biography, autobiography, and fiction, I hope to have provided as complete a portrait of John Rechy as the limitations of these genres allow.

During my three-year writing odyssey I encountered many people without whose help I could not have accomplished this feat and to whom I owe my sincerest thanks. Most importantly, John Rechy himself, who talked to me without limitations or conditions. Because so much of his work is autobiographical, many of the pieces to the puzzle of his life are in his fiction. It was a tremendous asset to be able to converse with Rechy about the true incidents and inspirations behind the stories he re-creates so vividly in his large body of work.

As our discussions progressed—in the living room of his Los Angeles apartment—Rechy became increasingly open with me, but he never told me how to tell his tale. If we didn't see eye to eye on something, he allowed me the freedom to develop my interpretation of events—though he never left me wondering about his opinion on the subject. For example, Rechy disagrees with my reading of the Johnny Rio character in *Numbers*. We debated the matter for some time, and I include his rebuttal in the text.

A personality as complex and compelling as Rechy's is bound to make a distinctive impression on many people during the course of his life. Rechy has moved through so many different worlds—some public, some shadowy—that I felt I had to see his life through the eyes of people who knew him in the locales, social scenes, and cultural eras where his influence was strongest. Many of my contacts wished to remain anonymous, and I have respected their wishes in all instances. I am grateful to all of them, wherever they may be now (and for some of them, that could be anywhere).

Rechy's sister, Blanche Rechy Ludwig, freely shared her memories and her knowledge of Rechy family history in numerous letters and phone conversations. Her genuine sweetness and good humor made it clear why she is so loved by her brother. Alfredo Jordan, a childhood friend of the Rechy family, was a treasure trove of background information. His wonderfully detailed correspondence enriched the chapters on Rechy's early years.

Rechy chose his friends wisely. Bill Regan is such a smart, kind, and sensitive soul—even in leather—that it's easy to see why he inspired such a memorable character in *City of Night*. Renowned author Gavin Lambert, another friend who inspired Rechy, was full of insight and wit—and was great fun to visit. I also enjoyed my conversations with the wonderful writer Felice Picano, who shared his recollections of Rechy from both before and after the two became friends. Russcll Barnard kindly contributed his thoughts about what it's like to be one of Rechy's students. I also extend my heartfelt thanks to Michael Snyder for his enthusiasm and support in this project.

Rechy has a knack for surrounding himself with creative, interesting women. There are three whom I have come to consider Rechy's three graces: Melodie Johnson Howe, Zella Riley, and Marsha Kinder. All of them gave generously of their time and memories. Kinder also allowed me to examine the research she has done for her interactive CD-ROM on Rechy's life and work, *Mysteries and Desire: Searching the Worlds of John Rechy*. Her research led me to a videotaped interview with Rechy's oldest brother, the suave and eloquent Robert Rechy.

Another dynamic lady I spoke with is Wendy Elliot Hyland, who contributed her Rechy recollections with tremendous style and humor.

For contributing information, recollections, creativity, and intelligence to this project I extend my warmest thanks to Nancy Hamilton, Rechy's contemporary at Texas Western College (now the University of Texas at El Paso), to Rechy's longtime agent Georges Borchardt, and to Floriano Vecchi, who was all class and sophistication on the phone even though my first call was late. It was a great privilege to interview the respected editor Michael Denneny, whose thoughts about Rechy's influence on contemporary literature were a revelation. Writer and poet Edward Field shared his thoughts on Alfred Chester's caustic review of Rechy's first novel. Edward later became a personal friend. Don Bachardy, an artist whose talent I greatly admire, was very forthcoming with his memories and opinions.

For valuable details that enlivened my final portrait of Rechy, I also thank Don Allen, Michael Kearns, Paula Shtrum, Robert Santana, Doreen Black, Tony Staffor, and James Mortenson. I also wish to thank Bill Brownell, Steve Stewart, Elena Nelson-Howe, Monica Trasandes, Jim Parish, Stewart Penn, Charles Ortleb, Ernest Cunningham, Bianca Rossini, Sammy LaBella, Sally Kirkland, Carol Vitale, and Neil Derrick.

I am terribly grateful to Laura L. Frakes, the community library manager at the County of Los Angeles Public Library, for her patient assistance, and to Misha Schott and the staff at the Gay Archives in Los Angeles, who allowed me access to their files and copy machine.

And I owe deepest thanks to Scott Brassart, my first editor at Alyson. He made me feel comfortable from day one with his joviality. In his enthusiasm for the book, Scott always knew when I needed a boost of confidence, good cheer, and the occasional kick in the ass. Terri Fabris, another editor I worked closely with, is everything a writer could hope for: smart, astute, fun, patient, and more pleasantly calming than a tranquilizer—with no side effects. Angela Brown, Alyson's senior editor, was a great help and a great pleasure to work with. I would also like to thank Nick Street for his hard work and contributions.

Newspaper and magazine articles, interviews, and essays that were particularly valuable are: "The Mastery and Genius of John Rechy" by Jonathan Kirsch, *Los Angeles Times*, November 18, 2001, "The Romantic Egotist" by Scott Timberg, *New Times Los Angeles*, February 24, 2000; "Don't Fuck with a Legend" by Matthew Kennedy, *Genre*, July 2000; "Sexual Outlaw" by Jameson Currier, *New York Blade News*, April 2, 1999; "A Writer's Return to the City of Night" by Pamela Warrick, *Los Angeles Times*, September 1, 1999;

"Hotter Than Ever" by R. Hunter Garcia, *The Advocate*, September 14, 1999; "Come Again, John Rechy?" by James L. Bloor, *Frontiers*, October 15, 1999; "One More Night" by Jeff Johnson, *Impact News*, May 9, 1997; "Credit Where It's Overdue" by Pamela Warrick, *Los Angeles Times*, October 26, 1997; "Beyond the Night" by Charles Isherwood, *The Advocate*, October 15, 1996; "John Rechy, Rebellious Angel" by Karen Dale Wolman, *Frontiers*, August 17, 1990; "Looking Back Into the Life" by Chasen Gaver, *The Washington Blade*, July 1, 1988; "Taming of the Sexual Outlaw" by Gregg Barrios, *Los Angeles Times*, September 7, 1988; "The Real John Rechy" by Richard Laermer, *New York Native*, November 3, 1986; "John Rechy: America's Bad Boy of Literature" by Mike Varady, *Frontiers*, May 16, 1984; "A Sexual Outlaw Dances Before the Void" by Timothy Carlson, *Los Angeles Herald Examiner*, December 23, 1979; "John Rechy: A Sexual Outlaw Speaks Out" by Steven S. Mahan, *Los Angeles Free Press*, September 23 1977; "Interview with the Fabulous Miss Destiny" author unknown, *One*, September, 1964; "The Sorrows Of The Young Man" by Frank O'Hara, *Kulcher* Winter 1963; "Fruit Salad" by Alfred Chester, *The New York Review of Books,* vol. 1, no. 3, 1963.

I also found helpful *Patterns of Anarchy and Order in the Works of John Rechy* (1976), an insightful dissertation by Honora M. Lynch, and Jose R. Santana's perceptive essay, "Fictions of Masculinity in the Novels of John Rechy and Michael Nava," which he published on the Internet in 1999. Toward the end of my research I was lucky enough to get my hands on some of Rechy's private papers and unpublished manuscripts while they were being archived. These freshly unearthed treasures sparkled with priceless bits of information.

The writing of biographers Gerald Clarke, Patricia Bosworth, and Anthony Summers is a steady source of inspiration for me.

There are a number of people who had nothing to do with the contents of this book but had everything to do with its completion. The following people have sustained this author at various times and in various places, and I would like to thank them for their friendship, support, and love. In New York: Jeff Dymowski, Scott Lesko, Francine Civello, Mark Silverman, Andrew Harte, Lillian Acevedo, Vincent Curcio, Nelson Rasado, Anthony Casillo, Arlene LaBoccetta, Angela Fratianni, and my grandparents, and of course my parents Ralph and Gloria Casillo. In Los Angeles: Bernie Guzman, Greg Veneklasen, Rick Brooks, Marc Wynne, Mona Miles, Frank Fischer, John Conboy, and Steve Curtis. All of whom are my family.

PART ONE

SEEDS

I was born into a sea of clashing memories.
—John Rechy, *Contemporary Authors*

JOHN RECHY DEVELOPED IN an atmosphere of upheaval and confusion. The members of his family, who fled Mexico in 1910 during the Revolution, lived dramatic, frantic, and constantly changing lives. Deaths, remarriages, and sudden poverty added to the disorder of the Rechy family tree. Documents were lost or destroyed or simply not kept. As the Rechys moved from place to place, not leaving much of a trail, history was changed and legends were created.

This ambiguous history has worked to Rechy's advantage and has made it easy for him to constantly reinvent himself. With roots that were not easily traced he could present a variety of personas to the world, embellishing his background as it best suited his masterpiece—the creation of himself. Like some of our great movie stars—Marilyn Monroe, for instance (with whom he has had a longtime fascination)—Rechy developed his facades to separate and protect his private self from his public image.

Rechy is a sensitive, creative man who likes to read and write and draw. An artistic man who adores the movies. A man who loved his mother and who loves his brothers and sisters. A man who, early in his life, was so conflicted by his homosexuality that, as he grew, he buried his sexuality under a handsome, impenetrable mask and an armor of well-oiled rippling muscles. A man whose vulnerability and intelligence allowed him to examine the seediness of his life and to write about it with a lyrical sensitivity. This is the John Rechy who evolved into a famous and highly praised author and a beloved teacher.

On the streets, though, from New York to Los Angeles, John Rechy was for sale: tough, impervious, and utterly masculine—all that is worth having in the homosexual cruising world. His obsession with remaining a sexually desirable hustler by preserving the handsomeness of his face and the hardness of his body is, through a series of novels, one of the best-documented cases of extreme narcissism in modern literature. By polishing this street-tough persona and writing about it in books such as *Numbers, Rushes, The Sexual Outlaw*, and his masterwork, *City of Night*, Rechy became one of the most renowned hustlers of the 20th century.

From a very early age Rechy observed things intensely, taking in bits and pieces of characteristics from the people he scrutinized and from people out of books and movies. Rechy absorbed the characteristics he liked while mentally crossing a line through the rest.

Other than his immediate family, John Rechy never got to know any of his relatives. His grandparents were dead before he was born or else tucked away in a far country. For his personal history he relied on the various accounts he'd heard from his parents and siblings. As an adult he would say, "I inherited ghosts that roamed the memories of others and floated into mine." Throughout his childhood he felt those ghosts swirling around him in the stories he heard and instantly embellished. Even as a child he composed stories in his head.

Rechy's paternal grandfather, Juan Francisco Rechy, a suave, sophisticated Scottish man born in Spain, was a respected doctor in the early 1900s. Dr. Rechy's wife, Maria, was a strong-willed, haughty, independent Spanish woman. Maria's arrogance may have derived from the fact that she was light-skinned and blue-eyed. In those days in Latin American countries, the fairness of one's skin, the lightness of one's hair and eyes, and the degree to which one's features looked Caucasian could determine one's class, one's value in society. Juan Francisco and his fair-skinned wife moved from Spain to Mexico City, where they quickly rose in prominence. They lived next door to the Capital Building, where the doctor treated high-ranking officials, enabling Maria to socialize in the high-society circles to which she felt she belonged. Eventually Juan Francisco became the personal physician to President Porfirio Diáz, and the couple often attended extravagant parties at the palace.

Their son, Roberto Sixto, who would become John Rechy's father, was born soon after the move to Mexico City. Roberto was the kind of son influential families hoped for: He was attractive, bright, and unusually talented—particularly in the area of music. By the age of 9 he could play almost any instrument, and his parents often brought him along to entertain at parties. At the age of 10 he gave his first concert—playing Mozart and Beethoven for President Diáz.

As the son of Mexico City's most prominent doctor, Roberto lived a life of privilege. He attended The University of Mexico City, where he excelled in musical studies, and his combination of brilliance and dashing looks made him very popular among the ladies. His reputation as a rogue equaled his fame as a musician. Even though it was a family of strong passions and extreme temperaments—family legend tells of the time Maria shot at her son during an argument—there was no doubt among the elder Rechys that Roberto would become an important figure in the world of music. Their confidence in him was validated when Roberto became the director of the Mexican Imperial Symphony, a group with whom he traveled extensively throughout the world.

Roberto's first marriage, to a German woman named Mary, further advanced the upward social climb of the Rechy family. Maria was especially pleased with her son's choice. A blond-haired, blue-eyed foreign woman would make a prized addition to the lineage.

Soon a son was born to Roberto and Mary. They named him Jon. (Years later Roberto would have another son, Juan, who became "John" and who grew up to be John Rechy.)

Unfortunately, marriage and fatherhood did not stop Roberto's wandering eye. Years later, in *City of Night* (1963), John Rechy would describe his father as "traveling from Mexico to California spreading his seed." Well into John's adulthood various strangers emerged claiming to be Roberto's child.

Under President Porfirio Díaz's regime, prosperous families like the Rechys were able to accumulate wealth and power, while the masses in the cities and the countryside remained impoverished. Roberto, however, was a champion of the downtrodden. He was one of the first to question the segregation of blacks and Mexicans in the Southwest, at times refusing to perform in segregated territories.

In 1910 the oppression of the Mexican people by the Díaz regime resulted in a violent, bloody revolution.

Roberto and Mary, along with Roberto's parents, fled the country and settled in El Paso, Texas. As he had in Mexico City, Juan Francisco Rechy became the most highly respected physician in El Paso, specializing in pulmonary diseases. But unlike what he had done in Mexico, Juan did not limit his practice to the rich. He became known for his generosity and kindness to the poor. "At the time, the regular charge for a visit was two dollars," grandson Robert Rechy says. "Most people didn't have two dollars to pay, so he would just treat them for free."

Roberto and Mary, unfortunately, didn't fare as well in their new country. As a musician, Roberto was virtually unknown in Texas. He continued to play, but could no longer make his living at it. Instead, he was forced to help out in his father's pharmacy—quite a change for a man who only a short time before had been touring the world with a prestigious symphony.

The first of many tragedies that plagued Roberto throughout his life happened when his first-born son, Jon, died at the age of 7 from a severe case of food poisoning. The loss of his son, the decline in his social standing, and the persistence of his infidelity took a severe toll on his marriage. Shortly after Jon's death, Roberto and Mary divorced.

Soon after the divorce, however, Roberto met a new woman who made him feel optimistic.

• • •

Family legend says Roberto met Guadalupe Flores when Guadalupe's youngest brother threw a baseball through the window of the Rechy pharmacy. Roberto chased the boy all the way home and it was there that he encountered the sister. Immediately all thoughts of the broken store window were discarded. With her long dark hair and green eyes, Guadalupe was the most beautiful woman Roberto had ever seen.

Guadalupe came from a working class family in Chihuahua, Mexico. The four daughters of the family were known as "the Beautiful Flores Sisters."

"When they walked into a dance hall everyone stopped and looked," one family historian says, "especially at Guadalupe." The Flores family had also settled in El Paso after fleeing the revolution in Mexico. Guadalupe's parents, Antonio and Dolores, had owned and operated a small hotel in Chihuahua where their four young daughters worked. One night Pancho Villa stormed into the hotel and commanded Antonio, "I want the entire second floor of the hotel cleared for the men and me." Then he added, "As soon as we're settled, I want all four of your girls up in our rooms."

Antonio answered, "Yes, General! Of course, General!" He gave Pancho Villa and his men the rooms. But as soon as the revolutionaries were safely out of sight, Antonio had a relative take the girls into the hills to hide while he prepared for a hasty escape. "Grab as much as you can and load it into the coach," he ordered his wife and sons. So carrying their belongings in their arms—including a trunk-load of Mexican money, which was by then worthless—the Flores family escaped into darkness, heading for

Juárez. Some ended up in Juárez, and others found themselves in El Paso, Texas, where they decided to settle.

Although Roberto's music career was in decline by the time he met Guadalupe, he was able to impress the young woman with his imposing air, imaginative personality, and elegant manners. They were soon married.

Maria did not approve of her son's second marriage. Although her days as a guest in the home of President Díaz were long over, she still considered herself "aristocracy" and felt that Guadalupe, no matter how lovely, was "just a common woman from Chihuahua." After all, it was well known that she went only as far as third grade before going to work in her parents' hotel. Maria called Guadalupe an "Indian," and viewed her as beneath the Rechy family name.

But Roberto and Guadalupe were happy—at least in the first years of their marriage. They would eventually have six children together in perfect girl-boy, girl-boy, girl-boy order. Their first child was born in 1915, a daughter they named Valeska, followed in 1918 by a son, Robert. In 1921 came Blanca (Blanche), another son Yvan in 1924, and Olga in 1928. Three years later, the birth of little Juan—John Rechy—would finish out the pattern. As his family grew, Roberto tried to stay involved in classical music, but in those days people were thinking of survival, not art.

Times were hard in El Paso and it was difficult for any man to make a living, let alone a foreigner. Roberto tried his hand at composing music for the movie industry, and when that led nowhere he founded a newspaper. But he was run out of business for championing minorities and protesting poor working conditions. In addition to his own music he continued to write movie scores; but his only profits came from giving lessons to the untalented children of the neighborhood and from selling pianos and sheet music at a local shop.

When Dr. Juan Rechy died, Roberto lost the family pharmacy. He later worked briefly as a caretaker for a public park, but eventually he was fired and had to take a job as a hospital custodian.

The man who had once gathered an audience at the palace now gathered bloodied bandages and human waste. The job did not bring in much money, and he had barely enough to pay for rent and groceries. Roberto was broken. He would come home late at night and work on his orchestrations, surrounded by the sheet music nobody was interested in, tapping his melodies out feverishly with his fingers on the table.

Adding to the family's woes, Roberto and Guadalupe's first-born daughter Valeska became mysteriously ill and died suddenly. She was only 12. Several days before she died, she had seen a truck back up into a small boy, crushing him to death against a wall. According to Mexican folklore, the sight of something terrifying can cause a sudden death. Family members believed this is what happened.

By the time Olga was born in 1928, Roberto had the sadness of a man who longed for greatness, gambled, and lost with his life. Nearing 50, he had been married twice, had buried two children, and had suffered through the slow disintegration of his great career in classical music. Sometimes while listening to a symphony on the radio, he would suddenly get up and begin to conduct, tears streaming down his cheeks.

Outside the home Roberto could still be a congenial man. But inside the home his brutal, domineering behavior terrified his children—especially the younger ones, who hadn't had the chance to know him in his kinder days. "He was a total Jekyll and Hyde," his daughter Blanche recalls. She remembers him grabbing a fistful of her hair and yanking so hard she feared it would rip from her head. Overcome with a sudden rage, Roberto would scream out, "I am respected! Known!" And Guadalupe, still in a deep depression over the death of Valeska, would go to him and try to soothe him, to make him feel like the important man he once was.

In 1930, still dealing with the loss of Valeska and dire concerns about finances, another problem presented itself in the Rechy household: Guadalupe was pregnant again.

Meanwhile, Roberto's mother was dying. After the death of

Juan Francisco, Maria's health deteriorated rapidly. For a while, thanks to her husband's savings and some valuable property she let slip away—"spitefully," Blanche says—Maria was able to live independently from her son. This was important to her because she had never accepted Guadalupe as a daughter-in-law. She could not see Guadalupe as a good, kind-hearted woman. Guadalupe and her children were "too dark," lacking the complexion of "true Spaniards." Only Robert*, Guadalupe's light-skinned, blue-eyed oldest son, was an acceptable shade. Maria adored him.

When Maria's money ran out and she became too ill to care for herself, the proud but destitute old woman grudgingly turned to her son and his family for help.

"She's my mother," Roberto said to Guadalupe. "What can I do with her?"

"Bring her here," Guadalupe replied without hesitation.

So the great dying lady went to live with the Rechys in their tiny house, which was already overcrowded with children—and with another on the way. And the pregnant Guadalupe took care of her—the woman who had despised her for years. And Blanche—who had also been the focus of Maria's hostility—helped to change the sheets and to faithfully empty and clean the bedpans. Still, Maria resented Blanche's even being in the same room with her.

Her grandmother's rejection had a lifelong effect on Blanche (who had changed her name from Blanca to the more Caucasian-sounding name). Maria unmercifully taunted her granddaughter at the irony of both "Blanca" and "Blanche" meaning "white." In adulthood, Blanche denounces her grandmother, declaring, "That woman was no Spanish aristocrat. I looked into her dark eyes, and I realized that she was simply an Indian woman with pretensions of grandeur!" Perhaps this memory is Blanche's revenge on a woman whose prejudices caused her so much pain. On the other

---

*Maria had no way of knowing that Olga—who was just an infant then—would also grow up to be light-skinned and quintessentially Spanish-looking.

hand, being an Indian would explain Maria's fanatical obsession with the eye and hair color of her descendants. Robert, whom Maria adored, insists his grandmother was blue-eyed and Spanish.

Maria did finally have a change of heart. As she lay dying she called to Guadalupe.

"I hope it's not too late," the old lady sighed. She was crying. Guadalupe, eight months pregnant and carrying very big, sat at her mother-in-law's bedside, straining to hear. "Forgive me," Maria whispered. "I have behaved very ugly toward you, and I never accepted your daughters because they are dark. But I wish I had gotten to know you. It is you who have shown me what true love is."

Just before she died, Maria asked Guadalupe—if she was carrying a son—to name him Juan Francisco, after her husband, the respected doctor and the child's paternal grandfather.

• • •

Juan Francisco Rechy—who would one day become famous as the writer, John Rechy—was born into a house of decay and death on March 10, 1931.

From the day he was born, the family had high hopes that the new baby might bring some much-needed joy into their home. His sister Blanche remembers John as being "a beautiful little baby." He had the light eyes, fair complexion, and, as an infant, the blond hair that would have endeared him to Maria, had she lived to appraise him. Guadalupe honored her mother-in-law's dying request by naming the child after her late husband Juan Francisco. The family called him "the Little Angel."

By the time Juan Francisco was born the family was poor enough that the oldest son, Robert, 13 at the time, was forced to go to work. Yet the poverty in El Paso and Juárez was such that the Rechy children didn't consider themselves poor. "We weren't actually hurting," Robert Rechy remembers, "because we never missed a meal and we always managed to pay the rent." Although he was small-framed, Robert got a job from a neighbor who was in the business of delivering blocks of ice to stores and homes. Robert soon grew strong enough to carry the heaviest blocks. Years later, Robert would give up a college scholarship to continue working to support his younger siblings. It was Robert who became a second father to John; "a real father figure," Rechy would always say.

Even before he could walk, little Juan's imagination was hard at work. "We didn't have a lot of toys," Blanche recalls, "but whatever we gave him, he would play with and entertain himself for hours. He was such a good baby. He would never cry."

Rechy, however, would remember things differently. In an essay written for *Contemporary Authors Autobiography Series*, he recalled that during his childhood a gloom hung heavily in the air of the Rechy household. "Death exists only for the living," he wrote, hinting that the aura of his grandmother's slow death still lingered in the house. And there were other ghosts as well.

One of Rechy's earliest memories is of the family taking flowers to the graves of Jon, his father's son from his first marriage, and Valeska, the first-born child with Guadalupe. Every year on November 1, the Day of the Dead, hundreds of people traveled to the sprawling Evergreen Cemetery on the north side of town to spend the day at the gravesides of their loved ones. The air over the entire city became heavy with the cloying smell of chrysanthemums.

Juan Francisco Rechy would stare in fascination at the tombstone of his half-brother, dead before Juan himself was born, but who shared the same name. (The name on his half-brother's tombstone reads Jon Francisco.) Every evening on the Day of the Dead, the church bells tolled to remind the living to take a moment to remember and pray for the souls that might still be trapped in purgatory.

Later, when shown photographs of his dead half-brother, John realized that they shared more than the same name. They looked remarkably alike—two cherubic boys with light eyes and blond curls. Rechy found himself burdened with the first of many roles he felt obligated to live up to: taking the place of his lost half-brother whose name and face he shared.

And because Guadalupe never completely recovered from the death of Valeska, John was also haunted by the memory of an older sister he never knew. "My mother would call my sisters 'Valeska' all the time," he says. "Not a day passed that my mother wasn't crying over that lost child."

Of his other parent he would have a harsher memory. "I knew only this," John Rechy wrote bitterly for *Contemporary Authors*, "he was my father and he hated me."

The 1930s were not easy times to be growing up in El Paso. The Great Depression was raging across the country in full force, destroying fortunes and driving many people into extreme poverty for the first time in their lives. Money continued to be a problem for the Rechys and they were forced to move to a destitute neighborhood, into a small, dilapidated house at 1115 Wyoming Street. John would always remember the peeling paper on the walls, the scampering cockroaches, the filthy brown water that filled up the bathtub, the stench of rot. Tramps, on their way west, roamed the neighborhood looking for a day's work in return for something to eat. And each day the angry West Texas winds blew around the same stale air, the same choking dust, the same old boredom.

These are the winds that recurred years later, again and again, in a number of Rechy's books, whenever he sought an image to foreshadow violent psychological turbulence, as in the novel *This Day's Death* (1969):

Last night the wind blew across empty miles of Texas desert, and raged along the streets, sheets of dust suddenly suspended by a shifting current glided eerily toward the ground, trees crouched to Escape the swallowing funnels.

John Rechy's early childhood was characterized by an intense and terrible feeling of isolation he felt powerless to escape. He wasn't like the other boys in his neighborhood, and—more confusing to him—he didn't want to be like them. Rather, very early on he felt "a dislike of ordinary people." He says, "I spent most of my time alone. I drew a lot of pictures. And I wrote, secretly. And I kept to myself. I hardly ever had any friends."

His aversion to "ordinary people" stemmed from the fact that he himself was not ordinary. He was solemn and serious and projected an imposing maturity that was unsettling in one so young. His family remembers that he was unusually intuitive and perceptive about people.

Regardless of these qualities, his father Roberto made it clear that he did not like the fact that his son was not outgoing and athletic like his two older brothers. Roberto saw John as a sullen, introverted, and brooding creature. As other children played in each other's backyards, John sat for hours on the front porch of their crumbling house with his head on his doting mother's lap, daydreaming. As he lay there she would dab her fingers on her tongue and curl his long lashes with saliva.

Rechy wrote in *The Sexual Outlaw* in 1977 (and often repeated in interviews):

> Unlike black people who are born to black parents, Jewish people who are born into the Jewish religion or Hispanics who are born to Hispanics, we homosexuals are the only minority born into the enemy camp, so we have to hide. Homosexuals, male and female, have it particularly hard. I think that heightens our isolation, our loneliness, and our unique sensibility as camouflage.

John's father was relentless on the subject of sports. Robert and Yvan had turned out to be outstanding athletes, a distinction that delighted their father, but that left John feeling inadequate. Yvan in particular distinguished himself as an athlete; eventually he was inducted into the El Paso Athletic Hall of Fame. Roberto desperately wanted John, who was slightly built, to be robust and athletic and participate in the neighborhood games like his two older brothers. Indeed, had John been more like his brothers, his relationship with his father might have been less complicated.

"My older brothers were my father's heroes," Rechy says. "He became an umpire, at times, at their games, and if anybody so much as raised their voice to one of my brothers he'd beat him up. He was an aggressive son of a bitch when it came to defending them."

Rechy's brother Robert remembers, "It really bothered John a lot that my father wanted him to be like us."

On top of his lack of interest in sports, John enjoyed recreations that were "not masculine" in his father's eyes—drawing and writing. Blanche remembers him designing dresses for their sister Olga. After John's designs were complete, Blanche would go to Juárez to buy material to have the dresses made. "He created a yellow one that was like a butterfly," Blanche recalls. "Everyone would say, 'Where did you get that dress?' And Olga would say proudly, 'My brother designed it, and my sister took it to have it made.'" This sort of thing exasperated Roberto.

Roberto was homophobic in the extreme, and he saw homosexuality everywhere. He probably suspected it in his artistic son, who was an uncommonly beautiful little boy and who was, by his own admission years later, "a weird child." Rechy explains: "I felt this because I was estranged, felt a part of nothing I saw."

Young John did, however, develop crushes on pretty girls in the neighborhood. He remembers a little girl named Gloria who became the focus of the town's attention after her father killed her mother. The little girl was whisked away by relatives without John ever having a chance to say goodbye to her. There was another girl he admired from afar, Mary Jane, who looked like Shirley Temple, a star he adored. But his biggest crush was on a little blond girl named Barbara, a name Rechy uses throughout his novels for beautiful, unreachable female characters.

Nevertheless, Roberto regarded his melancholy, youngest son as an intruder sent to live in his midst.

To John his father seemed impenetrable. He watched in silent fear as his father expressed his exasperation with him through a smoldering rage that would often suddenly escalate into a savage outburst. Roberto played solitaire hour after hour, angrily slapping down the cards. These hours were the worst for the family. They listened to the slap of each card, waiting for the inevitable—when Roberto would leap up and shout and throw furniture.

In *City of Night*, Rechy describes how the protagonist's father erupted brutally and unpredictably over almost anything. "In an instant he overturns the table—food and plates thrust to the floor. He would smash bottles, menacing us with the sharpfanged edges. He had an old sword which he kept hidden threateningly about the house."

Although the narrator of *City of Night* declares, "I cant blame my father—for anything," the seeds of terror, inadequacy, and anger Rechy's father planted in his child cannot be overestimated. Rechy grew up in the shadow of a father whose expectations he couldn't possibly live up to. "My father was always pushing me," he says. "But nothing I could ever do would satisfy him. Nothing."

John wanted to be an object of admiration to his father—to be like his brothers. He didn't want to be viewed as a problem that needed figuring out. Knowing that his father, the man who gave him life, was disillusioned and perplexed by him, stirred up a desire to excel, to prove himself. It also forced Rechy to separate himself from people because he feared being judged inadequate in the average person's eyes. At the same time, he both felt and acted superior. An aloof demeanor, he learned, could adorn his physical appearance. The two qualities worked hand-in-hand, adding a new dimension to people's fascination with him.

John had little in common with others anyway; he preferred to play by himself. So his perception of "play" became different. His childhood became a fusion of dreams and reality. Alone, he could draw and pretend and create his own fantasy world where he made his own rules, established his own ideals, determined his own accepted patterns of behavior. In the private world of his imagination, he found a place where it was safe.

When Juan Francisco Rechy was five years old, his mother told him that he had to start school. He was terrified of going out into the world, leaving her behind, even for brief periods. "What will happen if the robbers come or the house burns? Who will save you?" he asked.

"You will," she replied. "You will know if anything threatens me, and you will save me." And for the rest of her life Rechy would be there for his mother, trying—without really knowing how—to save her.

To his siblings, John seemed unusually sensitive and compassionate. Blanche remembers him crying over the death of anything. He couldn't even bear to see his mother swat flies. "But why do you have to kill them?" he would ask in tears.

"They're only bugs. They're pests," his mother would say.

"But they want to live too," he would argue.

He was also affected by the tiny dead squirrels and birds he'd sometimes find in his back yard. "I gave many creatures a good Christian burial," he recalls with a laugh.

The death that had the greatest impact on him, however, was that of his beloved dog Winnie. Rechy re-creates this important event in the initial chapter of *City of Night*, and it sets in motion the events that follow. As the protagonist's dog lies dying near the side of the house, the boy—trying to cope with his first personal loss—tells his mother he won't be sad when Winnie (Rechy could not even bring himself to change the dog's name) dies because she will go to Heaven, "and I'll see her there."

In real life, when Winnie died, Guadalupe, who was a deeply religious woman, explained that dogs—not having souls—didn't go to heaven. "She's dead, that's all," the protagonist's mother says. "The body just disappears, becomes dirt."

The idea of nothingness filled John with horror and fear. How could something so important, so loved become nothing? It was unfathomable.

In his first novel, *City of Night*, Rechy writes:

I was very religious then. I went to Mass regularly, to Confession. I prayed nightly. And I prayed now for my dead dog: God would make an exception. He would let her into Heaven.

I stand watching my brother dig that hole in the backyard. He put the dead dog in and covered it. I made a cross and brought flowers. Knelt. Made the sign of the cross: "Let her into Heaven..."

In the days that followed—I dont know exactly how much later—we could smell the body rotting....The day was a ferocious Texas summerday with the threat of rain: thunder—but no rain. The sky lit up through the cracked clouds, and lightning snapped at the world like a whip. My older brother said we hadnt buried Winnie deep enough.

So he dug up the body, and I stand by him as he shovels the dirt in our backyard (littered with papers and bottles covering the weeds which occasionally we pulled, trying several times to grow grass—but it never grew). Finally the body appeared. I turned away quickly. I had seen the decaying face of death. My mother was right. Soon Winnie will blend into the dirt. There was no soul, the body would rot, and there would be Nothing left of Winnie.

Chapter Two

My father willed me deep memories too... In my memories
I discover this: My father's eyes were always filled with tears!
—perhaps unseen tears.
—John Rechy, *Contemporary Authors*

IN LATE 1936, WHEN JOHN was 5, his father was given an opportunity once again to express his creative side, which seemed likely, for a while at least, to make him less angry. In a stroke of inspiration, Father Francisco Pacheco, the head priest of the neighborhood parish, El Calvario Church, engaged Roberto as the director of cultural activities for the parish. The job consisted mostly of putting on musical skits and plays in the church basement.

Roberto Rechy had a completely different personality when away from his family. He maintained his regal bearing, and exuded an air of importance and charm. Being put in charge of parish productions allowed him to befriend the parishioners. His dealings with the community left a lasting impression.

"The father was such an interesting man," recalls Alfredo Jordan, a childhood friend of John's sister Olga. "My father used to think that he was a magician; he had such magical ideas. He and my grandfather used to talk about things like theology, the Arabian Nights, and the prerevolutionary Mexican aristocracy. Things that people in our village normally didn't talk about. My grandfather used to say, 'This man is somebody who is very important. When he's talking, keep your mouth shut and listen.'"

Energized by putting his creative talent to use, even in so humble an arena, Roberto started a theatrical company for the culture-starved community, using local talent to play the leads. He approached each production with artistic zeal. He convinced the neighborhood men to play in the band and organized the poor Mexican women from his village for supporting roles in his productions. Roberto worked with them on their singing and taught them to minuet. He even involved Guadalupe by having her design and sew the elaborate costumes. She wouldn't perform in the shows, but would often talk quietly at the rehearsals with the other wives.

The entire community was electrified by the newly energized Roberto Rechy, whose flamboyant shows, staged in the church basement in a ghetto between the stockyard and the West Texas desert, came across as a combination of pure surrealism and masterful kitsch. To the community, the shows became the bright focus of an otherwise drab existence.

"Mr. Rechy changed our lives," Alfredo Jordan states matter-of-factly. "It was quite an anomaly in West Texas during the Depression. Dust and wind and boredom and along comes Mr. Rechy, and he presents us with plays and music and dances from Russia. From Spain he had dances with castanets."

Alfredo and his family often took part in Roberto's productions, and he vividly remembers the experience. "He devised and staged a sort of masque in which men and women dressed in French costumes of the late 17th and early 18th century and danced minuets and other court dances from Versailles. Can you imagine this tableau in the basement of a church in the middle of windy West Texas during the Great Depression? The Mexican men wore white silk stockings and shoes with buckles, silk knee britches. The women wore huge powdered wigs like Norma Shearer in Marie Antoinette."

Roberto's young son, John, also made a striking impression on the community. His aloofness, along with his arresting looks, gave him a compelling mystique that he seemed to exude effortlessly. Even as a little boy he telegraphed enormous sexuality. Men and women stopped to stare at him on the street.

Alfredo Jordan who, at 10, was five years older than John, remembers being so enraptured with the child—his silent intensity—that he would follow him around. Over 60 years later he says he "never forgot John because he was so handsome and so beautiful, and yet so distant. I was fascinated by him. He didn't belong to us. He was not part of us. He didn't speak. He didn't want to play. He seemed unattainable. But he kept looking at us. And also, in retrospect, he was not involved with his father. He always seemed as if he was observing us. I didn't care, but I'm sure other people did, because he kept his distance—he studied us as if we were objects. You couldn't approach him, and he wouldn't approach you, but you kept following him. You couldn't help yourself."

Surely most of the other boys his age would have excluded this seemingly strange, haughty boy who was delicate and remote. So instead John rejected them first. He separated himself with an air of absolute indifference before he could be excluded. As a result, he always seemed to be judging others.

Roberto left El Calvario Church to become the artistic director of another parish, Guardian Angel Church. There he staged operas and had a children's theater group. Working in the theater, Roberto transformed into a man whose behavior was in stark contrast to what his family had come to expect from him at home. His daughter Blanche, whom he cast as a gypsy girl in *Carmen*, remembers, "Every time I see any of my grandchildren on the stage, I imagine my daddy looking up at them from the audience and beaming."

Because his father was such a completely changed man when involved in his productions, even John would sometimes agree to perform. "For a time I was the star of his children's productions,"

Rechy remembers. "Another anomaly about my father: He wrote skits with me in mind." Coached by his sister Blanche, John would expertly perform the Shirley Temple song, "Come Along and Follow Me to the Bottom of the Sea."

"He was so cute when he did that," Blanche remembers. Friends recall that a sweet, seductive quality hung heavily over the child, who beckoned his audience to follow him to the sea. "Every week there was a group of older ladies that would go to the theater just to see him perform. During one show, when he was sick, they didn't even want to buy a ticket." The show just didn't seem worth it if they couldn't follow little John to the bottom of the sea.

At the age of 8 he had a leading role in a play titled *El Monje Blanco* (The White Monk), an allegory about the boy—played by Rechy—who became Jesus Christ. Rechy remembers, "During intermission I would run out to be hugged by women in tears—to the point that someone was assigned to keep me from rushing out. Soon after, a movie was to be made with the great Mexican film star María Félix. I was up for the role of the boy, but my father would not allow the move to Mexico City."

Still, John loved being admired and thought of show business as a way to escape. He started to believe that all of life was performance, a role-play, in which you became whatever you appeared to be. He wrote a letter to Shirley Temple suggesting that he should become her partner. "I was always precocious and could write very well," he explains. The 7-year-old Rechy had a plan. Shirley would say "yes" and summon him to Hollywood. They'd star together, and soon John would so outshine Shirley that she would retire and he'd become the cute dancing kid in the movies everyone loved. "She must have suspected something of my design," the adult Rechy observes dryly, "because the bitch never answered."

Still, there was the loneliness.

Loneliness is one of the great motivators. In John there developed a yearning to have someone to connect with. To have someone understand him completely, his feelings, his dreams. He felt the stirrings of something important in him, but for the time being everything seemed to be stuck in a limbo. Being outstanding would get him noticed and perhaps bring to him people with whom he could have some sort of bond. So the boy persevered in his writing and drawing and excelled in school. He would write and illustrate stories, always with the title "Long Ago." His loneliness also compelled him to build up a steely, untouchable exterior that kept the enemies of the world—everyone—at a distance. In adulthood the beautiful outsider would slowly metamorphose into the sexual outlaw.

John was not, of course, totally isolated. He was aware of his mother's devotion and he in turn had a deep attachment to her. There was also another relative Rechy remembers fondly, "My favorite aunt, actually my mother's aunt, claimed to have 'mystical powers.' She loved me because I was Anglo-looking; and so she took me to the movies." Tia Ana had a small restaurant called, in English, "The Such is Life." Later John found out that his colorful aunt had been a bootlegger in "dry" Texas and that the *federales* had raided The Such is Life, which was a front for her lucrative business. "She was jailed for a few months," Rechy says, "and came out as resplendent as ever."

Also, John's brothers and sisters were devoted to him—and he loved them—but he knew early on he wasn't like them. The social ease of his sisters and the athleticism of his brothers didn't come naturally to John. All he could do was study and observe.

John was closest with his sister Olga. She in return was extremely protective of her "little brother," especially because he was so moony and moody. Olga was very good at sports. On the rare occasions John was coaxed into playing baseball in a vacant Texas field, he was always assigned to the outfield. There, he could daydream while the baseball game went on. One afternoon, John was doing just that when he heard his sister say, "Jump and catch it!" Responding to her commanding voice, John did jump, and he caught the ball—winning the game. Olga was overjoyed. John was the baseball hero for that day—but only that day.

Eventually, Olga turned into a beauty, pursued by scores of handsome young men. "I was very jealous," Rechy says. "Because she would often sit on the porch with one or another of them, I put up an electric connection and lit up the porch. She then began taking walks with her boyfriends. So I followed them, pretending to be reading from a book as I walked in the dark night."

John's siblings were a cushion for him, but anyone outside of his immediate family unit was frightening. Friends noticed the dissimilarity. "He was not playful, aggressive, or sociable," a family friend remembers. "Certainly completely different from Blanche and Olga, who were amenable and approachable."

John's brothers and sisters sensed he was ill at ease in the world, but he was still the baby and they coddled and indulged him, looking the other way when his behavior seemed odd—like the time he hid in the crawl space under the house when relatives came to visit rather than be exposed to their scrutiny.

In his unhappiness he turned to God, clutching tightly to the image of Him as a protector and savior. At night he would stand in the backyard looking up at the stars, praying fervently. As time went by, his list of grievances grew longer and longer until, finally, he would merely say in his mind, *You already know why I'm praying.*

The adult Rechy channeled some of his early pain into novels like *Marilyn's Daughter* (1988), his fictitious creation of an imagined daughter of Marilyn Monroe and Robert Kennedy. In the novel, he describes the young Monroe as having "discovered that there must be a terrible wound somewhere inside her body. Only *she* had it. Sometimes she'd locate it inside her stomach, sometimes in her heart, a deep pit that was 'empty' yet still hurt—a cold 'painless' aching, she described it in her mind."

Meanwhile, John yearned to connect with the magical, creative side of his father. He was aware of his father's sophisticated reputation with outsiders, so why couldn't his father share some of himself with his son? "Everybody knew him, everybody loved him—Professor Rechy," he recalls with bitterness. The public Roberto was sophisticated and congenial, but the father John continued to encounter at home was a dark, cruel man.

In spite of Roberto's brooding nature, he left a faint lascivious trail that was easy enough for young John to follow. John had discovered Roberto's collection of "girlie" magazines early on, and the minute he was alone in the house he would run to his father's secret stash and stare for hours, enthralled with the voluptuous seminaked bodies. This was dirty. This was interesting. The photos made him feel sexy, as did observing his father around the sensuous, theatrical women he cast in his stage productions—some of whom resembled the ladies in the magazines. Watching Roberto interact with these women enabled John to catch glimpses of the rogue in his father.

In his novel *The Miraculous Day of Amalia Gómez* (1991), Rechy has an adulterous character confess:

> "My women. Yes, I need my women...Because I don't feel complete...It's like something was taken from me long ago, I don't even know what—so I go looking for it in women, lots of women."

From inside Roberto a small jet of love for his son sometimes shot through the hatred. As John wrote in *City of Night*, "After the violence my father would break down and cry. Just wail." Later he would come home laden with toys for John and an armful of fresh flowers for Guadalupe. Gifts. Material things. An attempt to say, "I do love you."

Once in a moment of tenderness Roberto gave John his ruby ring that had been converted from a tiepin—only to take it back the following day. Another afternoon while John was sitting on the front porch his father came up from behind and put his hand on his shoulder. "You're my son, and I love you," he blurted. But coming from a man who had caused him so much pain, the admission was too late. John could not respond.

A few years later, when John became interested in the movies, his father would allow him to cut school to spend hours in the darkened theater. Roberto then reprimanded John's teacher for punishing him for truancy. "Don't you ever tell my son what to do," he admonished the startled teacher. Yet face-to-face his father would not, could not, acknowledge John's extraordinary qualities. He would force them to remain strangers.

Like many wives of the day, Guadalupe turned a blind eye to her husband's infidelities. But the fact that his father was blatantly having affairs with the very sexy women who surrounded him angered John, and at the same time stirred up his budding sexuality. He was aroused by his father's exploits. At night he would lie in bed devising heated and confused fantasies involving the women in his father's productions.

While his sexuality remained baffling to him, John found a way to express some of his hidden feelings in his sketches. Some of his early drawings are quite erotic. Poised, sexy women with hands on their hips, projecting a brazen sexuality. One drawing is uncanny in its foreshadowing. It depicts a prostitute under a street light and a street sign that reads SALEM ALLEY. Many years later Rechy worked as a male prostitute and was known for hustling on Selma Street in Hollywood.

Was he sexually attracted to this type of woman or merely fascinated? Rechy wasn't sure. Certainly by convincing himself that he desired the female body, he persuaded himself that he was "normal." In his father's world, men desired women. "My realization of being gay was long coming," Rechy says. "I can look back and say, 'Oh, sure, that was already there,' but consciously it took years to come out."

In *City of Night*, Rechy writes of the protagonist's mother that she "never once understood the terror between my father and me." Part of Roberto's terror of his son, it seems, is that John—for all his strangeness—reminded Roberto of himself. Father and son were alike in more ways than either could recognize. In retrospect, it seems inconceivable that a man who loved music and wrote operas could not appreciate his artistically sensitive son, a sullen boy who spent his days creating fantasies. Instead, he saw a boy who refused to be taken outside and taught how to throw a ball.

Roberto was, in his own eyes, an intensely masculine man. He loved sports, despite his life in the artistic world of theater and music. (His obituary noted that he was well known in El Paso athletic circles.) But the reflection of himself that he saw in John was an image without the masculine trappings so important to male identity in the Latino culture.

Roberto may not have shown such antagonism toward John because they were so different, but, perversely, because they were so alike. It is very possible Roberto focused his anger on John because he was a reflection of Roberto's sensitive side and, in some unacknowledged way, his more feminine side. In those early years John was condemned to that terrible isolation only a child can feel when the adult world seems bleak and foreign and unlearnable. And for that small child, the reasons for these barriers were incomprehensible.

His father's homophobia made it essential for young John to learn to project a "masculine" image. In the '30s and '40s in the Chicano culture, adherence to gender roles was even more rigidly observed than today. As a result, Rechy didn't allow himself to play with the neighborhood girls or with dolls. Rechy's youthful mind wouldn't even consider it. But he did create dolls, in a sense, on paper. Along with his early erotic drawings—in which he reproduced the scantily clad women from his father's girlie magazines, then further undressed them—are sketches of glamorous women in fancy gowns, with elbow-length gloves and carefully styled hair.

In his dream world he could draw pictures and write stories in which he controlled the characters' destinies. At the same time, he couldn't bear the thought of anything feminine in himself, a characteristic that has remained with him throughout his life. Once a journalist described the adult John Rechy as "a great beauty" and Rechy exclaimed, "No, no, no!...say I'm handsome, masculine, sexy...but not a great beauty."

Another way he projected his masculinity was to adopt a

perfectly reserved demeanor. This is common among Chicano men. In his book *El Laberinto de la Soledad*, Mexican essayist Octavio Paz analyzes masculine identity in Mexican men:

> Old or adolescent, Creole or *mestizo*, laborer or college educated, the Mexican man appears to me as a being who encloses and preserves himself. The ideal of manliness consists of never opening up. Those who open are cowards. For us, in contrast to other countries, opening is a weakness—the Mexican man may bend over himself—but will never open up, in other words, will never allow the outer world to penetrate his intimacy. Women are inferior beings, because they open up when they give themselves...like on their sex, on the opening, a wound that will never close.

Later in life, Rechy played out this Chicano conception of masculinity sexually—as a hustler he would always be the one doing the penetrating, adamantly refusing to "open up" to another man.

It was during Rechy's childhood that the seeds for the "butch" street hustler, the impenetrable loner were planted.

Being thought of as masculine became so important to John as a young boy that his entire world revolved around constructing and perfecting a flawless mask. This made it imperative that his insecurities remain unacknowledged, even to himself. And it was in his silence that he attained his masculinity. He couldn't give his father no-hitters, but if masculinity also meant being stoic, certainly he could keep his emotions buried.

But in his silence, a budding rage festered. "As my father's violence intensified, I was sure he would attempt to kill me, or worse, my mother, as he threatened often. He also threatened to disfigure my 'pretty face' so no one would ever look at me. I was about 12, 13 when I decided I would beat him to it. I did research at the library on poisons and tried to find out what happened to children who killed their fathers. I decided he wasn't worth the risk. Still,

I would try to thwart him at every sinister turn. The tension between us grew so that for months we did not speak to each other, but each time I encountered him I would stare at him, unbudging, with hatred."

Roberto's inability to relate to his youngest son, to connect with him, to show him love, drew Guadalupe closer to John. More and more the youngest Rechy turned to his mother for comfort, clinging to her for safety. This was a woman he would describe as having "nothing brutal about her, only a crushing tenderness, as powerful as the hatred I would discover later in my father." "Crushing" being a crucial word in this description. Guadalupe recognized John's separateness and intuitively sensed that her dreamy little boy was deeply unhappy about something unspoken. As a result she drew John nearer to her and protected him with the kind of love only a mother can give. And, while the love between mother and child is an awesome power, it is also an awesome danger. Guadalupe's love would influence John's life to an extent that was as far-reaching and consequential as his father's hatred.

• • •

For a man who spent his life obsessed with physical beauty—attaining it for himself and describing it in others—it is important to John Rechy that his mother was a startlingly beautiful woman. "Her eyes are true green," one of the parish wives marveled after seeing Guadalupe for the first time. She was a deeply religious woman but she was also quite engaging company for the women of the community, often trading recipes and reminiscing about the old days in Mexico.

John was constantly at her side. "Strangely, I loved to sit and look at her as she fixed the food—or did the laundry," he wrote in *City of Night.* "She washed our clothes outside in an aluminum tub, and I would watch her hanging up the clean sheets flapping in the wind." Neighbors remember John showing up at his father's rehearsals holding her hand. Leaning into her. Gazing up at her as if the mere sight of her offered him protection. And she was devoted to him, keeping him close to shelter him from a world she sensed didn't understand him. Guadalupe Flores Rechy channeled her energies into being a good wife and mother, and John Rechy may well have had her devotion in mind when he described the mother character, years later, in his novel *This Day's Death*:

> When they were sick—from colds accompanied by fever in that drafty house (and she nailed boards to broken windows, ferociously challenging the wind—yet still they got colds and fever which seized Jim as a child, before he developed his body to resist all illness)—when they were sick, she spread love over them like balm or salve. Even that was done with ferocity: Although she smiled the gentle smile they would carry forever in their memories. She defied sleep then until she knew they were well. Exhausted, she collapsed in bed for a few hours, only to pull herself, gray from sleeplessness and by now feverish herself, to care for them again. Furiously—but wearing that beautiful smile—she washed their clothes in a tin tub—because dirt, bringing sickness to her children, was an enemy she must personally eradicate. They would help her carry the tub outside after she had heated the water on the stove. The water, hot enough to purify her children's clothes, scorched her hands red. She merely rubbed oil on them—and ironed that same night.

Although written with great appreciation and love, Rechy's remembrance is peppered with words like "ferocity" and "furiously," hinting that the result of the mother's affection wasn't always positive, upon which he elaborates in a later passage:

> The children grew to expect these acts of her love: Because it was what they were born into; it was all they knew: the churning ocean of her love in which they swam. Even when

they resisted drowning in it, they loved her back with an equal rage, intensity, need—as the source of their lives—because her love was by now like a physical thing which bathed them, nourished them, lulled them to sleep, stirred them awake.

Friends of the family also remember Guadalupe's devotion to her children—to John in particular—yet, like John, the first thing anyone mentions when remembering Guadalupe is her great beauty, her flawless skin, her lush, dark hair, and especially her mysterious green eyes—like Spanish olives. Oddly, though, Guadalupe never really appears beautiful in her photographs. The fault may lie in the limitations of photography, or perhaps in Guadalupe's inability to project her true self. It is almost as if she was embarrassed by her beauty and tried to present a serious and stern attitude—a suitable Catholic wife's demeanor—for the camera's scrutiny. "She was very beautiful," Rechy remarks when going through old photographs, "but the pictures don't show that."

Guadalupe's wifely demeanor and calm exterior hid internal loneliness, longings, and fears. In this way John and his mother were alike. Out of all her children, John was the one to whom Guadalupe felt closest. He was vulnerable, he was quiet, he stayed at home with her and wanted all the affection she longed to give, and to give all the affection she longed for. Unlike Roberto, Guadalupe encouraged John's artistic side. It was his mother to whom he would show his drawings and read his stories.

"She loved me very much," Rechy remembers wistfully. "I was very special to her. I was happiest when I was with her. Like the time my father went to Mexico for over a week—perhaps the happiest time of my childhood; my mother made sandwiches, and she and I and Olga went on a picnic to a nearby park. It was wonderful! Then we went to the movies. But I knew eventually my father would come back, and he did, and when I saw him getting out of the cab, I knew that time of happiness would be crushed again by his rage." Another time, shortly after Blanche was married, Rechy and his mother were again preparing for a picnic and Roberto—who was working on his music—suddenly lunged at John with a knife. John's new brother-in-law had to restrain Roberto.

Roberto knew his son hated him, and his revenge was to threaten to separate John from Guadalupe. At night he would taunt John, predicting that he "will kill my mother in bed, and in the morning, when I go wake her, she'll be dead and I'll be left alone with him." John became so fearful of losing his mother that, if she was not feeling well, he would stand by her bed and monitor her breathing as she slept.

Roberto was not only cruel and sometimes aggressively hostile to John but also to Guadalupe. He icily observed his son replacing him as Guadalupe's emotional confidante and—as his relationship with Guadalupe deteriorated—her surrogate husband. A condition that is emphasized by the fact that, for as long as John can remember, Roberto and Guadalupe had separate bedrooms.

Only in her 40s, with a husband much older than herself, Guadalupe found herself trapped in a marriage with a disturbed, sadistic, and violent man. She felt, in her own loneliness, a need for a love that protected. John sensed this in her and attempted to shield his mother from her husband, a man he would later call "an unusual enemy." Yet John could only watch helplessly as Roberto, raging, accused her of intentionally bringing about his downfall. In his fury he would threaten to burn down the house and everyone in it.

Certainly their mutual fear of Roberto bound John and his mother together, but there was a more complex side to their love. Along with Guadalupe's anxiety over her husband's brutality was her constant and unresolved grief over the loss of her first-born daughter, Valeska. She never got over that. Roberto did not provide the support she needed, so she clung urgently to her "baby" John. He filled the emotional space his father was supposed to fill. But love that starts out as a need often turns into something insatiable. Instead of finding independence and strength in each other's protection, the two merged their hungers.

Mother and son gripped on to each other so tightly that their love, which had started out as tenderness, ultimately became devouring. Guadalupe's fierce devotion encompassed John with a complicated love, leaving the child without much breathing room. In her delicate, tender way, she made him totally dependent on her. That dependence soon bordered on addiction.

John's love for Guadalupe was so integral that only years later was he able to explore, in his fiction, its damaging effects. In *This Day's Death* he writes about an adult mother and son relationship, but it is clear their mutual dependency started many years earlier:

> She needed him urgently, and she grasped strongly. He felt her frail engulfing strength, and instinctively he resisted as one resists drowning. Aware of his resistance, that frail strength became more powerful. Soon he needed her—as much to cling back to as to resist. And so it went, the symmetrical construction of the terrible trap.

Meanwhile, Roberto's jealousy of John's relationship with Guadalupe, his love-hate jumble of feelings toward his son, and his bewilderment and exasperation in general may have taken on a more horrifying expression.

Throughout Rechy's published writings there are strong implications of sexual abuse in his childhood. He often speaks passionately on the subject of molestation by a family member. In 2001, for instance, he wrote an angry essay rebuking the journalist Dominick Dunne, who had been critical of Lyle and Eric Menendez in his coverage of their trial. The two brothers were found guilty in 1996 of murdering their parents, gunning the couple down as they watched television. During their imprisonment the brothers claimed that their father had been sexually abusing them for years, a defense many people, including Dominick Dunne, disbelieved:

> Mr. Dunne doubted that there had been any molestation whatsoever in the Menendez case, although some of us who

may be knowledgeable in the area heard the unmistakable ring of truth in the testimony of the two young men about molestation by their father (whatever else they may have lied about), details that could be reported only by those who may have experienced something of the sort—including the horror that may lie behind a closed door that threatens to open at any moment, when, on the other side, there is someone—in this case Father Menendez—who may rush out to terrorize.

Here, Rechy clearly intimates that he is among the "some of us" familiar with incest, and that he heard the ring of truth in the brothers' testimony.

Nearly 30 years before that article, in the first chapter of *City of Night*, which is, by Rechy's own admission, as close to autobiography as anything he's ever written, Rechy wrote:

When I was about eight years old, my father taught me this:
He would say to me: "Give me a thousand," and I knew this meant I should hop on his lap and then he would fondle me—intimately—and he'd give me a penny, sometimes a nickel.

This is an extraordinarily revealing admission from a man who for many years was only able to express his sexuality through prostitution, going from man to man for profit. But years later Rechy is still unable to admit anything sexual actually occurred during these games of "give me a thousand." Or, at least, he found it difficult to verbalize. "I don't think so. I don't think so," he murmurs, looking down at the floor when asked if his father abused him sexually. "That area is so...weird."

Even more astonishingly, the passage in *City of Night* continues:

At times when his friends—old gray men—came to our house, they would ask for "a thousand." And I would jump on their laps too. And I would get nickel after nickel, going around the table.

As an adult, Rechy claims that while he wasn't aroused by the game, he wasn't appalled or frightened either. Instead, he found a strange comfort in the arms of these men. Looking back on the "give me a thousand" experiences, Rechy says, "I felt very warm and loved, whatever their intention. That is when I felt it the most in my childhood, other than from my mother. But that is when I felt entirely loved."

Rechy readily admits that his father was a "son of a bitch," that he was "brutal," that he was "cruel." But, although his closest friends believe he was undoubtedly sexually abused as a child, Rechy himself abruptly stops short of making that accusation. Sexual abuse would, however, be at least one explanation for his lifelong obsession with hustling: A lonely and isolated boy feels loved and secure only when being fondled by his father and his father's mature friends, and afterward he is rewarded, sowing the seeds for his future belief that his beauty could inspire tenderness and that sensual physical contact with him was valuable and would be rewarded. Even by someone who rebuffed him otherwise—his own father.

Confronted with this theory as an adult, Rechy argues, "No, I don't think that explains anything. I always pull away from anything that explains too patly, and you know it makes it too pat." Rechy gives a more innocent interpretation of the erotic game. "The reason that that is so befuddled in my mind," he explains, "is that Mexican men are very affectionate in a particular way that can easily be misinterpreted."

Toward the end of *City of Night*, the protagonist sums up the legacy of feelings his father's game left him, stating that the memory would be remembered as, "reassuring me, in that strange way—so briefly!—that he did...want me." It is possible that these moments are among the few memories Rechy has of pleasing his father, and that he remembers them as innocent so as not to tarnish them.

"Give me a thousand" games were not John Rechy's only childhood sexual or sensual experiences. He remembers a handsome drifter, one of the hundreds of tramps and hobos who spilled out "like flies" into the neighborhood from the nearby railroad tracks.

"We lived about two blocks away from the railroad tracks," Robert Rechy says, "and at that time tramps were coming all the way from the eastern part of the country, traveling west to Los Angeles. They would get off the train in El Paso because they heard it was a place where they could get something to eat."

Rechy's mother took pity on the homeless men and women and prepared food that she served on plates especially reserved for the hobos on a wooden table on the back porch. "Every time they knocked, my mama would go to the door and feed them beans and rice and tortillas along with hot coffee," Robert says. "We couldn't understand how they all knew to stop at our house. Later we found out that they would mark the street in front of a house to let others know that they could get something to eat because we were friendly people. When they passed through the neighborhood, the first place they would stop was at our house."

Robert remembers that the hobos were friendly, though he is aware that John viewed them quite differently. "Johnny was very young, very small," he says. "The tramps looked awful at the time. While they were traveling, there was the smoke from the train and that would make them very dirty. John, who appreciated beauty, resented them. He didn't resent the way my mama treated them, but he resented the way they looked."

Even back then young John was deeply curious, a little spy who loved to be a fly on the wall. He observed the lean, grimy strangers who paraded to his home with the same bewildered fascination with which he looked at his father's dirty magazines. Most of them were harmless, just out-of-work people displaced by the Depression. But to Rechy's sensitive eyes they were sinister and mysterious, advertising their hunger—and then hunching over the meals his mother prepared for them. At times the child's fascination was so great he would wander down to the tracks where the hobos huddled in dark freight trains. Rechy would watch them there, silent and wary. He made up a word ("pet-eh") to describe the strange, fetid odor that sometimes drifted from the freight cars. He still remembers that smell.

On one occasion John was intrigued by a particular drifter who had strolled up to his mother's back door looking for something to eat. In *Contemporary Authors*, Rechy described the young stranger as "a dirtied angel" who stood out among the other tramps. The good-looking hobo sat on the porch alone, hungrily shoveling in the food John's mother had given him. John stood quietly in the garage—watching, waiting. He felt fear and excitement. "Was there an attraction?" John Rechy wonders as an adult trying to comprehend the incident. "Even at that early age, I'm sure there was a fascination." Yes, he was enthralled, but at the same time he was terrified of the sensations the stranger aroused. Rather than keeping them buried, however, he opted to explore them.

This memory is blurred. Perhaps John made his presence known to the drifter. ("I seem to remember that he was kind, that he did see me.") The recollection then jumps to the freight trains. Rechy says, "I've tried to remember, yet I don't know how much I tried to conceal. Something happened. What? I don't know. I remember only a freight car, lots of shadows, figures of people moving. That's all." The incident remains as obscured in Rechy's memory as the sensual games he played with his father and his father's friends. "All these memories of the hobo just tumble into something very ambiguous. Something happened in a freight car. Sometimes the memory is violent, but sometimes it's not."

It's possible that Rechy's memory forces him to remember the incident as violent as a way of denying that he was a curious participant. As an adult when he wrote about it for *Contemporary Authors*, the encounter is shadowed with innuendo. Whatever the details, the result was indelible; for years afterward Rechy experienced periods where he felt compelled to go to skid rows and walk and walk, observing the hobo communities with a mixture of anger and sadness, trying to comprehend their mystery, the fascination he had for them. He did it in New York and Chicago and later in Los Angeles. His friend Marsha Kinder sometimes accompanied him on these excursions. "He had obsessive nightmares about it," she recalls. "It was a recurring dream, the tramps. I remember I used to ride to Main Street with him and he became a different person—really obsessed with it." Rechy remembers that as he drove he was consumed with feelings of fascination, outrage, and hatred, and then sometimes "a brief warm peace."

CHAPTER THREE

I would sit by the window looking at the people that
passed. I felt miraculously separated from the world outside:
separated by the pane, the screen through which,
nevertheless—uninvolved—I could see the world.
—John Rechy, *City of Night*

ON TOP OF HIS SEXUAL CONFUSION in these formative years, John
Rechy was forced to deal with his ethnic alienation. The difference between the way he looked on the outside—Anglo—and
what he knew himself to be—Mexican—added to the turmoil of
his divided self. At the time in El Paso, Rechy remembers there
was fierce discrimination against Mexicans, much of which he saw
first-hand. His brother Yvan and sister Blanche were both dark,
and so they felt the discrimination most directly, even from their
own family. Blanche, for instance, had been treated horribly by her
grandmother. And her brothers often teased her, saying that she
wasn't a blood relative, but just "left on the doorstep in a basket,"
until, in tears, she went to her mother to be reassured.

John, on the other hand, didn't look Mexican. His finely chis-
eled features, fair skin, and light eyes set him apart. Hence, he was
separated from other Mexicans by his appearance—and from the
Anglos by his family.

In their household the Rechys spoke only Spanish. His

father spoke English with a thick accent. When John started school, he didn't speak a word of English. It was his kindergarten teacher who changed his name from Juan to John. Every time she said "one" the 5-year-old thought she was saying Juan and walked up to her. Exasperated, she changed his name to John, which soon became Johnny. Some of his early drawings are signed "Johnny Rechy."

Rechy would direct angry memories at the way his "gringo" teachers treated him into his 1991 novel *The Miraculous Day of Amalia Gómez*. The impoverished character, Amalia, is often mistreated by her teachers. "God wants you to speak in English," an angry nun scolds the child. "And he doesn't want you to speak with a Mexican accent." And although the Anglo children in the novel are also poor, they are treated kindly; it is the Mexican children, like Amalia, who must endure the humiliation of having their hair checked for lice.

In spite of the discrimination John flourished academically. From kindergarten through seventh grade he was on the honor roll and achieved a steady stream of straight A's. By the time he was 10, he had started writing novels. One of his earliest attempts was a long book about Marie Antoinette that he worked on for years. Later he began a novel, *Pablo!*—about a Mexican boy who longs to be a dancer. (Rechy would rewrite this novel many times over the years, although he chose not to publish it.) Roberto was proud of John's intellect but could not bring himself to express those feelings directly. It was to his oldest son, Robert, that he exclaimed about John, "My son is going to be something great!"

Father and son remained strangers. John, too, found it impossible to talk to his father. He instead wrote stories in which his father was the main character, the villain. "Horrible stories," he recalls. In these childhood fantasies a young boy would murder his father. Young John would hide these writings where he was sure his father could find them.

At the same time, John discovered a way to expand his secret fantasy life—at the movies. Some of the most wonderful times of his early years were spent alone at the Texas Grand Theater, where they had thrilling "Revival Week," a film festival that brought back the more popular movies from the past and ran a different one every day for a week. John would skip school and sit in the dark theater watching fantasy come to life on the screen. He was captivated by the remarkably alluring women and the dashing men who pursued them. Sometimes, as Rechy recalls, the drama occurred in the audience. "When I was about 10, I went to see a movie called *The Dark Command*, with John Wayne and Claire Trevor," he says. "It was a weekday, I had cut classes, and there were no more than 10 people in the cavernous theater. An older man sat next to me. That made me very uncomfortable, but I didn't move because I had become scared. He pushed his arm against mine, and when I jerked away he showed me some money he had held in his hand—a 50-cent piece! That scared me even more, and I ran out. He rushed out too, I'm sure afraid."

The incident didn't stop John from going to the movies ("Nothing could stop me from Thrilling Revival Week.") and soon he was again happily attending matinees. Curiously, his father allowed, even encouraged John to cut classes to go to the movies. He may not have approved of all of his strange son's habits, but he didn't want anyone interfering with the boy's independence. This, perhaps, was Roberto's way of trying to show his son some semblance of acceptance.

John didn't have a word yet for how the male leads in these movies made him feel. "I had to have had sexual feelings for those actors, but I think it was all so repressed and contained. In retrospect, I could say, 'Yes, I was attracted to Alan Ladd.' I must have been. I wanted to be just like him, but at the same time I was attracted to Veronica Lake. Jon Hall. I mean, these were very sexy male figures. Consciously, I wanted to be like them. But, you know, all that stuff is mixed with desire."

Along with idolizing the men in the movies, Rechy sat for hours studying the glamorous screen lives of Joan Crawford,

Greta Garbo, Rita Hayworth, and his favorite, Hedy Lamarr, the exotic actress with jet-black hair and blue eyes, who spoke with an accent and lured a man to his doom in *Algiers*. But Rechy's feelings toward the actresses were ambiguous. Did he desire them sexually? Did he wish to be like these femmes fatales? Certainly he longed to be desired as they were, and he preferred the enticing women whose screen personas mixed an aloof beauty with wanton sexuality. When he saw *Snow White*, for example, he dismissed the goody-goody Snow White as banal and uninteresting. Instead he developed a crush on the wicked, narcissistic Queen with her fervent lust to be the fairest of them all. "I couldn't stop drawing her," he recalls.

For the rest of his life, Rechy would see the world as if looking through a movie camera. All around him, in the movies, in his father's acting troupes, in the sexy magazines he read in secret, John saw that beauty was power—and he would search out beauty with a precise and judgmental eye. His loneliness turned into a crucial need to possess a masculine version of it.

Still, nothing he saw on the screen, in magazines, or in real life quite fit as a prototype for his unique physicality and personality, so he began to develop his own version of a male sex symbol. Most of the women he admired—Rechy says he had crushes on them—like Hedy Lamarr, were sexual objects to be indulged, desired, and pursued. Their beauty brought them lives filled with passion and adventure. The men who coveted these ladies were dominant and strong. By combining these images, the desirable, catered-to woman and the lusty, powerful man, Rechy eventually created his persona as a hustler.

To be sexually desirable became his lifelong obsession. What the young boy learned from movies was that beautiful people were accepted and sought after and worthy. With his astonishing appearance, Rechy realized he could be one of those accepted, sought after, worthy people. His father had always made him feel so helpless. He longed to exercise the power of his physical desirability. The way John looked became the focus of John's world, more important than how he behaved, and even the way he wrote, drew, and performed. He needed to be perceived as desirable. That would be his ticket to survival.

As a teenager, Rechy expressed his divided self within the extreme contrasts of his high school life and home life. Clearly, some degree of his isolation stemmed from the buried knowledge of his homosexuality. In *The Sexual Outlaw* (1977), he writes, "Threatened by rejection by the straight world of parents, friends, teachers, the gay child finds fear of detection a factor in his early life; he hates what creates it, his homosexuality." But other issues also explain his separation and anxiety, such as poverty and his Mexican heritage.

"The bigotry against Mexicans was phenomenal," he explains. "I could have become popular, but there were so many problems I had—of identity. The whole Mexican thing was very big. The so-called Mexican kids were wary of me, because I didn't look like what they expected. And with the Anglo kids I constantly had to be on my guard in case someone would say something against Mexicans and then I would have to defend myself. It was always a very schizophrenic existence for me. People thought I was ashamed at being Mexican. That's nonsense. I didn't want to be hurt. I was trying to escape unnecessary pain."

Rechy tells an anecdote illustrating how terrified he was of people finding out about his home life. Again, he viewed his Mexican heritage and his poverty as the reasons for his fears. "I wasn't invited to parties because I ran home directly after school. I didn't want anyone to know where I lived. For a time I gave the wrong address. There was a time when I did start getting some invitations, and it became very painful because they were from kids from the upper side of the hill and I was from the lower. And there was a very pretty house on our block—ours was decrepit— and I gave that address, and when someone was going to pick me up I ran to that house and waited on the steps of that house. And they picked me up. But then the horror happened. One of my new friends decided to drop in one day: to the wrong house. It was just one of those obliterating things. It happens, and then you think you'll never recover, but of course you do and you even talk about it."

Rechy was able to avoid becoming a high school scapegoat by excelling in every area his talents allowed. "I had a devouring need to be number one," he says. "I wanted to be everything." His plan was to make himself so superior, in every way possible, that his achievements would raise him above his contemporaries, intimidate them, and keep them from turning him into their token adolescent outcast. As an adult, Rechy would tell one of his writing classes: "I've never fitted in. I've always felt ostracized by everyone. And now I don't feel that I belong anywhere, except as an artist, and I'm glad of it. Who'd want to join a group?"

As a teenager John began to live a sort of Cinderella existence, leading two lives, with a day self and a night self. He directed his energy toward his school hours—where he could excel, at least academically. His father's contemptuous treatment had conditioned him to feel subconsciously inferior. To make himself better than everyone else became his ambition. He boasted that his ambition was to "write a great novel" that rivaled Kathleen Winsor's *Forever Amber*. He was determined to become president of everything in his power: the honor society, the writer's society, and the editor of the paper. Each new accomplishment was, however, a flawed victory.

Rechy's desire to excel contrasted starkly with his inability to connect with his contemporaries. Strangled, he became a member of clubs without ever gaining popularity among other students. They were aware of him. They wondered about him. But he wasn't one of them. He became successful without becoming popular. As he puts it, "It was the outsider penetrating as an outsider. I never became part of the group." But he would remember with glee the time his high school paper, *The Tattler*, commented in an editorial, "We've had enough of three students being at the top of everything—let's give the others a chance."

Rechy was delighted that his name was listed among the three high achievers.

"I think maybe I intimidated people," Rechy muses. "I don't mean by being negative—but simply by being really different. I was extremely intelligent. The teachers loved me. Some of them too much. Two of them tried to seduce me. There was a very buxom teacher, very tall—my Latin teacher—who was very fond of coming over to talk to me while I sat at my desk. She wore a tight dress that revealed her ample breasts, and she bent over so that they were almost in my face. I became aroused. I didn't know what I know now—that she was doing that on purpose—and so I was terrified that she would discover that I had a hard-on. Around the same time there was a math teacher, a fussy man, who loved to ask me to go to the board to write out math problems. He would get very close to me."

Years later, in 1957, during one of the times John returned to El Paso briefly to see his mother, he went to San Jacinto Plaza, which was a cruising arena. There, his math teacher from way back tried to pick him up. "Obviously he didn't recognize me, thought I was transient," Rechy says.

Though the sexual vibrations he gave off sometimes confused him, John continued to rely on his physicality as a buffer. "I was good-looking—which was my salvation," he says. "But I was never popular in the way of going out to the pep rallies and all of that. I detested those. When I went to the football games, because my father thought that I should, I kept to myself. I didn't have any friends, really."

When the bell rang signaling the end of the school day John withdrew into the safety of his shell once again. "My life ended when school was out," he says.

He kept to himself, acquiring an air of godlike indifference. He continued to spend much of his time at the movies. But mostly he read: Greek tragedies, Dostoevsky, García Lorca, Rimbaud, Emily Brontë, Nietzsche, Swift, Faulkner, as well as popular novelists such as Margaret Mitchell and Ben Ames Williams.

Rechy says he read, "at least one book a week when I was in my early teens. I read everything, plays, histories—especially about the French Revolution—and novels. My brother Robert used to joke that I was going to go blind because, often, I'd be reading on the porch and before I knew it, the day had gone dark."

In 1945, when Rechy was 14, he began to notice a slow shift in power in his relationship with his father. "I was just a kid and he was already a very old man," he recalls. Suddenly, it was John who sometimes took the upper hand in cruelty. Once when they were crossing the street his father stumbled on his cane and fell in the middle of the road. Instead of immediately helping the old man to his feet John rushed to the sidewalk, silently hoping a car would come along and run his father over. It was only after several seconds of pondering that John returned to the street and lifted his father from the ground, handing him his cane and steadying him on his feet. Even at that point there were no words. They walked the rest of the way home in silence, with nothing but a smoldering rage between them.

Between these two walls of rage Guadalupe remained in the center. "I very much wanted her not to love him," Rechy remembers. "I tried to get my mother to leave my father. I told her that I would quit school and support her, but she wouldn't do it." Rechy re-created one of their continual arguments in *This Day's Death*:

"Leave him, I can support you now, look, I've got enough money and I'll quit school and work full-time and I'll take care of you."
She branded him with a look of horror.
"He's your father, he's my husband," she said.
He was able to say, "You love that man?"
"He's my husband," she insisted quietly.
"You love him?!" he demanded.
"He's your father!" she said.

In his teens John suddenly stopped finding comfort in religion, blaming the Church for his mother's refusal to get out of the marriage. "Their attitudes, I felt, kept my mother a prisoner. My mother in another time would have been a very creative woman. She was stifled by the hypocrisy of the Catholic Church." In *This Day's Death* Rechy writes, "Did she really love him? Or did she choose to remain with him because of the stifling Mexican Catholicism that painfully extracted from her an arbitrary devotion to her husband?"

Up to this point, along with John's mother there had always been God. But now with his grip on faith slipping, John began to focus his anger toward religion. He had grown up with the Catholic Church, the mysteries in its statues and icons, the "painted saints with painted tears who writhe in gorgeous agony," and the most startling image, "Christ posing on his cross." These are visions that dominate many of his later works. In *Bodies and Souls* (1984), for instance, the character Manny wants a "full frontal" nude Jesus tattooed on his torso. "Why aren't you naked," the teenager asks the icon on the altar of his local church. "Why don't you ever reveal yourself?"

Rechy found further reason to turn against the church as he grew more aware of, and became more confused by, his own maturing sexuality. "Their hypocritical attitudes toward sexuality I would say is the major cause for sexual repression," he says. "Their feelings of antihomosexuality. And most of them are obviously homosexuals."

How lonely life is. Especially if you've lost God—a God with whom you were once close. Rechy began to turn away from his "savior" when the church began to make him feel guilty about feelings he experienced but was still unable to name. His attitude was not to bow down and ask forgiveness. Better, he thought, to one day storm heaven and protest. So he stopped going to Mass. The adult Rechy jokes, "In church during the wailing and mourning, you thought, *This has nothing to do with me. I want to be dancing with Shirley Temple.*" But as a teenager, the decision to stop praying was a serious one. "The God that would allow this vast unhappiness was a God I would rebel against," he wrote in *City of Night*.

Later, as a young man, Rechy continuously fell into experiences that strengthened his feelings about hypocrisy in the Catholic Church: "At one point in my life I met a young priest who was a friend of a gay friend of mine," he remembers. "I lost track of the priest until, one night in Los Angeles, he had managed to get my number and he called, late at night, to tell me his sexual feelings for me. He had clearly been drinking, and he sounded desperate to admit what he had been hiding. I felt very sorry for him."

In 1977 John made his contempt for Catholicism very clear, still railing against the marks the church's rituals had left on him when he wrote of his early memories in *The Sexual Outlaw*:

> You had to tell your "trespasses" to a faceless whispering voice that kept insisting, "How many times did you commit that sin? How many times? Locked in guilt even when you had no cause to feel guilty. After confession and fasting, came the Sunday morning purification. Communion! You knelt to receive the wafer that was the precious body of Christ. It was all over so quickly, especially since there had been so much agony in confession and fasting! And you knew that soon, too soon, you'd be huddled kneeling guiltily in the darkness again before that mysterious little screen window of the confessional and addressing the faceless presence: Bless me Father, for I have sinned.

In recent years, Rechy's anger at God in general and at the Catholic Church in particular has mellowed into wry bemusement. "I have always admired Christ's oblique muscles," he told one of his private classes. "They're very difficult to get. If you have those, you have points going for you. Jesus must have done 700 sit ups a day to get those abdominals."

As the young Rechy turned his face from God, he turned it

toward the mirror. It was there he found the one person he could trust, who would love him, and who would never hurt or abandon him. Much has been made, through the years, about John Rechy's narcissism. He jokes about it. His friends laugh about it. And he writes about it constantly, starting with his first book *City of Night*:

> From my father's inexplicable hatred of me and my mother's blind, carnivorous love, I fled to the Mirror. I would stand before it thinking: I have only Me!...I became obsessed with age. At 17, I dreaded growing old. Old age is something that must never happen to me. The image of myself in the mirror must never fade into someone I cant look at.

With a journalism scholarship and with financial help from his brother Robert who worked in a pool hall, Rechy entered Texas Western College (now University of Texas at El Paso), where he majored in English with a minor in French. "It nestles in the desert; we climbed rocks to get to class," he later wrote in *City of Night*. Rechy has never forgotten his brother's sacrifice. "Given another series of accidents, my brother might have become the writer. But being the oldest, he had to sacrifice his education because we could not otherwise survive on what my father was able to earn." To lessen the financial burden on his family, John Rechy also worked after school in the call-office of a laundry and cleaners, and later as a copy boy at a newspaper.

Rechy was still very much a loner, and was viewed by his classmates as separate and mysterious. Silence was still a good defense. He knew well the power of mystery. He didn't tell his classmates or teachers he was part Mexican, and he didn't tell them he was poor. The face he presented his peers was very much one of his own design. He again used a false home address so he couldn't be traced back to his shabby neighborhood.

His fellow college students watched him with the same kind of curiosity as the people who watched him walk by on the streets as a boy. But by now his prettiness had matured into a striking handsomeness.

It was his arresting looks that got him noticed by the fraternity SAE. Sigma Alpha Epsilon was notorious as a sexy, macho fraternity. At Texas Western membership to SAE was reserved for college jocks and moneyed Texans—the very good-looking athletic people. John was noticed by two such guys, SAE members Jeff Koontz and Ralph Glen (both names are pseudonyms). They recognized that John, with his aloof good looks and classy demeanor, could be an asset to the exclusive fraternity. Because of his light eyes and refined features—combined with the fake home address—they had no idea the real John Rechy was Mexican and poor, qualities that would have led them to immediately snub him.

The two strapping frat brothers invited Rechy to visit Koontz's family on a ranch in Balmorhea, Texas. After a night of adolescent horseplay, culminating in the three guys wrestling on the rug in their jockey shorts, the fraternity jocks slept side-by-side in the large bed. Adding to his queasy sexual tension was John's confusing ethnic and financial charade. The following day he found out that the only movie theater in town separated Mexicans from Anglos, and didn't allow Blacks in at all. Rechy refused to go in.

At dinner with his would-be fraternity brother's family, a Koontz relative complained that she would rather not eat while the Mexican maid was still in the room. Rechy could not stomach this final indignity. He stood and looked directly at the woman. "I don't want to fuck up your dinner," he stated. Then, as the stunned dinner guests looked on, he strode from the house.

"There was no way I was going to go through this," he says, adding, "There was no way I was going to join this fraternity. I didn't have the money. They would have discovered me. They would not have had me." Once again Rechy decided to do the rejecting before being rejected.

After that incident, he retreated and rebelled. He wrapped his sex appeal around himself like a blanket for protection. He began dressing in an aggressively sexual way. For example, he'd take an ordinary T-shirt, pull it down till it scooped, then wear it with tight muslin pants. And he designed other daring shirts and had his mother make them for him. Very open. Very sexy. His mother did not object. Instead, she seemed to be proud of her son's erotic appeal and individuality.

Rechy remembers: "A lot of stuff that International Male has now, I designed years ago. I'd say, 'Mother, I need to go tomorrow to college like this,' and I'd show her a picture. She'd make a pattern on me. She'd fit them on me. And she'd be sewing till midnight—literally—to finish them. A favorite shirt of mine dipped down to my navel, form fitted, no buttons. Now remember this was in the '50s, and I was walking around the campus like that, and it caused quite a stir."

Ralph Glen, the fraternity jock who stayed friends with Rechy in spite of his growing reputation for being weird, warned him, "Something's happening to you, and people are talking. You'd better watch it."

Rechy's writing also took a controversial turn. He wrote a paper "proving" that John Milton was on the side of the rebel angels and had succeeded in justifying the ways of man to God. Inspired by that success, he wrote an epic poem in which humankind, led by Jesus, turns the final judgment day around and puts God on trial. In the end, God throws himself into hell.

John had also been working as editor of the school magazine, and now he had ideas of turning it into a radical literary periodical, much like his father had done with his renegade newspaper. Instead of the usual harmless bits and pieces of news clipped and pasted from other publications, Rechy wrote pieces like "Modern Art: A Broken Mirror." His parody of Eliot's "The Wasteland," in which he satirized the stupidity of college activities (even illustrating the piece with caricatures of the students involved) led to his removal.

"By then," Rechy says, "everyone was saying, 'He's a fucking queer.'" His peers, however, might have been surprised to discover that the overtly erotic character, with a cynical sneer for his contemporaries, was still a virgin—less sexually active than most of them.

In contrast to the flamboyant image he projected at school, after hours he remained sullen and alone. In *Contemporary Authors* Rechy wrote:

> After classes in college, I often climbed the nearby Mount Cristo Rey, a barren rocky mountain bordered by the Rio Grande, usually waterless—the passageway by which *braceros* make their ways into the farms of Texas. At the top of the mountain is a giant Christ, an Indian Christ, looking down as the Border Patrol rounds up "illegals." Vast empty desert marked with cactuses. I climbed for hours, sweating. Once I climbed with a beautiful girl I was in love with. Was I? People said we resembled each other.

The beautiful girl who climbed with him was Julie Williams, a woman who became a major influence on his life and work, later recurring in a number of his novels as the "Barbara" character—the one heterosexual romantic interest of the male protagonist. In Julie, Rechy's narcissistic nature found the perfect mirror image. She was beautiful, and beauty Rechy understood. Beauty he could relate to. For awhile they became extremely close.

Julie was also a bohemian and rebellious. "Julie was a '60s person trapped in the '40s," remembers her friend Nancy Hamilton, who went on to become a journalist in El Paso. "She studied to be a bullfighter. Those were the times when girls wore garter belts for their stockings, short white gloves, and little hats to the many tea parties that went with being of the age where people were getting married and entertaining. Shorts and slacks were allowed to be worn by girls on campus only in physical education class."

Julie and John also related to each other because of their shared dislike for a parent. "Her mother was a very strange lady and drove Julie nuts," Hamilton remembers. "She'd put little notes everywhere reminding Julie to do things like 'turn off the lights when you leave a room.'" Julie's mother tried to control every detail of her daughter's life. One evening, when her mother arranged a date for her with a man she found boring, Julie sat on top of the refrigerator refusing to budge. When her date arrived he found Julie perched on the appliance. He sat there in the kitchen talking to her for a while before finally giving up and going home. Julie's mother fought back, though. When Rechy went to pick Julie up for a date, her mother, who was watering the lawn, tried to hose him down.

Rechy's relationship with Julie added to his aura of mystery and glamour. "The fellows I hung out with, the student journalists, were all crazy about Julie," Nancy Hamilton remembers.

Rechy first described his relationship with Julie when she made her initial appearance in *City of Night*—as two separate characters. In the opening chapter, like the narrator of the book, she is nameless, a beautiful girl he meets in college:

> I had only one friend: a wild-eyed girl who sometimes would climb the mountain with me. We were both 17, and I felt in her the same wordless unhappiness I felt within myself. We would walk and climb for hours without speaking. For a brief time I liked her intensely—without ever telling her. Yet I was beginning to feel, too, a remoteness toward people— more and more a craving for attention which I could not reciprocate: one sided, as if the need in me was so hungry that it couldnt share or give back in kind.

Later in *City of Night*, Julie returns in the guise of another character, this time as a friend of Rechy's protagonist, now a hustler in Los Angeles. In this section this Julie character is given a name. For the first time she is called Barbara. "With long ash-blond hair and hypnotic eyes. She always looked at you with a half-smile that was somehow wistful, as if for her the world, though sad, still amused her." As in real life, the two characters are drawn to each other by mutual loneliness and they spend quiet afternoons clinging to each other. In the book, before their love can turn into a full-fledged affair the character—no longer Julie—is made unreachable when she enters a lesbian lifestyle, reversing the real-life situation of John veering toward homosexuality. "Barbara dont need you guys any more... Shes got me," Barbara's female lover growls when the protagonist tries to see her.

During the same period that Rechy was spending a lot of time with Julie, he met Wilford Leach. Several years older than Rechy, Leach would later go on to become a prize-winning theater director. Rechy describes Leach and their relationship: "He was in the army and I was still in college. I often went to the public library, as I was still discovering new writers. I noticed Wilford looking at me—and he was there almost every time I was. I would then hurry out of the library. One night I was aware that he was following me. I let him catch up and his first words to me were, 'Are you a frustrated actor or a frustrated writer?' I said, 'I'm too young to be a frustrated anything.' 'Oh,' he said, 'some of the most frustrated people I know are young.'

"A very close friendship developed. This sounds crazy even to me now, but I wasn't aware that his main attraction to me was sexual. Well, maybe I knew, but it was that strange time for me. He became a most important part of my life. I showed him the novel I was again rewriting, *Pablo!* He gave me expert criticism. He was a kind of salvation for me, within the isolation of El Paso. He also introduced me to modern music."

Rechy introduced Leach to Julie, and Leach was immediately charmed by her; he called the two friends "Bobbsey Twins" and made plans to introduce the charismatic couple to a bigger arena, using their good looks as a conduit to success. Leach, while stationed in Texas, contacted the college, hoping to stage some productions there. He was already quite respected in the theater. He wanted John and Julie to star in his shows. He planned to direct *Dark of the Moon*, with John playing "The Witch Boy" and Julie portraying "Barbara Allen." He also wanted to do *Carousel* with

Julie and John in the leads. In Julie's apartment, he would rehearse them. "But I wasn't good at acting," Rechy remembers. "Only in real life! But Wilford said he'd coach me. Then my father got us a hall in a park for rehearsals. Julie would be doing ballet steps with a female friend. Wilford would be coaching me on acting."

However, Leach didn't get the assignment to direct locally, and then he was transferred. By now he had very deep feelings for John, which he longed to express. Rechy remembers, "The night before he left, he was—I know now—attempting to say something to me about his feelings. But I thwarted it. When he left I felt very lonesome, missed him very much. I was very depressed."

As for Rechy, his feelings for Julie were passionate and sexual, but conflicted. Yet, for a while, he imagined being married to her.

In *City of Night* Rechy re-creates a sexual experience that takes place one late afternoon, when, unable to wait any longer, the Julie/Barbara character seduces the protagonist in a boarded-up cabin. "But the discovery of sex with her, releasing as it had been, merely turned me further into myself." Whether sex occurred between Rechy and Julie in real life is a topic on which Rechy will not elaborate.

Either way, Rechy's relationship with Julie did nothing to alleviate his loneliness. As Rechy puts it, "Mutually we withdrew from each other."

Although Rechy was truly attracted to Julie, his attempt at a physical relationship with her was likely based on admiration, emotional connection, and an opportunity to "be" heterosexual. Perhaps it was to throw a blanket over what Wilford Leach was feeling for him. In those pre–gay pride days, homosexuality was still very much perceived as a perversion and sickness. Who wanted that? Better to be viewed as an elusive rebel. Well aware of the stigma, Rechy was thoroughly unwilling to explore the possibility of being homosexual.

So was John Rechy bisexual? In 1977 Rechy told the *Berkeley Barb* that he felt most bisexuals were cop-outs. "Bisexuality has become very chic and it's a subterfuge," he told the paper. "You say you're bisexual and then you don't have to say you're a homosexual. I think much of what is proclaimed bisexuality is not. And I object to it in part."

Nevertheless, for Rechy, expressing a physical attraction toward a woman was probably more than just an attempt to proclaim heterosexuality. Melodie Johnson Howe, one of several beautiful women Rechy surrounded himself with later in his life, says, "Unlike some homosexual men who never had sexual feelings for women, John always had just a little touch, and I think it confused him sometimes."

Rechy's close friend Marsha Kinder maintains that his attachment to his mother had at least a little to do with his failure to further his relationships with women, like Julie, early in his life. "It was hard for John to establish a romantically emotional attachment with any woman because that would be a threat to the loyalty to his mother," Kinder says. "He does talk about Julie in the early books, about a young woman that he was really attracted to. Whether his mother said it or he just internalized it and felt it, he felt that to pursue that relationship was a betrayal of his mother."

Regardless, Rechy continuously explored his feelings for Julie in his writing. In his novels, the Julie/Barbara character has come to represent the narrowly missed, unattainable heterosexual relationship that might have transformed him. In *City of Night*, when he attempts to look up the nameless girl upon returning home after his unfulfilling hustling experiences in New York and Los Angeles, he finds that she is now unattainable—gone away and married—just as in real life Julie won a fashion modeling award, married a "Marlon Brando type," and left town.

Meanwhile, Rechy's father was aging, ailing, and his behavior was more eccentric than ever. In the mornings Roberto hung around the courthouse, trying to get selected for jury duty so he could sit in court and enjoy the air conditioning. That was fine, it gave him something to do and got him away from the house.

But by the afternoon he was ogling pretty girls, following them lecherously down the street as they scurried away. Also, as he grew feebler, his personality softened. Perhaps because he regretted never getting to know the son who was, in so many ways, like him. "As difficult as it is to believe, my father gave me a typewriter," Rechy says. "He bought it for me! My ferocious father, that stranger, was acknowledging then, I suppose, that art would be for me, although it wasn't for him, a salvation."

By 1952 Rechy was beginning to feel smothered. There was nowhere in El Paso to go. The stain of his father was on everything, and John needed to develop his own identity. Rechy says that, while his siblings married very young, partially as a way to get away from their father, the only option he had, as he saw it, was to join the army. Yet he was torn. If he ran from his father, he'd also have to leave his mother.

One of Rechy's English teachers had offered to recommend him for a scholarship to Harvard. But Rechy did not feel ready for another academic experience. He needed something different to experience the personal growth he was longing for. So he volunteered to be drafted into the army. He told only his immediate family that he was going away. His goal was to begin completely anew, to wipe out all ties to his past, and so he destroyed most of his completed and incomplete manuscripts—the stories and poems he had been saving since childhood.

One of the few things he kept was his novel *Pablo!*, which by now had turned into a realistic fantasy—told by a narcissistic young narrator—about a beautiful woman who died. The story was based on Mayan legends. Rechy did a great deal of research on the sound patterns and symbolism of Mayan mythology. This unpublished novel—Rechy has since turned down offers to publish it—also foreshadows many themes that Rechy would explore in his mature novels: incest, religion, sex, fear of aging, and the desperate need to be desired. Pablo, like many of Rechy's later protagonists, is aware of his physical appeal, but here the idea of sexual gratification with any of his admirers repulses him:

> He had remembered, treasured, all the admiring furtive glances. But strangely he did not want any of these people who admired him, neither the young nor the old like the man with whom he stayed. Instead, he felt contempt, almost like revulsion for them, and yet he remembered every glance he received, every whisper, locking up these memories needfully, as a person stores food to keep from starvation.

In *Contemporary Authors* Rechy remembers the morning he left El Paso for the army:

> I get up early. My mother is already up. She has been crying. I hug her. My father is up, too! Is he crying? Yes, I remember it. He has just started to cry. We hadn't spoken to each other for months, locked silence replaced rage and curses.

Before John left, father and son looked at each other very hard, silent for a moment. Without the blinders of his hatred, John saw for the first time the broken old man his father had become—defeated, sad, crushed—and felt sympathy for him. Before John turned away, his father presented him with the ruby and gold ring he had given, then taken back from him years before.

This time Roberto did not take his ring back. He didn't have time and so never got the chance.

While in the army, it was his friend Wilford Leach to whom Rechy wrote almost constantly. When John was stationed in Kentucky at Camp Breckinridge, Leach came to visit him. There was no denying the erotic feelings from Leach, but Rechy still resisted. They spent a night together at a hotel, in separate beds. "This still baffles me," Rechy says in retrospect. "I suppose I was so expert at repressing these matters that I didn't grasp—or pretended not to grasp—his suggestions."

A few years later when Rechy was hustling in New York, he saw Leach again. But even then Rechy found it impossible to allow anything sexual to happen. Eventually Leach stopped wanting to have anything to do with him. Today Rechy understands how unready he was for any kind of abrupt initiation, but regrets having left so many feelings unspoken. "I continue to cherish him, to treasure him," he says of Leach. "I hope very much that I didn't hurt him. If I did, it was out of sheer stupidity and, I suppose, fear."

Rechy was stationed at Camp Breckenridge in Kentucky with the 101st Airborne Infantry Division. On November 22, 1952, Rechy's company was out doing physical tests, being told to do as many sit-ups as they could. Some of the soldiers, not in good shape, fell away quickly, others (like Rechy, of course) continued. John's combined spirit of fierce competition and egotism drove him to the point where he was the only one left doing the sit-ups. The sergeant in charge began counting aloud while everyone watched as Rechy passed a hundred and more. Then someone came from the orderly room saying that there was a message for John to call El Paso. His father had died. Rechy rushed home, borrowing money from the Red Cross because, like his brother Robert before him, he sent most of his army allotment to his mother and father.

The death of the man who had been such an ominous presence in his life did not free John from his lifelong oppression. The scars were too deep. "I went to the chapel where his body was laid out, and then beyond my control I started crying," Rechy says. "Because he was gone? I don't think so. I cried because there was no way now that I would ever experience having a father."

Rechy recorded his feelings about his father's death in *City of Night*:

And throughout the days that followed—and will follow forever—I will discover him in my memories, and hopelessly—through the infinite miles that separate life from death—try to understand his torture: in searching out the shape of my own.

In death Roberto remained to John as he was in life: a stranger. Many years later Rechy still looks back at his relationship with his father with a mixture of sadness and longing. "I regret that only hatred bound me and my father," he says. "I know his life must have been a nightmare, for him to lash out so brutally. I was cruel back to him, in later years. Could there have been another avenue taken? I do understand his pain now—all the loss—but I still cannot reconcile the cruelty, the years of unmitigated horror that he suffused with threats of violence. Still, I wish it might have been otherwise, while knowing that it couldn't have been."

If the death of his father added no relief to his own "torture," the army, also, did not quite provide the escape he had hoped for. Instead of finding freedom he found himself in the 101st Infantry Airborne Division surrounded by swaggering macho types seemingly devoid of sensitivity. Studying their blustering and stoic demeanor came in handy later on, though, when Rechy used some of those characteristics to create his own butch hustler image. But he despised the strict regimen of the army, the crassness and banality of its routines. Most of all he missed his life of creativity. Although he did sometimes manage to write in secret—mostly poems—he longed for the freedom to come and go as he pleased.

He was able to avoid some of the more unpleasant duties because of his intelligence. "I was very bright, and I was always trying to get out of army stuff—kitchen duty, guard duty. And it was my IQ that got me into this army school to teach in Germany. This was in Dachau, the site of the horrifying extermination of the Jews." Rechy wandered through the place and saw where the victims had left desperate messages. "I could only try to imagine what the actual horror had been like. That had a profound impact on my later life, politicizing me against all prejudice."

As students, they gave Rechy four soldiers who didn't know

how to write. "I was supposed to teach them to a fourth grade level in 10 weeks," Rechy says. "Impossible, of course. All the army cared about was getting it on the record, so I taught them how to write their names. But some of them got very involved with me, not sexually but emotionally, as you could imagine."

As he had in the past, Rechy dealt with his unhappiness over his environment by concentrating on his appearance. "I hated the army," he says. "But I was so attractive. I could dress up!" He even discovered tricks to convert the restrictive uniform code into a costume that made him feel more dazzling. "I was always trying to get out of the horrible army duties. I went in a private and came out a private. But I was the cutest thing. I never went in a planc to jump out or anything, but we inherited the goddamn uniform. And if anybody was made to wear the uniform it was me. I was always chosen to carry the flag. I was always the Colonel's orderly—that was the person who was chosen for looking really sharp and who got to spend the day with a Colonel traveling around in a jeep. It was the army's version of a kept boy. Only the best-looking got selected. And the uniform was terrific."

The men were allowed to blouse their pants over their boots. Soon John learned that if you tucked the pants in it would be no good, but if you bloused them over a rubber band it would look very attractive in a Hollywood sort of way. And he took advantage of the fact that his unit was allowed to wear scarves and caps. Caps were forbidden to be tilted, but John practiced till he found a way to wear his at an almost undetectable jaunty slant. And even though the soldiers were forbidden to have their jackets tailored, John went ahead and had his fitted to his 28-inch waist anyway.

In *The Miraculous Day of Amalia Gómez* Rechy used this memory of himself in the army when creating the strapping young soldier, Gabriel: "He wore a dashing blue scarf, allowed by his unit, and he bloused the pants of his uniform over cordovan-waxed boots. His shirts were tailored to fit his proud body, and he had eyes that looked greener because of his brown skin."

In spite of Rechy's natty appearance and cultivated manners, he managed to keep his sexuality deeply buried under his uniform. "I was in the army; people were constantly trying to come on to me without my knowing it." Even though the way he looked and what he projected screamed sex, Rechy kept his passions repressed. He had a habit—one he would continue through much of his life—of creating a very pervasive sexual atmosphere around him and then distancing himself from it.

For example, on a boat to Europe another private tried to come on to Rechy by hypnotizing him. Rechy's fear and avoidance prevented him from falling under the young man's spell. Then, in another attempt to draw Rechy out, the soldier wanted to play a game of association by giving Rechy words to unscramble. The letters he gave Rechy were YGA. As unbelievable as it seems, Rechy was unable to come up with the word *gay*. Rechy, a college graduate, sophisticated in language, played with the letters: YAG, YGA, all the while becoming more and more frustrated.

Rechy was still bogged down by the emotional baggage he dragged along with him from his childhood in El Paso. In a later novel, *The Coming of the Night*, Rechy has a character explain that discovering his homosexuality was like waking up into what he thought was a dream. And it was only a matter of time until Rechy, through a series of brief, close encounters, would experience his own awakening.

The first stirrings occurred during a leave in Paris. It was one of those budding sexual experiences when the universe conspires with you and everything falls into place. Rechy was wandering the Paris streets—"Alone. In the army I remained alone"—in love with the city, losing track of time, only to discover the trains stopped running at midnight. Yet he felt so at home in the dark Parisian streets that he didn't mind. Even the natives thought he was French, he blended in so well. He felt comfortable and was content to find his own way.

Then he turned a corner and walked into a dream.

Rechy found himself on St. Germain des Prés, past the Café de Flor, the famous outdoor cafe Jean-Paul Sartre had frequented. It was nearly 2 o'clock in the morning, and by then that block in Paris was occupied only by men. He walked down the block slowly, drifting. "There are very few things that I could say I remember as if I were there. Usually you've forgotten. But I can close my eyes and I see it: Everyone was in a slow motion dance and I fell into it." Through the years, this was a dance John Rechy would master.

That evening in Paris was the first time in his life that he was overtly and powerfully aware of the homosexual atmosphere, and there was no denying it was where he wanted to be. When a dark, attractive Frenchman approached, Rechy fell into easy conversation with him in French and Spanish. Before he could stop himself, he found himself inviting the stranger to his room.

Rechy's sexual feelings were ready to burst out, but his subconscious mind made one last ardent effort to keep them securely locked in. As he and the Frenchman continued to converse to the best of their ability, the atmosphere in Rechy's room became sensual and expectant. The stranger leaned in to Rechy, but when the Frenchman touched him Rechy's panic leaped forward.

"Listen," Rechy said suddenly. "You have to get out."

"Are you crazy?" the man asked in broken English. He was indignant. "I came all this way—and now you tell me to leave?"

"I'm sorry, but you have to go."

"What's the matter with you?"

"You, um...see...it's not you," Rechy stammered. "It's the woman downstairs. I'm pretty sure she saw me bringing you up here, and it's not allowed."

The man was furious, and rightfully so, but John finally managed to convince him that he could lose the room if the landlady found out he had a late-night guest.

Rechy managed to avoid that homosexual encounter, but it was becoming impossible for him to deny his desire for other men. This encounter didn't become muddled or buried; in fact, he viewed the entire incident clearly, and for the first time in his life he found no hidden excuses for the homoerotic experience except that he wanted it to happen. Suddenly he understood: The emotions he had struggled with all of his life—the loneliness, the isolation, and the fear—seemed to have an explanation. He had a name for it now; dare he think it? Naming it would not make it any less threatening, and he still didn't have the slightest idea how he would deal with it. The walls he had spent his lifetime putting up were too strong now to be brought down by a one-time near-miss with an attractive Frenchman. The notion of consensual sex with another man was unthinkable. He wanted it, yes, but he couldn't accept it in himself. Not yet. If male-to-male sex was inevitable for him, Rechy was going to have to find a different way to express it.

Still, the experience did make a tiny chink in Rechy's armor. With his new self-discovery, he could no longer stand to be in the close quarters of the army. He applied to, and was accepted by, Columbia University in New York for graduate work and was given an honorable discharge.

At Columbia, however, on the basis of his unpublished novel *Pablo!*, Pearl S. Buck, the Pulitzer Prize–winning author of *The Good Earth*, rejected him for her creative writing class. She didn't feel she could deal with his material. Ironically, years later Rechy was invited to teach that very class, though he didn't accept the offer.

John had a few free months before he had to be in New York to start school, but he avoided going home to El Paso. He didn't even know how to confront himself, let alone his family, with his confusing sexual awakening. He spent a few months in Dallas at a YMCA. There, with his desires a little closer to the surface, he engaged in a few fleeting flirtations with the Y's inhabitants, still always stopping short. Most days he sunbathed and just generally checked out the other men. He befriended a good-looking young man and spent a brief amount of time chatting in his room, but, once again, he pulled away before anything intimate could be initiated. Rechy then fled to Neiman Marcus, where he bought his sister a blouse.

It was time, he knew, to go home before moving on. This became a pattern he would follow for many years, leaving and returning, leaving and returning. "Always dreading the moment of separation," he says. Yet he knew leaving his mother this time was necessary. He had reached a point in his life where he needed complete freedom. Rechy remembers, "Leaving was the most difficult. When I left, she was crying, and so was I. I was haunted by her beautiful green eyes and the tears I was responsible for, and as I moved farther away I wasn't at all sure that I wouldn't turn back. But I didn't."

Something new was forming in him. He knew it. He felt it. "The Little Angel," "Juan Francisco," "Johnny" was about to turn into "John Rechy," and he realized there was no way he could fully explore his new personality in El Paso. His budding identity would not be able to survive in his repressive hometown, a place that had taught him life is cold and judgmental. And so, after a brief visit he left El Paso and headed for a bigger arena, to a city that promised to be more permissive and adventurous but was also notoriously dangerous. In streets without love, one of the most potent weapons can be beauty. John Rechy, armed with this weapon, headed for New York.

He was ready to begin.

PART TWO

EXPLORING NIGHT

CHAPTER FOUR

*I surrendered to the world of Times Square, and like a hype
who needs more and more junk to keep going, I haunted that
world not only at night now but in the mornings, the afternoons...*
—John Rechy, *City of Night*

*Southern California, which is shaped somewhat like a coffin,
is a giant sanatorium with flowers where people come to be
cured of life itself in whatever way...*
—John Rechy, *City of Night*

"I'LL GIVE YOU 10 BUCKS, and I don't give a damn for you."

That one sentence, muttered in 1954 to the 23-year-old John
Rechy on a Manhattan street corner, penetrated the tiny chink in
his emotional armor and released a torrent of sexual feelings that
had been pent up since childhood. The notion hit him as a sort of
answer: Take money for sex! This was a way to explore sexuality
without admitting—at least to himself—his homosexuality. It was
as if Rechy's subconscious declared, "Well, if I'm going to have gay
experiences, someone is going to have to pay for it."

Rechy was not alone in using prostitution as a way of denying
his homosexual feelings. In the 1950s homosexuality was still
regarded by the American Psychiatric Association as a mental illness. There was a great sense of confusion about being gay and

about what constituted "manliness." Hustling gave Rechy a sense of control over his masculinity. "You could keep a distance from yourself and your desire," he explains, looking back on his early experiences as a hustler.

Many hustlers believe that as long as there is money involved, they're not compromising their heterosexuality. For example, Jim Carroll, the celebrated author of *The Basketball Diaries*, at one time hustled men to support his heroin habit, a practice he called "perversion for profit." When asked if he considered himself gay, however, Carroll replied, "No matter how beautiful the guy was, I always asked for the money. That's how I knew I was straight." Even though Carroll sometimes recognized the beauty of the men he hustled, the money separated the sexual act from any desire he might have felt. Rechy's contemporaries, the hustlers he met and then wrote about in *City of Night*, shared this belief.

For Rechy, hustling was only the first phase of his coming out—a process he admits took him years to complete. His first major step was taken in New York City that very day he was first solicited. Years later, Rechy recalls the course of events that led him to that particular street corner.

"I landed in New York and a hurricane was threatening. I only had 20 bucks in my pocket. I asked a cop at the station where I could find a room, and he recommended the Sloan House YMCA.* At the Y, I met this merchant marine in the shower—a big, hairy, good-looking guy.

He invited me to his room and ended up buying me hamburgers which, you know, wasn't enough. He was trying to come on to me, and I wouldn't, so he started mentioning money. Actually he said, 'Too bad I didn't run into you last night, because if I had met you then, you wouldn't be broke now. I met a kid down at a bar in the Village last night and I laid 50 bucks on him. And you're much better looking than him.'"

---

*In the 1970s the musical group the Village People immortalized this encounter—re-created in *City of Night*—and paid homage to Rechy with their song "YMCA."

Rechy tried not to lose his composure, but the mention of money stirred in him an internal hurricane that rivaled the one threatening New York. The merchant marine realized the reason for the young man's excitement, so as Rechy made his hasty retreat he added, "If you want to make a few bucks, try Times Square."

City of Night has often been called an exposé of the homosexual underground. And an underground is exactly what the gay scene was in the 1950s and '60s. The gay areas were generally unknown to the general population, shadowy spots confined to a few blocks in selected areas of big cities. Times Square was one place where homosexuals could discreetly cruise out in the open. Young hustlers lolled on busy street corners, casting stares like nets into the sea.

Thanks to the merchant marine, Rechy discovered the notorious strip on 42nd Street between 7th and 8th avenues. In the 1950s the neighborhood was a chaotic combination of menace and passion, a concrete maze of tall grayish buildings, flashy arcades, sloppy-joe stands, tough bars, and run-down movie houses that, at night, doubled as motels for the homeless. Rechy was mesmerized by these tawdry city streets teeming and steaming with an extraordinary cast of characters. He looked deep into hundreds of diverse faces, each radiating traces of hunger and fear and sex, sex, sex—but always masked with a layer of tense indifference. Rechy noted the vagrants, jaded prostitutes, anxious junkies, drug pushers, and the occasional cop on the beat calmly twirling his nightstick. And every few minutes a new mob of pretty midtown secretaries and dark-suited businessmen swarmed up from the subway station, charging into the frantic milieu to become the new supporting cast in scenes that continually played out on the sidewalks.

The impact was powerful and immediate. Rechy knew he was home.

For Rechy—a repressed homosexual Catholic coming firstly from the moralistic El Paso and secondly from the rigid, homophobic subculture known as the U.S. Army—Times Square seemed to be an adults-only version of Oz, a fairy-tale kingdom whose lurid denizens roamed the streets. It was a kingdom he had never before dreamed of, but that immediately gave him the kind of power he had always hoped to possess. Rechy's physicality instantly brought him to the top of the field, a position from which he could call the shots.

Amid this disorder and confusion, as if by radar, Rechy zeroed in on the interactions between the young hoody-looking guys lingering on corners and the shifty, middle-aged businessmen. He observed the studied casualness, the secret sex signals, the eye contact, and the hurried conversations. And he watched as the unlikely couples slunk off together. Rechy was fascinated. More than just a way for him to explore his sexuality while affirming his physical value, the characters and situations of the hustling world would eventually give him the subject matter he had been searching for in order to express his unique and smoldering talent.

Yet even through his initial excitement, Rechy couldn't have imagined how much of his adult life would be played out within the backdrop of the secretive and sexually-charged atmosphere of these streets—and streets just like them all over the country; the hours and days and years he would spend on shadowy corners hunting with his eyes, even while being hunted.

"I was pulled into that world so quickly," he recalls. "As if I rehearsed it in dreams, acted it out—without remembering. There I was on the street, I looked around and I had been observing the hustlers only for a few moments when I assumed the stance. And I had been there a few minutes when a Mr. Klein came by and spoke the words embedded in my mind: 'I'll give you 10 bucks and I don't give a damn for you.' Those were the first words I heard hustling. And it was as if I had always been listening for those words, waiting all my life. Like waking up. It was extraordinary. My God, getting paid for sex! We got in a cab, which kind of set the tone, and he took me to dinner."

Rechy had already eaten the greasy hamburgers with the merchant marine back at the YMCA but, as he said, "that wasn't enough." Part of the appeal of being bought sexually was that he could assert his worth, and he self-assuredly did so on his very first experience. Seated at a good restaurant with Mr. Klein, Rechy made a point of ordering the most expensive steak on the menu. During dinner Rechy sat mostly silent as his mind astutely took notes on his first "john," the arrogant Mr. Klein—scrutinizing the way he looked, the way he spoke, almost as if he knew this momentous event in his life would later be documented. "He was a labor organizer," Rechy recalls. "He was a sturdy, masculine man. And he was a cocky son of a bitch. I admired him then, and I admire him now."

"Nobody pulls shit on me, boy," he told the young Rechy.

In *City of Night*, Rechy changed Mr. Klein's name, disguising him as "Mr. King." The narrator memorably describes what happened after dinner as the older gentleman attempts to seduce the novice hustler:

> "Why are you so nervous, aint you been with a cocksucker before?—that's what I am, pal and I aint ashamed of it." He got into a purple robe and I lay back and fix my eyes on a picture on the wall—rainclouds, a sad tree draped in something like moss—a skeleton vine, I think. If I squint, the tree looks like a shawled Mexican woman.

In spite of the distraction of the painting and the connotation of a "shawled Mexican woman," by this time the young hustler had traveled too far to turn back, and Mr. King/Klein manages to relax him enough to, at last, go through with the encounter. "I try to stop thinking.... I feel him touch my body—hesitantly at first, despite his bravado; and then more freely, intimately."

Rechy had been initiated. As he recounts in his first novel, hustler and client agree to meet again between the two concrete lions that guard the steps leading to the great Library on 42nd Street—an image Rechy found so striking he named a chapter "Between Two Lions." By then Rechy had come to see Manhattan as a concrete jungle and the cement lions as symbolizing the hungry predators who roamed the area—including Mr.

Klein and Rechy himself, carefully circling each other on rough city terrain.

On their second meeting, Mr. Klein slowly unraveled, revealing the broken, lonely middle-aged man his "I don't give a damn" exterior concealed. Taken with Rechy's naïveté, Mr. Klein began to wonder whether a relationship with the handsome youth might be a way to end his addiction to the streets and a revolving door of boys who didn't give a damn for *him*. By acquiring a boy—not yet jaded—for his very own, Klein could once and for all give up cruising the Times Square streets, streets he felt had swallowed him. After another meeting, he asked Rechy to live with him. According to the version Rechy provides in *City of Night*, Klein/King muttered, "I—uh—kinda—like you," and went on to explain that the unnamed hustler can even sleep in a separate bed. "I won't bother you," he added, "except sometimes."

At this point in his journey, however, the young hustler is far from ready for intimacy without the separating factor of money. "Two needs of my time then," Rechy wrote in *Contemporary Authors*, were "to be desired powerfully and not to be expected to care." Mr. Klein had crossed a line when he started to want Rechy to care. The next time they were set to meet Rechy stood Klein up—leaving him hungrily waiting between the two lions at the library.

Both men had been playing roles, but Rechy clearly saw in Klein the sad combination of pride, weakness, and lust. "I was very aware of his pain every minute that I was with him," Rechy says. "And I couldn't stand it sometimes. At the time I probably thought that I didn't want to get involved with somebody that much. I simply saw that this man was so vulnerable and that he wanted from me something that I would not be able to give him. So I pulled away rather than proceed to act on false expectations."

After that first day, Rechy quickly mastered what did and didn't sell on the streets. He discovered that what the men paying for sex usually wanted was the unattainable. The most valued qualities were masculinity and mystery. They wanted their boys to be dumb, uneducated sex objects, like the neighborhood ruffians of their childhood or the aggressive jocks from high school. As a result, Rechy learned to hide his complicated psychology behind an austere and impenetrable facade. How easy it was to become someone else. "My voice would change, my posture would change, my accent would become tougher," he remembers. "It was a performance, and a good one. I came to feel that I was what I appeared to be at any set time. My appearance changed radically from encounter to encounter. My age, younger—I perceived signals, and I became what they wanted. I see this—and it fascinates and bewilders me—in photographs of me taken during the same session, that I could look different from moment to moment, depending on signals given."

Although he was nearly 24, Rechy looked years younger. Many mistook him for a teenager, which made him all the more desirable. But it was Rechy's inscrutable toughness, his aloof apathy that made him such a hot commodity on the streets and that allowed him to survive from season to season with the ever-changing crop of boys.

With John there was never the slightest hint that the act was exchanged for any reason other than money. As he expertly transformed himself into the fantasy, he kept his past, his ambitions, his true character a secret. No matter what he felt for his clients, he remained absolutely detached. Otherwise the fantasy he created could be broken in an instant. This was a lesson he had learned very quickly. Once he went home with a client and, as the man undressed, Rechy leafed through a novel by Colette. "You read?" the man asked incredulously. When Rechy admitted that, yes, he did read on occasion, the john gave him a fiver and told him to leave.

Rechy grew adept at playing straight. When he was still hustling in his 30s he told a reporter, "In hustling, I'm often picked up by someone who wants me to be straight and I get the message right away. If the person asks, for example, 'Have you been married?' then I get the signals. And not only will I say yes, which is not true, but I will elaborate on it and say I'm separated and now living with my girlfriend somewhere."

When he was just starting out, however, the paradox was that, although he quickly and easily assumed the tough-guy exterior, on the inside he was the sensitive boy from El Paso, very much the inexperienced prostitute with the heart of gold.

Early in his hustling career, perhaps the second or third time he made himself available, a gentleman approached him and asked, "Just one thing, how big is your cock?" John was utterly baffled by the question. "I didn't know that there was much of a difference in the size and shape of cocks in different men," Rechy says. "I guess he saw the confusion on my face, and so he said, 'You don't have one of these tiny cocks, do you?' The concept of big or small cocks confused me. I said, 'Wait a second. I don't understand. I swear to God I don't understand.' Here I was hustling and I didn't realize that size mattered. I suppose one of the reasons for my bafflement was that I hadn't really been looking at other cocks. I did go with that man, though, and he wasn't disappointed, I'm very pleased to say."

But like a beginner artist yearning to become a master painter, John Rechy continued to learn. He could live out a private life now and, for the first time, was accountable to no one. "I just loved everything about hustling," he says. Often he would return to the streets in the mornings and afternoons.

To satisfy his appetite for culture, John took advantage of New York's museums and especially the theater. He saw Bert Lahr in *Waiting for Godot*, Siobon McKenna in *Saint Joan*, Julie Harris in *The Lark*, Ben Gazzara and Barbara Bel Geddes in *Cat on a Hot Tin Roof*, Tallulah Bankhead in *A Streetcar Named Desire*, and Eartha Kitt in Capote's *House of Flowers*. He also attended ballet and modern dance performances—Martha Graham, and Pearl Lang in *Letter to the World*. "I always went alone," Rechy says, "because that was another life."

Although he haunted the museums and the theaters, he was particularly enthralled by the secret experiences, the little-known adventures that developed on street corners and to which most of the busy inhabitants passing by were totally oblivious. He loved every encounter the streets brought him—each challenge, inconsistency, and possibility. But with every trick there was always a sadness that he quickly pushed away as soon as another opportunity came along.

Some of Rechy's friends contend that he was never a true hustler because although he took the money, it was never an act of need: "We're talking about a guy who was selective," a long-time acquaintance observed. "I think John was more interested in who was approaching him than he was about making money. We use the word hustler, but he wasn't a true hustler. There's something buried deep in him that made him do that. And being a talented and creative person, he turned it into a style, a way of being, a way of thinking."

Rechy, despite the fact that he was having contact with different men daily, didn't go crazy in exploring his sexuality. What he would do was extremely limited. He found most of his sexual fulfillment in the standing around and waiting—the hunt followed by the conquest—rather than the act itself. As he revealed in a 1999 interview (with the author):

Q: What exactly did sex entail for a hustler in New York? I mean what did you do?
J.R.: Now, listen, I can only answer for myself because the street is rife with stories and postures. Who knows other than the persons involved? We all have to pretend certain things. At that time hustlers were supposed to be straight. Obvious nonsense. We pretended that to each other. This incredible subterfuge. Myself, in hustling situations, I was always known at the time as "trade." And I'm very proud to tell you I was very honest about it. When I discovered that people had other desires I became extremely honest about what would be involved.

Well, let me give you an example of how naive I am. Trade? Does that mean that men would pay to give you blow jobs?
Right. But this was not just me. This was a vast part of hustling in the day. There were some people who would actually say, "Now, you're not going to touch me, are you?"

Would you give a blow job for money?
No.

Would you fuck someone?
No.

Would you kiss?
No.

So the only thing you did was get a blow job?
That's all.

And people paid for that?
That's right.

Did you enjoy it? Did you enjoy the actual sex as well as the chase?
The subterfuge was supposed to be that hustlers didn't enjoy the sex. That's nonsense. I delighted in it. The fact of the matter is, I loved the attention on my body. I loved that. Now remember we're talking about hustling—not when I was cruising later in life and money wasn't involved. Then the strictures were not as rigid.

But that was pretty much your sex life?
That was my sex life at the time. That was my sex life. Remember it was the same for other butch hustlers, not just me. Every now and then I'd go into a movie theater and do it for free, but my sexuality would still be the same.

How many tricks would you do for a night in Times Square?
I never went for multiple numbers a night. Because, do
remember, with me it never really was about making the
money. The money was a thrill, sure. But it was never, "God,
I gotta go now and make a buck."

So after you scored you would leave, that was it?
I'm sure that I'd go back as many as three times now and
then. But mostly whatever it was I needed had been satisfied. I would very often carry the money in my pocket and
not spend it.

Rechy instilled some of his own attitudes and experiences in
the hustler character, Nick, in his novel *The Coming of the Night*:

The guy lowered his own pants and Nick looked away from
the flabby flesh, shut his eyes. He preferred it when old
guys didn't even take off their clothes, man.
He felt the man's cock poking at his ass.
Nick's eyes flashed open. He pushed the man away.
"What the hell? I told you I don't get fucked."
"What do you do?"
"Didn'ya hear me out there? I told you all I do is get
blown. Now you go ahead and blow me."
"Shit. And what do I get?"
"You get to suck my dick. I told you out there, man.
Didn'ya hear me? You can jerk off while you blow me. Go
ahead now, blow me—that's all, just fuckin' blow me."
The man's head bent down and sucked Nick's cock.

This is not to say that Rechy was always successful selling his
limited bag of sexual tricks. Some men rejected him for his lack of
versatility. "That's all you do?" one offended man asked. When
Rechy replied, yes, that was it, the irate man snarled, "Why don't
you go home, fuck yourself, and pay yourself generously."

For the egotistical hustler there was also the extreme pain of not being desirable at all times. Rechy remembers, "There are for all hustlers, as there were for me, those nights when nothing, nothing works. When you move from one proposed encounter to another and it all fails—signals go off, expectations and otherwise, amount of money not agreed upon, then another possibility and that doesn't work either. Those are the nightmare nights. No matter how great-looking or sexy you are, times when you're not on the line, your whole stance is on the line. You become desperate, reckless. No one is ever immune in that world. Those times are the worst—hustling or cruising—end when it's beginning to dawn and yet not one single connection has worked out."

In spite of the drawbacks, hustling continued to be an essential element of his life's blood; he needed to sell his "self" in order to explore, to grow, and to be sexual.

As he went along in New York, Rechy recorded in his mind the "nightworld" he discovered, later transforming into literature the sad and eccentric characters he would immortalize in the early sections of *City of Night*. Characters like Pete, the cocksure hustler outfitted with his army fatigue cap, pulled down low to his eyes, and a baggy army jacket, swaggering up and down Times Square calling everyone "sport," or "spote" as he pronounces it.

Rechy and Pete would meet casually on the Times Square sidewalks and swap hustling stories. Sometimes the two young hustlers would share a trick. Rechy re-created their dual hustling experiences a few years later in *City of Night*. Scenes like the one with the effeminate elderly man whose particular kink was to become the two young men's doting mother in a bizarre role-play. In the book, Pete and the nameless protagonist ride the subway to Queens to the man's fussy little apartment where he cooks them dinner, watches over them as they nap, and raptly observes them as they play a naked game of checkers.

Scenes like this in *City of Night* followed real life as closely as memory would allow. Rechy reveals, "When Pete and I played out that scene with the man who wanted to be our mother, there was a real excitement in the air between the two of us. It was incredibly erotic; we were getting paid and we were lying there without any clothes on." This gave the two young men—who played "straight" on the streets—an opportunity to avidly observe each other. But the attraction the two young men felt for each other had to remain unspoken. The payment from the nelly mama acted as the perfect smoke screen for their desire. To show lust for each other would have broken the rules of the game—their fantasy of themselves as well as the older man's fantasy of what they were.

The hustler "Pete" in *City of Night* was in real life also named Pete. Rechy did not change the young man's name when he came to write about him, although he did soften his character by combining memories of the real Pete with those of another hustler who had refined his street toughness to a classier image. The result is a memorable character who projects a snappy, wise-ass charm as a subterfuge for concealed yearnings. Rechy and the real Pete formed a cautious friendship. There was a definite physical attraction between the two young men, but their chosen roles at the time prevented any tenderness. They hid their feelings with a blasé hipster demeanor.

However, like Mr. Klein, Pete recognized that there was something hidden in John, something receptive and mysterious that separated him from the other hustlers. This delicate something led Pete to believe that a more serious relationship with Rechy might be his salvation. For his part, Rechy was surprised to discover that under Pete's bravado, he hid a desire for compassion and acceptance.

Rechy remembers an exchange that he did not write about in *City of Night*: "Once Pete was walking along the Broadway strip with me, and there was a line before the box office of a play; several men looked at us. Pete said to me, 'You think they're looking at us and knowing?' I didn't understand exactly what he meant and didn't ask. 'Knowing' that we were hustlers? Or, 'knowing'—or suspecting—that we were a couple?"

Rechy did, however, document an encounter between him and Pete that actually took place in John's bedroom. (Gore Vidal wrote to Rechy, stating that this passage was his favorite in *City of Night*, and it remains one of Rechy's favorites as well.) Up to this point in the book, both characters have been relating to each other's masks; now, in the narrator's seedy apartment, they face each other, raw and uncertain. In the achingly tender scene, Pete for once drops his jaunty facade and makes a veiled plea for normalcy and love:

> "maybe—you know—I was just thinking—shacking up with another guy for a while—we could hustle together, really make the scores. It wouldnt be hard: I know lots of scores. Theyd stop digging me; dig you; so on—I mean, whoever it was, we would keep going like that.... I was even thinking— Christ—well—that fuckin street—it bugs me—sometimes I get nightmares about those toilets—I mean, all those fags—and—well—if I got a job, even—and split the rent with someone—well—"

In the grubby, cramped room one can feel the agitated loneliness, the claustrophobic despair, the fear and longing in this young boy, unable to verbalize his desires. Of course, in a flash of panic the protagonist abruptly stops short Pete's confession by exclaiming, "It's after midnight."

This prompts Pete to blurt out urgently, "Can I spend the night here?"

Although, by now, the protagonist has learned to speak the street vernacular and to interact in an untouchable manner, underneath he is still the compassionate little boy who wanted to please his father and who couldn't stand to see his mother swat flies. Rechy, both as the unnamed narrator and in real life, was truly frightened of what might happen if he and Pete spent the night together. If sex transpired without payment they'd be forced to admit what they were—not only to themselves, but to each other.

Yet, ultimately, Rechy responded to Pete's pain and agreed to let his friend stay the night.

The two young hustlers spent the evening together fitfully on opposite corners of a tiny bed. And when Pete gave in to his feelings and tentatively reached for Rechy's hand in the dark, whatever intimacy they felt for each other was shattered under the crushing weight of physical contact. In Pete's frightening grip, their budding attraction was immediately strangled. They both jumped out of bed and fled the apartment in opposite directions. For a short while after, the friendship lingered briefly in ruins, but eventually the two hustlers started avoiding each other.

As Rechy saw it, everyone he interacted with in his dark terrain experienced moments of frightening isolation and loneliness. Undercurrents of these feelings lie hidden beneath the Teflon exteriors of all of the characters in *City of Night*, flowing along with them as the characters drift through the underground searching for some sort of emotional connection—only to reel back terrified and frozen when it is presented.

The real-life Rechy was determined not to show his own sadness. He kept his true self separate from the people he encountered in his "nightworld" the same way he remained apart from others in school and in the army—by quietly passing by without becoming an integral part of their lives. At times he would have liked to become more involved with the people he met, but the persona he had created would not allow it. He had to keep his distance. That was one of the tricks of his trade. John Rechy was neither cold nor unfeeling; but the character he was playing was.

Whenever John felt himself becoming too sucked in by the streets, he pulled away slightly and led a split life. Sometimes, to keep one hand in the real world, he would take a day job. For a while he worked writing press releases for a group called the American Heritage Foundation that sponsored the Crusade for Freedom. He quit when he found out they were an extreme right-wing organization. He also did some temporary work through agencies, sometimes writing legal briefs. (Rechy received some training in the army when he was sent to court-reporting school to record courts-martial.)

Taking a day job now and then afforded Rechy some protection. While his outcast contemporaries were forced to do their high-wire act without a safety net, Rechy knew he could always escape the streets and make a living elsewhere. Usually, what he earned from his day jobs he sent to his mother. Out of respect, though, Rechy never gave Guadalupe any of the money he made as a hustler.

If one of Rechy's jobs did not allow him to come dressed in character, he'd leave for the office in the mornings in dress clothes carrying a satchel with his street attire. After work he'd change in the subway bathrooms into his standard jeans and T-shirt, ready for the streets.

There were, however, times when his two lives collided. Like the day Julie Williams, his college love-interest, ran into him on the sidewalk. Julie was coming out of a movie theater with a date when she spotted Rechy on the corner. They exclaimed and embraced, but Julie quickly hurried along. She was hip enough to realize Rechy was hustling.

After a time the few blocks that make up Times Square began to look smaller and smaller. Once a hustler worked those streets for only a few weeks, he was already considered a regular, causing his value to go down because, by then, a new supply of fresh meat had arrived, eager and ready and wrapped in the excitement of newness. For Rechy, the people and experiences that seemed so exciting a short time before quickly became tired. When faces started blending together and he couldn't remember whom he had talked to, whom he had been with, or whom he simply recognized from the neighborhood, Rechy knew that, at least for a while, his time in Manhattan was coming to an end.

Rechy left New York and headed back to his mother in El Paso, continuing his pattern of a remarkable adventure followed by a brief return to safe territory for rest and reflection. This time, however, he was instantly struck by the changes—in himself and the city. Everything was different now—smaller, less interesting. After only a few nights in his hometown he allowed himself to be picked up for $10 by a stranger in the men's room of a local movie theater, something that would have been unthinkable in El Paso a few months before. The resulting guilt made him vow to keep his two lives completely separate whenever he was in El Paso—a promise he would not keep. For now, though, he knew he wouldn't stay long.

While he was there, he concentrated on family and on putting to rest some past obligations. He and his mother chose a marble tombstone to replace the plain marker on his father's grave, and a few days later Rechy visited the cemetery alone. "Within that ground, his body had decayed," Rechy writes in *City of Night*. "He lived only in my thoughts of him." Thoughts of death led to thoughts of things lost. In an account that occurs in *City of Night* and that Rechy confirms really happened, he went to look at his old neighborhood to see the house he grew up in. It had all changed. He tried to look in the backyard where his beloved dog Winnie's remains were long before buried, but a fence blocked his view. This fed into Rechy's obsession: Things change; things die. These thoughts of loss mingled with the memory of the recent short interludes with his hustling contacts back in New York. The memory of them burned in him. "Do they also remember me?" he wondered. Rechy wanted things locked in time. He not only wanted to be remembered, he wanted the people who had touched him in his journey toward himself to also be remembered.

• • •

Rechy found an extension of the underground "nightworld" he had discovered in Times Square in the streets and bars and parks of Los Angeles—especially downtown. And he discovered a new source of inspiration when he came into contact with the flamboyant drag queens of that city. In Rechy's eyes these coy, flouncing young boys in makeup and ruffles were not unlike the heroines from Tennessee Williams's plays. Sometimes comic, sometimes tragic, always entertaining, they lived in a make-believe world of dreams and illusions.

In the '50s and '60s, for a man to dress up as a woman or to be "masquerading," as it was called then, was illegal. Observing the drag queens in downtown Los Angeles bars, Rechy recognized a tragic nobility in these social outcasts. "They were defiant and brave," he says. In *POPism: The Warhol '60s*, Andy Warhol has noted that drag queens weren't even accepted in freak circles until 1967. Yet, even before then, they were determined to be themselves, do their thing, always with the very real possibility of being arrested hanging over them. As one denizen of this outcast society would remember: "Part of the purpose of our conduct and dress was to force our personalities as far into the faces of the rest of the world as we possibly can. We say, 'Take us or leave us.' In a way our position is more manly than that of any other part of the male homosexual population. Wouldn't you think that we would gain some respect from this open stand?"

Rechy would go to the bars specifically to observe the drag queens. The dramatics of it all appealed to him. The queens would come to the bar and pause theatrically at the door in some sort of unisex outfit. They'd squint into the smoke-filled darkness scanning for undercover cops. If all was safe, an amazing transformation would take place. Collars would fly up, shirts tied above the navel, pants rolled up toreador style, and—with one brazen swipe of a lipstick—mouths crimsoned. Thus transformed, the queens would sashay into the bar to hoots and catcalls of approval from the stud hustlers.

But if the atmosphere was not dangerous when a drag queen first arrived, it didn't always stay safe. Even as far back as the late 1950s, Rechy witnessed many riots between police and drag queens. The danger presented itself not only in the clubs but sometimes in the after-hours hangouts. One late night at Cooper's Doughnuts in downtown L.A., a rumor quickly swept through the shop that the place was going to be raided. Everybody pushed chairs against the doors to keep the cops out, and when they did arrive the colorful patrons put up a fight, throwing doughnuts and screeching. After such incidents, headlines would scream, "Queers Busted!"

"Stonewall, as wonderful as it was, wasn't really the beginning," Rechy says.

One of the most extraordinary and touching drag queens Rechy met in L.A. was a 23-year-old cross-dresser who had been raised in a mining camp. At the age of 6 the young boy moved to California with his parents, which is when he started dressing in his mother's clothes—unable to understand why his mother continued to dress him as a boy. (Today this individual might be classified as transgendered rather than as a drag queen.) Hoping for understanding and love, at an early age he decided to come out to his parents. Predictably for the times, they rejected him. "This is a pain that is most devastating," he would say. "I wanted my parents to love me, and I had hoped that we could be friends."

The boy grew up to become a sad and lonely creature who covered her torment with a hyperactive energy, rapid-fire chatter, and a caustic wit sharpened in Pershing Square—a park in downtown Los Angeles.

Pershing Square, like Times Square, squeezed together an amazing assortment of bizarre inhabitants. Preachers mixed freely with winos, tough chicks, and transitory male hustlers. And, of course, the queens—dressed as femininely as they could get away with in public. This young person immediately found a home among the other societal misfits. Unlike Rechy, who masked his true self with the tough-guy garb of jeans and T-shirts, she costumed herself as a coquettish woman and called her transformed persona "Miss Destiny."

Miss Destiny! Miss Destiny! The fabulous Miss Destiny! With her quick quips and her flamboyant mannerisms, laughing giddily one moment, crying in despair the next, quoting and misquoting

Shakespeare, talking—nonstop—of her yearnings and burnings, dreaming of the day she will fulfill her life's greatest ambition: to be a beautiful bride at her own fabulous wedding. Miss Destiny's destiny, though, was to become Rechy's tragicomic muse and one of the most memorable characters in *City of Night*.

Rechy had his first encounter with Destiny in Pershing Square Park, a setting that would later feed a wealth of material into Rechy's imagination.* "Pershing Square," Miss Destiny once said, "is the meeting place of all those who have somehow emancipated themselves from the straitjacket of conventional behavior. Most of us who hang in and around this tiny square in L.A., whether hetero or homo, are considered crackpots. You many not believe it, but most Pershing Square characters are rather simple, defenseless persons. We say what we feel at any moment, even when we know it is against our interests. Naturally where you have such naïveté you also have the exploiters."

Rechy—one of those who had emancipated himself from the straitjacket of conventional behavior—was sitting on a bench in Pershing Square with another hustler, the cowboy stud Chuck (who became a major character in *City of Night*), when Miss Destiny came sashaying down the path, outshining everyone. Even in Pershing Square she stood out. Rechy vividly describes her entrance (for, as he informs us, drag queens always refer to themselves as female):

Indeed, indeed! here comes Miss Destiny! fluttering out of the shadows into the dimlights along the ledges like a giant firefly—flirting, calling out to everyone: "Hello, darling, I love you—I love you too, dear—so very much—ummmm!" Kisses flung recklessly into the wind... Now Miss Destiny is a youngman possibly 20 but quite as possibly 18 and very probably 25, with false I.D. like everyone else in case she is underage: a slim young queen with masses and masses of

*Although, through all these experiences, Rechy says, "I had no intention of writing about them. In private when I wrote, they were stories that had no relation whatsoever to that world. I was living on the streets. Never, while I was there, did I consider writing about them."

curly red hair (which she fondly calls her "rair"), oh, and it tumbles gaily over a pale skinny face almost smothering it at times. Unpredictably occasionally she comes on with crazy Southern sounds cultivated, you will learn, all the way from northern Pennsylvania.

Unlike most of the other characters in *City of Night*, Miss Destiny is educated. She has actually been to college, where she naturally studied drama. More literate than the queens and studs surrounding her, when she makes a comment she believes is out of their league, she explains it for them via a rapid aside, for example: "That's from Shakespeare, my dears—a very great writer who wrote ladies' roles for drag queens in his time."

It is Miss Destiny who, like some demented social director for eccentrics, introduced Rechy to the array of characters he celebrated in the Los Angeles chapters of *City of Night*.

Unlike his New York period, during which time Rechy quickly removed himself from the characters who came crashing into his life, in Los Angeles he actually became a part of an outcast group of hustlers and drag queens, however peripherally. He'd have chance encounters with them in darkened bars, or on a park bench some late lazy afternoon, and they would tell him their stories. This was unlimited fuel for the fire in his imagination. The ones he became closest with had their peculiar personalities documented in *City of Night*.

The hustlers, like Chuck and Tiger and Skipper, played the role of the tough male stud. Like Rechy, they felt that to receive blow jobs from men did not compromise their heterosexuality as long as they got paid. In contrast, there was Darling Dolly Dane, Lola, and Trudi.* The stud hustlers often took advantage of the queens. Miss Destiny explains:

The male hustler, rough or otherwise, needs a gullible, generous-natured person to prey upon, and the queen

---

*Trudi later enjoyed brief notoriety as one of the first publicized transsexuals in the United States, appearing in the pages of *Tattler* magazine.

who wants to believe in dreamy things like love—in fact wants desperately to be loved—is the hustler's easy and repeated victim. The hustler is one of those strange and pitiful creatures who cannot easily make out sexually. Somehow he is not adequate to the male role with a woman and, on the other hand, he is not able to stand up to the terrible competition and demand required for sex with another man. The homosexual who has no doubts about his masculinity usually demands as much maleness from his sexual partners as does any woman—maybe more. The hustler suspects he is a failure in this department. And although he keeps his secret well, he turns toward the easy marks, and the queen is the one person who will treat him like a man. After all, the queen wants to believe she is getting a "real man" (a heterosexual to her way of thinking) in bed. This, in turn, makes the queen feel that much more feminine. So she plays the game.

The brooding narrator of *City of Night*, however, stays away from this kind of role playing, even when Miss Destiny pleads, "Marry me please, dear."

When *City of Night* came out a few years later, Miss Destiny was one of the few characters from Rechy's world who actually read the book, recognized herself (How could she not? So striking was her personality that Rechy didn't even change her name.) and cashed in on her 15 minutes of fame by giving a cover interview to the gay magazine *One*.

The interview stands as a testament to Rechy's powers of observation and description. Miss Destiny, documented by a journalist for *One*, comes across very much like her fictional self as re-created by John Rechy. As she speaks a steady stream of consciousness, her words could easily fit into any of Miss Destiny's monologues in *City of Night*. Her observation skills seem to be as sharp as John Rechy's. During the interview she turns the tables and describes Rechy and the other hustlers she hung out with:

> The male hustlers are a peculiar breed of the homosexual even more difficult to diagnose than the queen...By selling himself, he protects the feeling of sexual normality so dear to his self-esteem, while he has the pleasure of having sex with another man...If you will recall, John Rechy in *City of Night* tries to make out that the studs go out with the young chicks once in awhile to prove their masculinity. Nothing could be farther than the truth. The hustlers are even afraid of the Main Street floozies. If they do make out it is *usually* with one of the freak girls who can't do better. The *City of Night* hustlers—Skipper, Buddy, and Chuck, and even Rechy himself—have not likely been to bed with a woman in their lives...When I first saw Rechy he looked butch. He wore blue jeans; for the year that he hung around he never wore anything else. And he was kind of cute with lots of curly light brown hair. Of course, like the rest pulling the butch act, he tried to make like a man, and, of course, I loved it because that was exactly what I wanted to see in him.

When the *One* interview came out in 1964 Rechy was furious with Miss Destiny—although when confronted with a ragged copy of *One* magazine years later Rechy exclaimed, "Brava, Miss Destiny!"

Rechy was already extremely vulnerable about aging, and Los Angeles, a city where a person's value is almost exclusively based on youthful good looks, heightened his awareness of the cruelty of lost youth. In *City of Night* Rechy had one character express the collective L.A. attitude to a hustler:

> "You're too old for me anyway," he said. "I prefer them very young and very, very dumb, dear...In their 20s, they've already been had too often—and in too many ways.

Living on the outskirts of the Hollywood scene, Rechy encountered an assortment of male characters who had once been highly desirable but were by then fading. In writing about the wannabe actors, dancers, and models he befriended, Rechy found perfect expression for his terror of growing older. Men like the character Rechy ultimately called "Lance O'Hara."

Rechy had a brief fling with the real-life man behind the Lance character, a man notorious in Hollywood's homosexual circles. In the book, Lance is an aging "great beauty," a one-time minor actor in the movies, and a legend in the homosexual show business world. Rechy first heard the story of Lance through bits and pieces of gossip passed around in bars and clubs by the catty chorus boys and extras who existed on the show-business sidelines. These fringe players had once envied the young beauty's desirability; now they hungrily awaited his downfall.

Rechy learned that years before, during Lance's acting career, he had become the obsession of a very rich, very old, very effeminate man—skinny, bony, with cheeks that "looked like caves." In the book he is scornfully called "Esmeralda Drake the Third," a name Lance himself came up with, ridiculing the old man for his prissy appearance and mannerisms. The elderly gent begged Lance to live with him and Lance agreed, but only if Esmeralda signed over his lavish house to him. The wealthy admirer eagerly agreed. Lance then threw a party in "his" new house and in front of the guests, astonishingly, ordered Esmeralda, "Get out of my house. I don't ever want to see you here again." With that, Lance cruelly left the old man banging the door all night with his cane. Years later, the fading Lance, wracked with guilt over his treatment of Esmeralda, is obsessed with a young hustler named Dean, who treats the great Lance scornfully, giving him a bitter taste of his own medicine.

When Rechy wrote about his two-day fling with Lance, he framed the story as a Greek tragedy with a chorus of gossiping gay men foretelling Lance's downfall and the revenge of Esmeralda Drake. But when it came to ending the chapter, Rechy couldn't bear to have Lance come to a tragic end as true modern psychology dictates. Having a fading beauty totally degraded and ruined was too upsetting for Rechy to endure, even in fiction—so he allowed Lance to save his dignity. Real life was not as kind.

Rechy says, "Years later, after *City of Night* and *Numbers* had come out, I was back on the scene hitchhiking. Without remembering me Lance picked me up again, and I went home with him. It was a very sad experience because by then he had aged badly and was not living in the beautiful place he had been before, although perhaps he kept the lesser place for his casual encounters. I hope so."

As disturbed as Rechy was by faded beauties like Lance, it is with the sad character of Skipper that he found the ideal model to personify his fear of aging. There was a real Skipper hanging around the scene in the late '50s, but when Rechy came to write about him for *City of Night*, Skipper became a symbol of the lost dreams of every used up young man like him. Ultimately Rechy combined a number of aging hopefuls he had actually met in and around Hollywood into that one character. In the chapter titled "A Very Beautiful Boy," Skipper is portrayed as a grim and wasted creature with his best years behind him. Although by normal standards he'd still be considered a young man, a mean-spirited bystander observes cattily, "I bet he's over thirty," and later adds, "I could have had him when he was Young and Pretty." And Rechy capitalizes "Young" and "Pretty" to be sure the reader is aware of the importance of these qualities.

With the persona of Skipper, Rechy accurately and poignantly captures the cruel lure of Hollywood and its effect on the thousands of confident young people who come to Los Angeles each year, equipped with pretty faces, hard bodies, and dreams of movie stardom as an escape from the mediocrity of their simple hometowns. Each one is sure that *he* is the one who will beat the odds. Often in this scene the hopefuls are given a few false starts and thrown enough crumbs by important people in return for sex to make them believe they're on their way—only to be tossed aside when the next desirable shipment arrives the following year.

In *City of Night*, the character of Skipper is discovered by a photographer. The photographer is based on Bob Mizer, a popular physique photographer of the day who created and published *Athletic Model Guild*, a soft-core body magazine that showcased beefcake shots ostensibly for fitness buffs and weight training enthusiasts but really for gay men.

Rechy himself was photographed by Mizer. Always ready for new forums to show off his body, he readily agreed to be photographed in various stages of elaborate undress. "It was hilarious to go into his studio off Wilshire Boulevard," Rechy recalls. "He liked to photograph us in extremely exotic settings; so it was like entering into a whole other world. His place had a Hawaiian setting; there were Greek settings, jungle settings. One day you might get handed a helmet and all of a sudden you were a Greek warrior. He also made these soft-core movies with guys in jockstraps. Very tame by today's standards."

Mizer also acted as a sort of Hollywood pimp, bringing young studs to the older gentlemen who coveted them. He had a clientele of affluent amateur photographers who would come to his studio looking for new male models to test-shoot. Mizer would pull out his latest stack of contact sheets showcasing "the boys," and his clients would select the one they would most like to "photograph." Then, in the most dignified way possible, Mizer would set up a meeting and make the introductions. "It was sort of like auditions," Rechy remembers.

Mizer had a good eye for the desirable, and a continuous stream of movie directors, talent scouts, and casting agents visited his studio, always on the lookout for the photographer's latest discoveries. Even the legendary movie maker George Cukor—a favorite director among stars like Katherine Hepburn and Greta Garbo—met many of his young companions via Mizer. And it was through these kinds of auditions that Skipper became one of the great director's protégés.

Although Rechy never names Cukor in *City of Night*, he gives the reader enough details to conclude that the character is based on the popular "women's" director responsible for such classic films as *The Women, Camille, The Philadelphia Story,* and *My Fair Lady.* Rechy wrote in *City of Night,* "I had heard the director's name; everyone in the world had. He is one of the kings. Later, in the Hollywood bars, when I would make the scene, I would hear the giddy fairies excitedly, enviously narrate who the director's newest 'discovery' was."

In the version told in *City of Night,* after seeing Skipper's nude photos the famous director tells the young man, "You're a very beautiful boy, and in this town that's All that matters." Skipper becomes the director's latest discovery and, for a while, lives with the director in his sumptuous house in the Hollywood Hills, mixing his drinks and acting as his current manservant-cum-showpiece. In return, Skipper is given a token extra part in a film, but, as Skipper puts it, "You couldn't—couldn't even see my face."*

The director eventually grows tired of the young actor and decides he "hasn't got the magic." He passes Skipper off to his friends, informing Skipper that he needs to study in order to really make it. That leads Skipper on a long road of being passed from man to man. "I lived with them all," he declares drunkenly in *City of Night,* "one right after the motherfucking other." Skipper steadily climbs down the ladder, from producers to teachers to Hollywood hangers-on, until he is what he appears to be in the pages of *City of Night*—a ravaged barfly hustling for drink money.

After *City of Night* came out, Cukor told friends that he was hurt by Rechy's brutal portrayal of him in the book. But Rechy was incensed by what he viewed as Cukor's callousness, his crafty manipulation. In the novel Rechy depicts Cukor as a user of beauty who wields his power in order to take advantage of a continuous supply of starry-eyed youths. Skipper is just one in a long line of boys who each, for a while, becomes one of the director's playthings, a temporary amusement added to dress up the decor of his spectacular mansion.

---

*Rechy says that the real Skipper can be glimpsed fleetingly, wearing swim trunks in a beach scene in the 1962 Cukor film *The Chapman Report.*

The writer Gavin Lambert, who was friends with both Rechy and Cukor at the time, tried to explain to Rechy that there are two sides to every story—that Skipper had been mean to Cukor and that the director was simply reacting to his cruelty. But Rechy would not hear of it. His sympathy remained with the younger man. In fact, Rechy had based his re-creation on an actual experience. He once observed Cukor up close when he was brought to the debonair director's home for one of his infamous "boy parties." Rechy had been invited by a friend of Cukor's, a businessman whose hobby was making 8mm films—short, black-and-white, male soft-core porn loops.

At the party Rechy witnessed firsthand how ruthless Cukor could be. Even when Cukor was trying to be charming—which wasn't often that night—Rechy noticed the sour condescension beneath his chatter. For the poolside dinner, Cukor served a watery stew and told the group of younger guests that Vivien Leigh would be coming for dinner the following evening and that she would be served a superior supper. He did a merciless imitation of Lana Turner on the witness stand testifying about the recent murder of her gigolo lover. When he was informed that Rechy was an aspiring writer, Cukor responded, "He'll never write anything that will ever get published."

"I, of course was playing the role of the silent hustler," Rechy explains, "but you must understand that I was always watching and listening from an entirely different perspective from the one Cukor assumed. The artist, the intelligent man in me, was always watching even when I was playing otherwise. And what I saw was nasty. It's something I don't even like to talk about because it was so demeaning. Truly. I was brought in on that day and I remember that Cukor was very suave and arrogant. Staying with him at his house was a young man—the man who became Skipper in my book. He was about 32 and fabulously handsome with a terrific body. Skipper was a real presence there, but by that time Cukor was through with him. He made that perfectly clear, ordering him around with such contempt. It was such a terrifying thing to watch because Skipper, this beautiful man, had been relegated to bartender. There were a few other young men present, me included, and we were all sitting near the pool witnessing all of this. Skipper was older than we were, but better looking than any of us—and I say that with all my vanity. In the course of the evening I heard the man who had brought me there whisper to Cukor, asking him if he could have Skipper. Cukor agreed. Skipper didn't object. That man who brought me there used to take nude movies and brag about how he had paid 50 cents to put some of his favorites on film. I saw all this. I absorbed it all."

Absorb it he did. And he transformed his observations masterfully in his writing. Under Rechy's scrutiny, Skipper, in his early 30s, is one of the most tragic characters in *City of Night*, used and discarded by a powerful man in Hollywood. While the director presumably goes on to further triumphs, Skipper pathetically clings to his glory days, avoiding the glare from a lighted match and instinctively flexing his muscles when someone eyes him:

> After being around him a few times, I began to avoid him; stifled by the knowledge of the sad, sad loss of Youth, of the terrible hints that life, perversely, makes one a caricature of oneself, a wandering persistent ghost of the young man that was, once—the attitudes of youth lingering after the youth itself was gone, played out. With Skipper, this loss was concentrated, emphasized because life had given him nothing but physical beauty, an ephemeral beauty relying on Youth.

Rechy was in his mid 20s when he began writing *City of Night*, and in his description of Skipper one can feel the author's dread of growing older. The thought that he might someday end up in a similar situation was too horrible for Rechy to bear. He began telling friends that he intended to preserve his appearance, that he would never grow old.

As in New York, Rechy sometimes felt it necessary to flee from the streets of Los Angeles and take a job in normal society.

"I had a duffel bag I had from the army and when one thing or another happened in a city—for example if somebody got too close to me—I would take whatever I could fit in that duffel bag and I'd be out of there." Years later Rechy would look back in amazement at how he managed to lead such a split existence.

"You'd see hustlers on the streets, and they thought they had it all," Rechy's friend Bill Regan remembers. "But this is where I give John a lot of credit—he knew the difference. When things got so rough and he couldn't hustle, he used to go down to a lawyer's office on Wilshire Boulevard in a leather jacket, jeans, and boots and prepare legal briefs. He hated doing it. But he never gave up his cover. He always was in character."

Sometimes, though, Rechy took a job where he actually had to dress in a jacket and tie. He worked for a while with the Attorney General's office on the Colorado River Litigation Topic—a big lawsuit Colorado was waging against Los Angeles. (Rechy worked for Los Angeles.) Working on the litigation of the briefs, he soon became the assistant to one of the higher officials who came from Washington. He was taken to San Francisco, all expenses paid. It was just the escape he needed from the seductive streets of Los Angeles, where he'd grown restless and anxious.

In San Francisco his offices were right across the street from a Market Street coffee shop that, at certain times, was a hustling spot. Even in a structured corporate setting Rechy found it difficult to give up the persona of his darker alter ego and he felt the constant pull of the streets beyond the window. He became so confident at his job that he began showing up in his customary Levi's, leather jacket, and boots—much to the staff's astonishment and chagrin. But his work was so good they put up with it. One night when he was working late the head attorney walked in and found Rechy working with his shirt off, tattered jeans' top button open, and barefoot.

Another idle afternoon while the staff was waiting for court to let out in order to begin the briefs, Rechy looked out the window and watched a young man getting picked up from among all the loitering guys who were obviously hustling. The call became too great. Rechy walked out of the office and headed for a new arena where he could explore the hustling scene.

It's fitting that Rechy's extraordinary years of discovery—traveling from place to place as a consummate voyeur (who eventually participates)—would climax in 1958 during Mardi Gras in New Orleans. The extravagant parades, garish costumes, and public displays of nudity eventually inspired Rechy to write in *City of Night*: "My journey begun on Times Square led me—inevitably—to the epiphany of Mardi Gras, my own Ash Wednesday."

The sexual repression of traditional society created a buildup of tension that peaked in an explosion of debauchery during carnival season. Traditionally a time of preparation for the Christian fast of Lent, Mardi Gras has instead become a testament to the excesses of humanity. In this annual festival, Rechy found the ideal backdrop for the concluding chapters of *City of Night*.

For Rechy, it was like walking into a hallucination—although it seemed unclear if the fantasy belonged to him or was the collective fantasy of the butch numbers, half-male and half-female queens, masked phantoms, rich daddies, and masculine vagrants who populated the streets, anxiously scurrying from place to place. Rechy writes:

> The mob frenzy is like an epidemic out of control, claiming more victims each darkening moment. I squeeze through the revelers, and I feel myself once again exploding with excitement. I move from bar to bar, drink to drink, from person to person—pushed along by that excitement which I know is suspended precariously over a threatening chasm of despair. But if I can go on!—hectically!—if I can retain my equilibrium on this level of excitement, of liquored sobriety!—then the swallowing void, though already yawning, can be avoided.

In the chapter "Jeremy: White Sheets," the last portrait in *City of Night*, the protagonist finds a moment of quiet in the midst of the carnival confusion when he spends some time with a stranger in a quiet hotel room, during which we discover what Rechy has learned about himself during his long journey as a "youngman." The character, Jeremy, who picks up the hustler during Mardi Gras, is himself young and handsome and smart. While they lie in bed together Jeremy forces the hustler to confront himself and the reasons why he's been running away from love:

> I had made the decision that it would be with many, many people—through many rooms, through many parks, through many streets and bars—that I would explore the world. And what, really, had prompted that decision? An attempt to shed the falsely, lulling, sheltered innocence of my childhood, yes. But had it also been, at least in part, fear?—a corrosive fear of vulnerability which with the world, with its early manifested coldness, had indoctrinated me; imbued in others: a world which you soon come to see as an emotional jungle; in which you learn very early that you are the sum-total of yourself—nothing more.

Other characters during the *City of Night* years had recognized the young hustler's sensitivity and vulnerability and felt that a relationship with him could be an escape from their own despair: Mr. King's offer for him to move in, Pete's suggestion that they share a room and become partners, Miss Destiny's plaintive plea for marriage. But Jeremy, with his good looks, intelligence, and stability, offers an almost ideal lifeline for the lonely drifter:

> "I'll be leaving New Orleans, right after Mardi Gras.... Back to New York. If you want, you can come with me...I'll help you," he went on softly. "I'll help you—in every way.... But it will involve giving of yourself. Loving back."

With these words Jeremy senses that the notion of love terrifies the hustler...and most of his terror stems from the fact that he doubts his ability to return Jeremy's love. Jeremy adds quickly, "I think that you could love me."

But for the protagonist, the price for love—returning love—is too high. While writing *City of Night*, Rechy still was not ready for that kind of relationship. To get too close to someone had come to represent entrapment, imprisonment, claustrophobia, and the possibility of being hurt.

Remembering his mother's love "like a stifling perfume," the protagonist flees to the bathroom mirror. "I'm still Young," he exclaims to himself. With his looks intact, the narrator feels that he will be OK without the costly safeguard of love. As long as he continues to be youthful and desirable he doesn't need anyone else. So instead of taking off with Jeremy, he takes the money he had offered as a sort of test, making it clear to Jeremy and himself that he chooses prostitution over monogamy. The narrator leaves Jeremy, thinking, *Maybe I could love you. But I wont.*

After this encounter, the hustler flees back into the carnival mayhem. He witnesses an angry fight between a hulking drag queen and a heterosexual couple on the streets of New Orleans. Unnerved by the violence, the protagonist tells himself that "very soon now it will be just another of many incidents quickly to be forgotten by those who have witnessed it..."

During the real incident behind his fictionalized one, Rechy carried on through the streets—the music, the voices, the crowds, the church bells, the bursts of laughter—sleeping only when he could no longer keep his eyes open, and then only for brief spells. He was popping bennies to give him energy, as if closing his eyes for too long of a time would hurl him into unspeakable danger. He spent days drifting from place to place, bar to bar, situation to situation.

This was the frenzied high point to his cross-country hustling odyssey—a sexual free-for-all where drugs, drinks, and sex mingled freely amongst the steady stream of monsters and clowns, red devils, and Scarlett O'Haras. Some of them offered him pills, which he swallowed. Some of them offered him money, for which he was swallowed. Rechy had reached a point where it no longer mattered what kind of pill he popped, and he finally swallowed one that gave him nightmarish hallucinations. Elbowing his way through the masses, he somehow managed to make his way to a rest room where he promptly passed out. Eventually he was helped up by a stranger.

He stumbled back to the streets thinking it was "deep night," but he had no real idea of what time it was. Rechy's next memory is of awakening in a movie theater sitting on a soiled velvet seat before a brightly colored cartoon. He noticed some bugs crawling on his arms, which he quickly brushed away. Through the gloom he could see there was an orgy going on several rows ahead.

Gradually, while Rechy's mind cleared, he became aware that his pants were down and someone was blowing him. "That wasn't all that difficult to understand," he remembers. "That's the kind of thing I was involved in. But it was the sense of not having control over what was happening to me that became a nightmare. And then I thought, *Jesus Christ, no!*"

For Rechy it was one of those moments—a defining one—when the sex is less important than the environment: One realizes where one is, and the place is no longer interesting—only filthy and contaminated, and one is not as beautiful as one thought one was. All Rechy wanted to do was get out.

Up until that point Rechy always felt like he had an out. He knew he had smarts. He could always flee, find employment, or move on when the streets became too much for him. But at this point, he was no longer a tourist in the city of night. He felt as if he had been outsmarted. The world he embraced had trapped him instead.

When he staggered out of the theater, Mardi Gras was over. The streets were silent. Rechy dully noted it was Ash Wednesday. In stark contrast to the tawdry throngs he had last seen, the people he saw now were stiff and somber-faced, with ashes smeared on their foreheads.

Suddenly Rechy had to escape. He didn't want to see anybody. He didn't want to tell anybody. He had clothes and some money scattered throughout the various places he had been staying, but he no longer wanted to go back to anyplace he had been. "I wanted to leave," he explains, "just myself, with nothing else associated with the Mardi Gras nightmare."

Not included in *City of Night* is what actually occurred after his lurid experience in the movie theater. Rechy headed straight for the Delta Airlines office and told the young woman behind the counter that he had to get out of New Orleans.

"How much is a ticket to El Paso?" he asked. He had some money in his pocket, but the young woman informed him that it wasn't enough. "I have to get out," Rechy whispered. Then, in an act of kindness that was rare in the world he had grown used to, the woman gave John the remainder of the fare plus money for a cab from the airport.

Rechy was overwhelmed with gratitude, and before he walked away he asked her name so he could send her the money from El Paso (which he did). "Miss Wingfield," she said in a startling moment, so poetic and beautiful to Rechy that he ultimately decided to leave it out of *City of Night*. He felt the occasion was too unreal to be believed in fiction. Yet, the name seemed like an omen that urged him to document what happened.

Just as he sought to give a "good Christian funeral" to the small dead bugs and tiny animals he would bury as a child, Rechy sought to memorialize the characters he had met during his voyage. While the other participants in this unfolding drama might allow these incidents to recede into the "cobweb-infested shadows of their minds," the writer in Rechy recognized that this was an extraordinary period in his life, populated by the fascinating characters of a thrilling and sensational odyssey. Already his mind must have been inventing ways to freeze them all in time, preserving himself, his cohorts, and his startling experiences for all eternity.

CHAPTER FIVE

Attracted to each other we often turn away in fear."
John Rechy, The Sexual Outlaw

IT WAS 1958, AND THE ODYSSEY was over. Rechy's exterior persona—the butch male hustler—had gradually developed and hard-
ened. But the young boy inside was exhausted and confused, and
longed for a nonsexual, noncompetitive environment. On the
brink of collapse, Rechy returned to El Paso and moved in with
his mother, who was living alone in a small one-bedroom house in
a government housing project. It distressed Rechy that his mother lived in such a place. But buoyed by the comfort and safety of
his mother's arms, he knew he could figure out a way to get them
both out.

Before he could do that, however, he needed to rest and collect
himself. On his first night back in El Paso, Rechy attempted to
organize in his mind the places he had been, the people he had
met, what he had learned, and how he had changed. The following day, with this jumble of information swirling around in his
head, he began a letter to a friend:

> Do you realize that a year ago in December I left for New
> York and came to El Paso and went to Los Angeles and
> Pershing Square then went to San Diego and La Jolla in the

sun and returned to Los Angeles and went to Laguna
Beach to a bar on the sand and San Francisco and came
back to Los Angeles and went back to the Orange Gate
and returned to Los Angeles and Pershing Square and went
to El Paso...and stopped in Phoenix one night and went
back to Pershing Square and on to San Francisco, and
Monterey and the shadow of James Dean because of the
movie, and Carmel where there's a house like a bird, and
back to El Paso where I was born, then Dallas with
Culture and Houston with A Million Population—and to
New Orleans where the world collapsed, and back, now, to
El Paso, grasping for God knows what?

The letter went on to describe in detail his experiences during
carnival season, and how the walls surrounding his self-made
underground kingdom had collapsed around him. Writing the letter helped Rechy conceive the story. And, in a decision that would
change literary history, he decided not to send the letter after all.
Instead, he pushed it aside and forgot about it for a while. "I was
so depressed," Rechy remembers. "I would simply lie on the
couch, trying not to move." Unsettling memories of the people he
had met in the previous months haunted him. It was as if they
spoke directly into his ear. "At night I couldn't sleep. I'd get up and
go outside, waiting for dawn."

A week later, when Rechy found the crumpled letter and read
through the discarded pages, he suspected his observations might
have some literary value. "That was the first time I considered
writing about those experiences," he says, "only then. And, I suppose, the idea contained the possibility of survival." Certainly survival for himself, but also a sort of survival for the people who had
marked his life—people who he suspected would be swallowed up
by the streets and forgotten.

He began to rewrite the letter, organizing events in his memory, shaping the disorder of emotional outbursts into a coherent
narrative. Rechy titled the finished product "Mardi Gras." Before

he had a chance to change his mind, he sent it out as a short story to two literary magazines: *Evergreen Review* and *New Directions*. To his surprise, both publications immediately accepted the story. His only problem was deciding which magazine to go with.

James Laughin, the editor at *New Directions*, told Rechy he'd have to hold on to "Mardi Gras" for nearly a year, since the magazine was only published annually. Meanwhile, Don Allen, who was a senior editor at Grove Press, as well as coeditor of *Evergreen Review*, was prepared to publish the story right away. Hence Rechy opted to go with *Evergreen*.

Evergreen Review was an alternative to the stuffier academic literary magazines of the time and was noted for showcasing unusual or overlooked talent. Allen had suggested starting *Evergreen* to Barney Rossett, Grove's publisher and editor-in-chief, as an outlet for new experimental fiction, such as Kerouac's *The Subterraneans,* Ginsberg's "Howl," and Burroughs's *Naked Lunch*. The magazine could test public reaction before actually publishing the work in book form. "I had done quite a bit of work with the *Partisan Review* and its anthologies," Allen says. "I thought there was room for a real magazine that did publish contemporary writers and less academic stuff. Barney seemed to feel the same way." They were right. *Evergreen Review* attracted a larger audience than either had expected and received submissions from some of the biggest literary names of the generation.

On accepting Rechy's "Mardi Gras," Allen wanted to know if, perhaps, it was part of a novel. Up to that point Rechy hadn't seriously considered writing a book about his hustling experiences. But thinking that Allen would only publish "Mardi Gras" if it was an excerpt, John quickly replied, "Oh, yes, yes, indeed, it's part of a novel." And then just to be safe he added, "and it's nearly half-finished."

In 1958 "Mardi Gras"—the story of a young hustler's experiences during Mardi Gras in New Orleans, written by a young hustler just back from Mardi Gras—appeared in Vol. 2, No. 5, the summer issue of *Evergreen Review*. At the time the magazine was publishing the likes of Beckett, Sartre, Kerouac, Ionesco, and

Artaud. Though "Mardi Gras" was the first piece Rechy published about his hustling experiences, it would eventually become the last chapter of *City of Night*.

The piece had an immediate and startling effect on the literary world. Noted author and *Washington Post* critic Carolyn See—who was at the time still primarily a homemaker—was astonished to read an account of a world she'd never known. "Here in these pages of the *Evergreen* was a kid, just a kid! With a fresh, beautiful, totally courageous, and totally cool, passionate and new voice, a boy-man twisting and pulling at the forms and contours of American language."

Rechy continued to write short pieces for *Evergreen Review*. Soon editors and readers were introduced to the hangouts and denizens of Rechy's private worlds. As his literary career began, however, Rechy was living in El Paso in his mother's house. When the call of his dark life became too irresistible, he recharged himself sexually in the local cruisy areas he had discovered since returning home. There was one particular area in the canyons where Rechy went to sunbathe.

Sometimes his dual identities clashed uncomfortably. His handsome oldest brother Robert had recently divorced and temporarily moved in with John and Guadalupe. Robert was aghast when mysterious men began telephoning for John. Who were these older-sounding men with cultured accents—calling and asking for his baby brother? How did they know Johnny, and what did they want? Later, when John showed Robert a story he had gotten published, Robert read it and flung it down on the table. "How could they publish things like this?" he demanded. Through his writing, Rechy's brothers and sisters became more aware of the kind of life he led while away on his excursions, but it was something they never talked about with him. Even with his multiple identities, Rechy was able to interact appropriately in all worlds, to show the side of him that people expected. To each spectator the side he revealed was the *real* John Rechy.

By mid 1958, Rechy was again living in downtown Los Angeles. Motivated by the reaction to Rechy writing in *Evergreen*, Don

Allen, who lived in New York, told John he'd like to come out to Los Angeles to meet him and "see some of the places." Rechy was ecstatic—a big Manhattan editor was flying out specifically to meet him. He didn't realize Allen suspected his work was not authentic. Allen thought an older, more experienced writer might be the author of "Mardi Gras" and the other pieces Rechy wrote— a suspicion critics would later echo.

Rechy mistakenly thought "some of the places" the editor wanted to see were the trendy Los Angeles spots, the swank hangouts of the Hollywood elite. Rechy had to confess, "I don't know much about those kinds of places." But Allen wanted to see the places Rechy had written about: the tawdry haunts of the unnamed hustler-narrator and the other characters who populated Rechy's fiction.

"Oh, my God! You want to see *those* places? Some of the settings?" Rechy exclaimed. "Of course! Of course!"

Allen soon came to regret his decision. A tour of the real underworld with Rechy was more than the mild-mannered, martini-drinking editor had bargained for. Even with Rechy as his guide, Allen became frightened of the seedy bars and cruisy streets.

"I showed him part of the setting of the novel I still had no intention of writing," Rechy recalled in the introduction he wrote in 1984 for a 20th anniversary edition of *City of Night*:

> I took this elegantly attired, slender New York editor into one of the most dangerous bars of the time (Ji-Ji's of the book). Pushers hovered outside like tattered paparazzi greeting the queens. Inside the bar, male-hustlers asserted tough poses. Don Allen said he thought perhaps the bar was a bit too crowded. As we drove away the police raided it.

Later, in the safer environment of a Beverly Hills apartment (Rechy had borrowed the place from an actor friend especially for this meeting), there was an awkward moment when Rechy felt Allen made a sexual advance. Rechy rebuffed his pass and for a moment believed he had ruined an important literary friendship. But Allen seemed unfazed by the rejection and asked to see the rest of the novel John was working on—assuming of course that there was a novel. There was none. Content with publishing the short pieces he had been working on, Rechy still had no intention of completing a book about his experiences. He hesitated to show Allen anything more.

Subsequently, Allen confessed that he had suspected there was no novel, but he urged Rechy to keep on writing. "John was a great writer to work with," Allen says. "He never needed a copy editor. He always knew what he wanted to write and went ahead and wrote it. All he needed sometimes was encouragement." Allen did indeed encourage Rechy to write other short pieces for *Evergreen*, and Allen continued to publish them.

Rechy says, "Don Allen became not only my champion and editor, but also my terrific friend, to whom I owe, in major part, the fact that I was able to become a published writer."

Rechy enjoyed working in the short-story format. Shorter pieces were not as intimidating as an entire novel. Each new piece he completed seemed to freeze a different important event—including the characters—in time. Writing was Rechy's chief weapon against death. He would live a little, write a little, observe a little, and transcribe a little. The stories that make up *City of Night* are the facts of Rechy's experiences as filtered through his inimitable poetic vision.

"Everything in *City of Night* is actually true," Rechy's friend Bill Regan asserts. "John would do so many rewrites trying to remember exactly how it happened. He'd get so torn about getting it right. One incident always occurs to me. He was on drugs and we drove out to Lake Arrowhead. When we got back, he was writing about it and he couldn't recall if the drive could be done in one day. I told him, 'Yes, it can.' But he wouldn't settle for that. John wanted to be sure, and he made me drive him up there and back so no one could question it in the book."

Through his writing Rechy re-created and preserved the uncommon characters that peopled his secret life. Men like the bedridden professor—a huge, bald-headed Buddha of a man, attended by a callous male nurse named Kenny (whom Rechy had met hustling). Kenny himself was a sometime hustler, sometime cruiser, and sometime buyer. Often when Kenny brought home a trick, the professor snatched the trick for himself. When Rechy came to write about the two of them, he placed the professor in New York, rather than in Los Angeles, and transformed Kenny into a sort of loving pimp and caretaker named Larry who brings boys home specifically for the professor's enjoyment. In *City of Night* (as in real life) the professor calls the young men Larry brings home to him "angels." It was in this way—when Kenny brought Rechy to meet the professor— that Rechy himself became one of the angels.

As recounted in the book, for several days this lonely man pays the nameless hustler $15 per session to sit by his bed and listen to stories of other angels who charged by the hour. Puffing on pastel-colored cigarettes, the professor reminisces about his passion for all the young men, and for one in particular named Robbie.

As the book's narrator sits by the bed listening to the peculiar professor's fairy tales, he is captivated by the man's kooky personality. The protagonist quickly realizes the professor's extravagant demeanor and air of ridiculous tragedy disguise a lifetime of subjection to humiliation and contempt. The real professor was a respected writer and an admired intellectual; Rechy wondered how such an esteemed academic in one life allowed himself to become such an absurd clown in another.

It became apparent through the professor's shaded stories that an endless line of angels consistently made a fool out of him, squeezing out of him large sums of money or gifts in exchange for a few kind words. The rules were simple: The professor played the part of the loving big brother, a wise mentor who gave money and presents in exchange for a fake friendship and the pleasure of sucking a young cock.

Yet the professor pathetically held on to the notion that he was important in his angels' lives. In *City of Night* he keeps photographs of each of them in an album he shows to the narrator. Deep down the Professor knows these young men use him. But they are the only type he is attracted to, so he clings desperately to the fantasy that each loved him in his own way. Better to have them under this false pretense than to never have them at all. He photographs the hustler—as the professor had photographed Rechy in real life—to add to his album of angels.

As with the others, at the end of each session the young hustler is expected to drop his pants and stand by the bed while the Professor fellates him. The narrator is intrigued enough to come back for several return engagements. But at their last meeting, when the professor attempts to kiss him with his rubbery lips, the young hustler pushes him away.

"When he tried to kiss me, I reacted immediately," Rechy says, remembering the real-life incident that inspired the scene in *City of Night*. "To me kissing is the most intimate act, and I really am in the mode of all prostitutes who disallow kissing. I always did then." In the novel, the rejection prompts the professor to unleash a firestorm of pent-up hatred—for the hustler and for all of the young men who came before him. He rages against the men who never desired him, never wanted his kiss. The professor demands that the Rechy character read his prestigious résumé out loud so that the room echoes with his list of accomplishments and awards.

"He was a very tragic figure," Rechy says. "He had a brilliant mind. The honors that man had, the awards and everything—but they meant nothing to him. I knew from his attitude toward me that he sought out people he knew would reject him. And then he lamented the exploitation. The people who pretended to love him. The people who could not love him."

In his humiliating moment of clarity, the enraged professor

damns his angels for sucking the life out of him, even as he loathes himself for his lifetime of waste and foolishness:

> "The angels! The voracious angels!" he shouted. "The ones who drained me—who never knew Me!—never respected Me. Love? Bought! Bought for the prospect of a trip to America, a wedding ring which I would never wear, pairs of shoes and bottles of wine—bought!"

The hypocrisy of the professor's plight was too irresistible for Rechy to pass up. Yet Rechy's genuine respect and fondness for the real professor remains. Years later he refused to name the man who inspired the character. "He was a very well-known figure," Rechy said. "Gore Vidal and Truman Capote were friends of his." But in his love life—given the kind of boys he craved—education and intellect meant nothing. And to them the professor was just an easy target.

Short pieces based on the professor and other characters, all of which would eventually become *City of Night*, continued to appear in *Evergreen Review*. Soon Rechy was contributing to other high-brow publications, such as the short-lived *Big Table*, which had recently broken away from the *Chicago Review* over a dispute about censorship. It was in *Big Table* that Rechy introduced the bewitching Miss Destiny character in 1959, after *Evergreen* rejected the piece in which she first appeared.

"I sent an early version of the Miss Destiny chapter to Don Allen, who admired it and wanted to publish it in *Evergreen Review*," Rechy recalls. "I never understood why Barney Rosset, the publisher, did not opt for using it. Don suggested I revise it. Moodily, I went to the roof of my Hope Street room, smoking some marijuana. It was night, and nearby church bells began to toll, and I looked toward Pershing Square. It was then that the metaphoric overtones now included in the Miss Destiny chapter—the references to pursuing angels—came to me. I rushed down to my room, and—high on the smoke—began revisions. Still, Barney did not accept the story for publication. Don believed in it and called me up to tell me about *Big Table*, and he sent the story to them for me. It was the Miss Destiny story that drew the attention of Norman Mailer, James Baldwin, Ken Keasey, et al." And so it was at *Big Table* that Rechy introduced the tale of Miss Destiny's fabulous wedding to the literary world.

Each new story was something of an event in literary circles. Rechy was elated when admiring letters arrived from established writers like Norman Mailer and James Baldwin.

In 1959, Rechy met the respected novelist and playwright Christopher Isherwood, who was living in Los Angeles and writing Hollywood films. Isherwood was best known for his tales about Berlin in the early 1930s, which were reissued as *The Berlin Stories* in 1946. The stories were based largely on his own life experiences and later formed the basis for the play and movie *Cabaret*. Isherwood had become a fan of Rechy's writing from the time of his earliest published stories. But after reading the Miss Destiny segment in *Big Table*, Isherwood became a champion of Rechy's work. "We sent our scouts out to find you," Isherwood whispered to Rechy on the night they met at Isherwood's house. "We" being Isherwood himself and his 27-year-old art-student boyfriend Don Bachardy. Rechy was, of course, flattered.

Isherwood's scouts were a couple of his friends: a young man who was Zsa Zsa Gabor's chauffeur and the driver's closeted lover, a handsome journalist at the *Los Angeles Times*. James Wright, a writer friend who often visited Rechy in his Hope Street hotel room, was also present at the house. "John made a theatrical appearance," Wright recalls. "His comportment was that of a very attractive boy. Instead of ordinary casual L.A. attire, he wore a red, filmy sport shirt, open at the waist, displaying a lovely torso, tight-fitting jeans, and a fetishistic necklace.... John's likeability and intelligence quickly won the day. Christopher, especially, was entranced."

Actually, Rechy hit it off with both Isherwood and Bachardy

and made plans to see them again. But the evening did not end smoothly. During the ride home (in a car driven by Zsa Zsa's chauffeur), the closeted journalist came on to Rechy, which of course miffed the journalist's chauffeur boyfriend. In a hissy fit worthy of his employer, the chauffeur stopped the car and began ranting at Rechy. This enraged the journalist, who began kicking at the windshield. The chauffeur, hysterical by now, screamed, "John Rechy, get out of this car now!"

Soon after their first meeting, Isherwood invited Rechy to dinner. Don Bachardy was away at school in London, so it was just Rechy and Isherwood.* After a meal at one of Isherwood's favorite restaurants, the two writers, who had been drinking a great deal, ended up back at Isherwood's charming canyonside house. In his hustling persona Rechy was continuously aware of the power of fantasy. He knew when to remain silent so that clients could read into him whatever they wished. But alone with Isherwood, as they sat by the fireplace, Rechy opened up and let some of his true self seep out, passionately giving his opinions on art and literature. Although they were both tipsy by then, Isherwood listened with somber attention. When Rechy finished talking, Isherwood said, "It's very late, John, why don't you spend the night?"

Rechy gratefully agreed to stay over, but was surprised when Isherwood led him to the master bedroom, making clear his expectation of sex. Certainly Rechy realized he was partially responsible for Isherwood's expectations. "Was I displeased that I was desirable to him?" Rechy asks. "Absolutely not. Maybe that was hypocritical. Because I wanted to be desired—that's the truth of it—but then I didn't want to act on it."

Although he had achieved a measure of literary recognition, whatever the situation, Rechy always dressed and acted provocatively. He craved the adoration of his peers, but once he won it he

---

*Rechy kept the details of this evening under wraps until the publication of Isherwood's gossipy diaries in 1997, which, Rechy says, savaged many of his friends.

withdrew sexually and wanted only to be respected as a writer. It would be years before he was able to gracefully reconcile these two aspects of his personality.

From his experience on the streets, Rechy knew how to brush off an overzealous admirer. But this was Christopher Isherwood—an older, more experienced writer whose work he admired. Rechy murmured that he couldn't possibly sleep in the same bed with him.

"Why not?" Isherwood demanded.

Rechy explained that he was unable to sleep in the same bed with anyone.

"Don't be silly," Isherwood replied. "It's an enormous bed. I thought you wouldn't mind sharing it."

Exhausted and not wanting to embarrass Isherwood by making a big deal out of the situation, Rechy agreed. He stripped down to his jockey shorts and lay at the far corner of the bed. In no time Isherwood was in Rechy's corner. There was no way Rechy could go through with it. He was simply not ready to merge the two worlds he was juggling. Besides, the absent Don Bachardy was also a friend.

"This isn't going to work," Rechy said.

"Oh, all right," the chagrined Isherwood exclaimed. He led Rechy to the guest room and testily retired to his own bedroom. Rechy was barely settled in the bed, however, when Isherwood couldn't resist his provocative guest down the hall. Driven by drink and testosterone, Isherwood soon slipped into the guest bed. At that point, Rechy had to push his host away, making it clear that sex was not a possibility. But by now it was also clear to Rechy that neither of them was going to get any sleep.

"I better go," he said.

Unapologetic, Isherwood attempted to hide his fury behind a sulking demeanor. "All right," he told Rechy. "You might as well go home." Rechy then reminded Isherwood that he had driven him there. Isherwood was unmoved, but Rechy persisted, not relishing the prospect of a long walk down the canyon—

onto Pacific Ocean Drive—and trying to hitch a ride in the dead of night. Grumbling, Isherwood agreed to drive him. But rather than take him all the way home, he dropped Rechy of at the bottom of the canyon. It was 3:00 in the morning. Tired and angry and without much money on him, Rechy found himself on Wilshire Boulevard in the middle of the night, with miles to go before he could sleep. He stuck out his thumb and luckily a cruising stranger soon picked him up. Rechy ended up hustling the driver in a gasoline service station that was closed for the night.

Years later, Thomas Wright—who was on friendly terms with both Isherwood and Rechy—observed, "Both Christopher and I were very attracted to John, but John's pattern was immutable: He was sexually interested only in transient strangers he couldn't care less about. His affectionate friendships with writers and other peers were a thing apart and platonic."

For Rechy, it was easier to make it with a stranger in the front seat of a car—quickly, efficiently, and anonymously, with the freedom to escape into the comfort of solitude. In Isherwood's company, John was a writer. An intellectual. An equal. But by continuing to dress and act provocatively he encouraged those in the literary world to see him as one of his own characters.

Fortunately, Isherwood did not hold a grudge for long, and soon he and Rechy were cheerfully socializing again. It was through Isherwood that Rechy met Dr. Evelyn Hooker, who in the 1950s conducted a series of studies researching the nature of homosexuality. Hooker became a pioneer of gay liberation, and the results of her research helped support the argument that homosexuality was not a mental illness.

Isherwood told Hooker that Rechy was extremely smart and talented, and that he was hustling the streets. Intrigued, Hooker called Rechy to ask if he would be a part of her study. In the beginning, Rechy refused to speak with her. Dr. Hooker, however, continued to court him, and when they finally met Rechy was charmed by the tall, intelligent, Eleanor Roosevelt look-alike. He agreed to be a subject for her research. He answered her questions and carefully filled in the questionnaire she was using at the time in studies that would go on to state that "homosexuals were not inherently abnormal" and that there was "no difference between the pathologies of homosexual and heterosexual men."*

It was an exciting time for Rechy. He always knew he would be an important writer. Now it was within his grasp. As his reputation grew, he began to receive book-contract offers from the likes of Dial and Random House. At the same time he was invited to write for other magazines, including *The Nation* and *Saturday Review*, to which he contributed essays on impoverished Mexicans and, later, rebelling GIs for Peace.

With a large body of work completed and his newer works being well received, Rechy decided the time was right to collect the shorter pieces and shape some of them into a complete novel. At first he called the manuscript *Storm Heaven and Protest.* Despite offers from other publishing houses, Rechy went with Grove Press, where Don Allen was senior editor. It was important to Rechy that Allen had been the first person to express unqualified enthusiasm for a book on Rechy's controversial subject matter. And at the time, Grove's president and publisher, Barney Rosset, was publishing the best modern authors—and battling censorship to do so.

However, a contract and an advance—$2,500—did not motivate Rechy to complete the book right away. Instead he returned to a world where he was already safe and established—the night cities, the sexual underground. He resumed what he called "the private, beautiful, and ugly magic of hustling." He still found this dark world irresistible.

"Because of that dichotomy of identification, I sometimes pushed myself to do acts that I regret enormously," Rechy says. "Trying to earn my full credentials for the street life, I forced myself to steal, and I did, four times. The first time, in New

---

*Only in 1973 did the American Psychiatric Association vote to remove homosexuality from its official diagnostic categories of mental illness.

Orleans, I didn't feel much, because I was picked up by three men and they treated me as if I wasn't there—talking about me in gaspy tones. We had all been drinking, and when they had passed out briefly, I went through their wallets. The second time, in Los Angeles, I went with a man who I felt made it clear he wanted me to steal from him, part of the distorted fantasy he harbored. I took money from him and then rushed back into the dingy hotel room to return it. I stole from another man at a hotel room in downtown Los Angeles. I justified it because he was trying to put me down while desiring me. I started demanding his wallet. But, thank God, I retrenched, and left without even asking him to pay me what we had agreed. The worst time was once when I was cruising and went home with a man. When he fell asleep I felt compelled to steal from him. With the exception of the first instance, in New Orleans, I often am jolted by what I did and feel an overwhelming guilt, and often, like now, the desire to confess, although I never feel absolved for the harm."

In conjunction with all his night crawling, Rechy kept the literary world within view, like a lighted doorway he could see at the end of the darkness. Bill Regan, who spent a lot of time with him during this period, says that Rechy "never had any question that he could write. That confidence level was always there. With his leather jacket and Levi's, he certainly didn't look like a writer. But he always thought he would be a famous writer...but he kept it very private. This was his own self-confidence level."

Whenever Rechy felt the night closing in on him he sent a lifeline to the literary world, where his friends eagerly waited to publish his next fictionalized dispatch. This escape hatch, however, made him feel somewhat guilty. He recognized that for many of his nocturnal companions there was no way out—whereas he was among them without being one of them.

• • •

In late 1959, Rechy was again temporarily living in downtown Los Angeles on the street ironically named Hope. In the early '50s his sister Olga had moved to nearby Torrance with her husband and children, and John would occasionally visit them. She would cook her Johnny delicious Mexican meals.

It wasn't so much that he felt himself being pulled in different directions; rather he kept various aspects of his life separate and contained. Each facet—family, career, hustling—was equally important to his development as a person. He inhabited each of his worlds as a separate persona, each crucial to his survival and feeding into his final metamorphosis.

Rechy remembers the pattern of his life at the time: "I would go to the huge public library just a few blocks away, and I would read books, newspapers, magazines. For a time I read a lot of plays, a lot of Shakespeare that I hadn't read in college. I discovered Chekhov. I loved the Greek myths. Later, I would use those in *Our Lady of Babylon* for the various retellings of the story of Helen and Paris, Medea and Jason. I sometimes read books on mathematics, fascinated by the mysteries they contained. I read Flaubert, and, thrillingly, James Joyce, making my way eventually to *Finnegan's Wake*—and, like everyone else, I stopped quickly. The next phase of the ritual occurred when the day began to darken. I would then head to Pershing Square to hustle. Often, I'd be invited by someone to have dinner at the Green Rose Cafeteria across the street. It was a dingy place, and I'd say, 'Oh, let's go somewhere better,' and then I'd suggest a terrific cafeteria, much more expensive, a few blocks away. The ritual might extend to my hitchhiking to Hollywood Boulevard to hustle there too. So it went: library, Pershing Square, Hollywood Boulevard."

While living on Hope Street, Rechy befriended another writer, Thomas Wright, who had moved to Los Angeles in the 1950s and had soon become part of the literary scene. Wright had read one of Rechy's short stories and asked a mutual friend to introduce them. Wright recalls, "John lived in a barren hotel room in the seedy depths of downtown Los Angeles. The only objects visible in it were a typewriter, a chair, a table, and a bed. That room was the scene of many trysts: I seldom stayed in it long without John's saying that in 20 minutes or so he 'had an engagement.' He offered me some typescripts of stories to read and said he wanted to make them into an episodic novel. The stories, openly homosexual, were stunningly good. A close friendship developed between us."

Rechy often struck out on solitary adventures, prowling the streets of Los Angeles. Sometimes, late in the afternoon, he would put on his hustling uniform—jeans and a T-shirt—and hitchhike down by MacArthur and Lafayette Parks, just to see where the day would take him. Or he might get on a bus and ride it to an unfamiliar destination, then hitch a ride home with a stranger. He wanted to experience the consequences of his choices. Certainly there was danger in the unknown, but Rechy found any hint of menace incredibly thrilling. Taking these risks fed his imagination and stimulated his sense of the inherent drama sometimes hidden in the mundane. Almost always, something unexpected happened.

Someone famous might give him a lift, like the time Spencer Tracy stopped his station wagon for him on Sunset Boulevard. Rechy sat in awe as the movie star drove in silence. There was no hint of anything sexual. "As far I know it was Spencer Tracy just giving a young kid a ride to wherever he was going," Rechy told friends.

Another time a stranger picked him up—he didn't indicate he knew Rechy was hustling—and offered to take him to the races. The man claimed he was superstitious and that he knew John would bring him luck. Rechy knew nothing about horse racing, but the man proposed that if Rechy would only pick the name of a lucky horse, Rechy could take half the winnings. A lucky charm Rechy was not, and the man lost money on every horse Rechy picked. Nevertheless, Rechy did go home with him, and the man did pay him—just not due to his choice of horses.

It was on another of these journeys to nowhere that Rechy met Bryce McKoy (a pseudonym)—a man who would change his life. McKoy became instrumental in helping John complete *City of Night*. On this particular evening Rechy was on Wilshire Boulevard. Although it was not hustling territory, he was always on the lookout for a possible score. When Bryce drove by and spotted Rechy, he made a quick U-turn. "Before someone else could snatch you up," he later told him. Bryce thought Rechy, who was 28, was 10 years younger. Rechy did nothing to correct him.

"I always played the fantasy," Rechy says. "If someone thought I was older than I was, and that had aroused the fantasy, I would go along with that. I was a fantasy player and that's where my intelligence came in."

Bryce was an attractive architect in his 40s. His tenderness and intelligence attracted Rechy, and the two began a cautious friendship. "He made me feel extremely special," Rechy recalls. "He took me to Pasadena, where he lived in a house with a pool. I happened to mention that I liked filet mignon, and we had it for breakfast, lunch, and dinner to the point that for a long time I couldn't stand it."

At the beginning of their relationship Rechy maintained his hustler persona, still living by his creed that to show intelligence to a client was to go down several notches in desirability. "In those days I was always posing, pretending, camouflaging...whatever you like, and every now and then the role would trap me." Entombed in his persona of the drifting young hustler, Rechy was unable to allow the relationship to move to a deeper level. Perhaps each fearing the loss of the other, they both continued to play the roles they had created on their first meeting.

"You know I never knew too much about his life beyond us," Rechy says. "He would pick me up on the weekends and he had a room there for me at his place. He had said, 'This is your room whenever you need it.' The thing is, it was never a strict hustling relationship." Instead Bryce gave Rechy money on the basis of his belief that this was a struggling young man in search of an identity. "That's why I wouldn't see him too much," Rechy says. "Because once they saw me in a different light I felt I'd end up rejected."

Despite their mutual fears, Bryce managed to penetrate Rechy's tough exterior—at least, to a partial degree—and recognized that he was indeed a promising young man. Of course, he did this without knowing Rechy had already graduated from college and was currently publishing short stories in highbrow literary magazines. Bryce was one of the few men Rechy picked up on the streets who saw beyond the sexual object. Even so, when John at last felt comfortable enough to drop his facade, he discovered how much honesty could change a relationship.

"We had a weekend in Malibu," Rechy says, "staying at a really beautiful place near the ocean. I can see it now. We sat outside for brunch...and then he started saying that he was very concerned about me. He said, 'Of course, you're very young, and I wonder what's going to happen to you, and I think a lot about your future.' He offered to put me through school. I already had a college degree! I had already been published. I had written 'Miss Destiny'...and, oh, I felt like such a fraud. He was assuming that I was not very educated. I played the role very well. I couldn't stand pretending after that... and so when he drove me back to the room I had on Hope Street, I asked him to wait, and he waited in the car and I went into my room and I brought out a copy of the Miss Destiny story that had recently been published in *Big Table*. I inscribed it to him. The most astonishing thing is, he didn't react. I gave it to him and told him I was going to be writing a book. All I remember is that I was stunned by his lack of reaction. I had expected him to say, 'This is you?!' That sort of thing. Nothing of the kind. It was as if I was a stranger."

Being so emotionally naked with Bryce made Rechy extremely uncomfortable. Now that his friend knew a bit about the real John Rechy, a real relationship might develop. To Rechy, this was a signal to flee. Although the encounter put a strain on their relationship, Bryce and Rechy continued to see each other. But Rechy was now more reluctant to be open.

Through his protagonist, Johnny Rio, Rechy attempted to confront his inability to commit to one person in his second novel, *Numbers* (1967):

What some might call insensitivity was, rather, a condition arising from the fact that Johnny's needs were so enormous: In those Los Angeles years, he longed, craved, needed to be admired, wanted, adored (and he was—abundantly); and as the symbol of his sexual power he "chose" (or perhaps it chose him) the act of men paying him to love his body without his reciprocating.

In his writing, as well as his in life on the streets, Rechy cultivated the reputation of being the tough, desirable loner who spurns those who desire any kind of emotional connection. Mystery, detachment, and aloofness were certainly part of Rechy's nature, qualities he cultivated during his lonely childhood. He viewed sex as a struggle for power, and for years he expected everyone he was sexual with to pay for it—making himself the winner.

However, during his *City of Night* period he *did* become close to one young man. He even allowed a tender, intimate relationship to develop—a relationship in which money was not involved.

In *City of Night*, Rechy describes this relationship through the narrator's encounter with a character called Dave. Dave is based on a man named Bill Regan, whom Rechy met in 1959. Regan was a handsome 24-year-old with a fondness for leather and motorcycles. Originally from Boston, he worked in a warehouse in Los Angeles at the time. "Whenever someone asks me how I met John I tell them to read *City of Night*," Regan says today. "It's pretty decisive." Rechy confirms that their meeting in the book is a true-to-life re-creation.

Rechy had been picked up by Regan's roommate, Kenny (the young male nurse who had originally introduced him to the professor). As mentioned earlier, Kenny also liked to dabble in street life, sometimes hustling himself, sometimes thieving. After picking up Rechy, Kenny took him on a shopping spree, using various stolen credit cards. Kenny then took Rechy back to the apartment of two friends, Bill Regan and a young Italian man named Carmen. At first sight Regan was quite taken with Rechy, who was clad in a leather jacket and engineer boots.

"I was lying on the couch when they came in," Regan recalls. "Kenny and Carmen were going to have a threesome with John and they asked if I wanted to come in. I said, 'No, I want him alone.'" Regan later said he could not stand the thought of sharing John. (Rechy disputes this, saying, "Kenny would never have suggested a threesome.")

A couple of weeks later, Regan encountered Rechy by chance on Hollywood Boulevard. "I had never picked up a hustler in my life, never had the desire to," Regan says. "That type of thing had never occurred to me, but I did want to know him. We talked for a while, and then I asked him straight out, 'Do you want to go home with me—alone?' And he accepted. And I had sex with him. Money was never involved."

The actual relationship was sexual, whereas in *City of Night*, Rechy suggests that, while Regan had wanted a sexual relationship, it was never allowed to develop:

> I went to his apartment with him when he asked me if I felt like talking some more.
>
> In the apartment, when he touched me, I told him quickly I had to leave.
>
> He looked at me steadily. Then he smiled. "Sure," he said. "Maybe youll want to go to Arrowhead with me tomorrow." Surprisingly, he was not annoyed that I put him off. "It's Sunday. I'll pick you up if you want to."
>
> I said yes, suddenly anxious to leave. As he drove me to the hotel on Hope Street, I felt certain I wouldnt be there when he came by.
>
> But I was.

Regan maintains (and Rechy concurs) that the relationship included sex from the first time Regan brought him back to the apartment. After that initial encounter they continued to see each other, including the trip to Arrowhead. But when it came to a romance, Regan says, "He resisted quite a bit. I could see I was interfering with his private life. But I did like him and I wanted to continue seeing him."

Although their sexual relationship lasted for five years and they spent a great deal of time together, even Regan finds it difficult to define the relationship. "It was a love affair without our actually becoming lovers," he says. Monogamy was out of the question. Rechy insisted on continuing with his life on the streets. "John always was very open with me," Regan says. "He always told me that he was out hustling, but I never judged him for it."

What Rechy needed more than anything else was an emotional attachment with someone outside of his family. "You have to understand that I was very lonely," Rechy says, "and I didn't have friends. It was probably my fault—I still was not very at ease with myself. I desperately wanted friendship but it couldn't be just anybody. I never made friends with guys I hustled with. Bill was so friendly, so witty. He became a very, very dear friend." With Regan, Rechy found a companion with whom he could let down his guard and be himself. If sex was necessary in order to nurture the friendship, then Rechy was willing to allow that to happen. "Bill was a friend who did desire me," he continues, "I had no difficulties with that. None at all. Yes, sex was involved. But it was the friendship that was important to me. I had dinner with him. I went to the movies with him."

Yet, even if he was comfortable with a sexual friendship, Rechy did put some limitations on it. Regan says, "I would get annoyed with him a little bit because I wasn't getting my way with him as much as I liked to, and we'd get into our little fights." Rechy continuously made it clear to Regan that he was not interested in a committed romantic attachment.

Sometimes Regan, dressed in full leather, encountered Rechy

outside of a bar. On these occasions, Regan spoke to John briefly, but then entered the bar alone. "He'd never go into a bar with me," Regan says. "He kept our lives separate. He didn't get to know any of my friends and didn't want to. I didn't take it personally. It was just part of his makeup."

Rechy was also up front with Regan about the men in his life, including Bryce McCoy, who was back on the scene and taking care of John—giving him money, taking him to dinner, buying him presents. John would tell Regan he was spending the weekend with Bryce, and that he would see Regan later in the week.

"When a person is hustling, like anyone else, they like to know they have a couple of people in their lives and I do feel that he always trusted me," Regan says. "What John saw in me is that I was a person he was very comfortable with because I was very real with him as a person. That's just the way it was. The hustling didn't have anything to do with it. I never gave John a dime, nor would he have ever asked for it."

Once the distinction was made about the kind of relationship they were involved in, Rechy was adamant that well-defined lines be drawn. If it wasn't a hustling-john relationship, Rechy also wanted to be clear that it wasn't a dating situation either. "Let me give you an example of how petty he would get with me," Regan says. "We'd go out to dinner, and it wasn't a question of who would pay for it. It was always that we had to split it right down the middle, to the point of splitting pennies. Because he wanted to have that distinction in the relationship—that was important to him."

Despite Rechy's idiosyncrasies, the two young men saw each other several times a week. John didn't have a car at the time, so Regan took him on long rides. Eventually Rechy even invited Regan out to dinner to meet his mother while she was in town visiting Olga in Torrance. Both women liked him a lot. "Bill had the kind of personality to win over anybody," Rechy says fondly.

Regan gave Rechy a leather jacket, which led to a running joke between the two of them. Regan would tease Rechy for sleeping with the jacket under his pillow, and Rechy would retort that he liked to sleep with his head elevated. Rechy still has the jacket.

Rechy wrote about the warmth and affection they shared. In *City of Night* he memorialized their visit to an animal circus in Santa Monica. Regan was disturbed to see a huge male elephant forced to do ridiculous dance routines as the audience roared with laughter:

> I see Dave stare solemnly at the elephant being led off the small arena, the flowered hat perched crookedly over one ear....
>
> "It's sad—that great big male elephant painted pink and that hat on his head," Dave said.
>
> Suddenly Im frighteningly moved by this young man beside me. I feel that impotent helplessness that comes when, through some perhaps casual remark, I see a person nakedly, sadly, pitifully revealed—as I see Dave now.

When confronted with complicated emotions, John Rechy's instinct was to flee. In his fiction he remained the unromantic drifter, always rejecting intimacy, dependent on no one. In *City of Night* the circus chapter ends when the fearful protagonist terminates the relationship because Dave expresses his growing feelings:

> Inside the apartment Dave said unexpectedly:
>
> "It sure is great to be with you!" He put his hand fondly on my shoulder, letting it rest there—the first time he had touched me this intimately since that first night.
>
> For a long moment I didnt move, feeling his hand increasingly heavier...I jerked away from him.
>
> The words erupted out of me: "Maybe so—but it's all stopping!"

Even when I saw the look of amazement on his face, even when I wanted to stop, even when I felt that compassion, tenderness, closeness to this youngman—even then, I knew, as much for me as for him, that I had to go on; that although inside, I was cringing at my own words, in hammerblows I have to destroy this friendship. "I mean—well—Ive spent too much time with you—thats all!"

The narrator then closes the door on the attachment:

Outside in the hall, I close the door behind me. I pause for a moment not knowing why. Then I walked out of the building quickly.

As Rechy grew older, he found it was not always so easy to disentangle himself from those who touched him. Although he would take off for long periods, he continued to return to Regan. Their friendship lasts to this day. (Regan is one of the men to whom Rechy dedicates his second novel, *Numbers*.)

"If you read the book *City of Night*, it talks about him walking out of the room," Regan says. "He actually did walk out of my apartment in Silver Lake, but he came back. And we had a couple more incidents. One time in particular I remember I was driving him back to the hotel and he hit me with a newspaper and he said, 'I don't want to see you anymore.' He had said that a few times but he would always come back. But this time he said it with real conviction. He ran up the stairs to his room and I figured, 'That's it.' I wrote it off. I started to drive away, and he came back, and he poked his head in the car and he said, 'I don't want it to end this way because if you leave now, I'll never see you again.' It wasn't till a few days later that I realized how much that meant to him."

Rechy agrees, saying, "Regan was my only friend."

In addition to his ongoing relationships with Bryce McKoy and Bill Regan, Rechy began to allow himself to fall into new kinds of experiences while hustling. Through this experimentation, he added new kinks to his role as a hustler—kinks that inspired some of the darker passages in *City of Night*.

Rechy was already familiar with the importance of masquerades and costumes and was aware of how his polished exterior contrasted with his emotions. In keeping up the subterfuge of the hustler, Rechy's costumes sometimes became more extreme. In his New York days Rechy had allowed a man to dress him up in full leather regalia and parade him around the city streets. Rechy had felt slightly silly, but it was good pay in exchange for being little more than a walking prop.

His fascination with masks led him to a curious relationship with a paunchy middle-aged man named Van, who became Neil in *City of Night*. Rechy met Van through Bill Regan. "Van had a house in Silver Lake," Regan remembers. "He was an older man. But he had this little attitude. John and he just didn't hit it off right. This guy would serve you tea and crumpets. And then he would start quoting things that were quite literary. And at one point he incorrectly quoted something as being by T.E. Lawrence. And John said, 'Don't you mean, D.H. Lawrence?' He couldn't resist correcting and surprising him, because this guy would pick up young kids and most of the kids didn't know what he was talking about. This Van had the ability to pick up very young kids. John was much more informed than his usual pickups, but he was fascinated with Van. You'd walk into his house and he'd say, 'What would you like to dress like?' John had so much fantasy about him, but he did not like the way that this guy would try to control people. He resented him that way."

In *City of Night*, Rechy disguised Van by changing his name to Neil and by moving him from Los Angeles to San Francisco. The narrator meets Neil in a club and is immediately intrigued by this man's extreme outfit: knee-length boots, a leather jacket with a bird insignia, and a chain around his shoulder. He accepts an invitation to Neil's house for lunch. The reserved

A drawing by 12-year-old John Rechy depicts a prostitute on the imaginary Salem Alley. Years later he hustled on a street named Selma in Hollywood, where he posed for this photo in 1978.
Photo © Tony Korody

"He looked like an angel to me—a cross between an angel and Tom Sawyer."
Above: Rechy's longtime partner Michael Snyder around the time of their first
meeting, 1979

Opposite page, clockwise from top left: Rechy walking with his sister Olga,
who is wearing the "butterfly dress" he designed for her, circa 1941; Rechy
with his beloved mother in the house he bought for her using the profits from
City of Night, 1964; The Rechy family, circa 1950. Back row: Olga, John,
Yvan, Robert, and Blanche. Seated: Guadalupe and Roberto

Clockwise from top left: This famous 1967 cover photo of Rechy from the hardback edition of *Numbers* caused readers to associate the author with his sexy protagonist, Johnny Rio; Bill Regan, the inspiration for the character Dave in *City of Night*, shared a warm friendship with Rechy in the early 1960s; John Rechy posing in front of one of his favorite objects.

From top: During the writing of *City of Night,* Rechy mastered the image that sold on the streets; snapshots taken by friend Bill Regan in 1961.

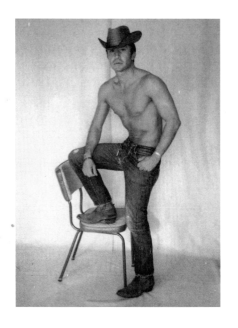

Circa 1969: Rechy enjoyed posing for the male physique magazines of the day.

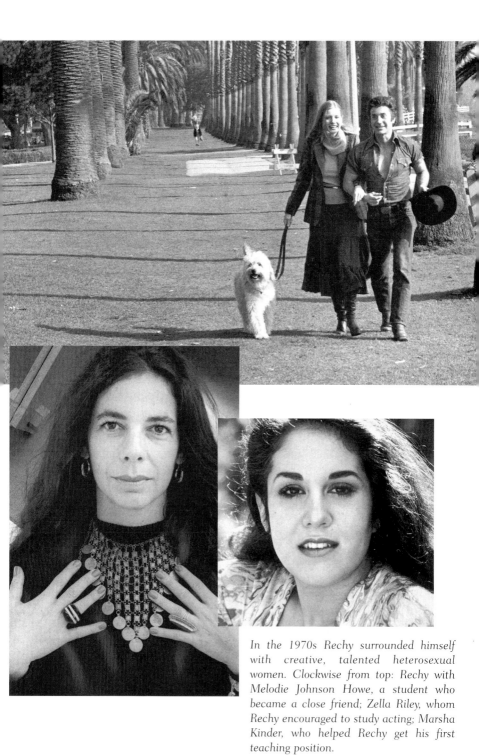

In the 1970s Rechy surrounded himself with creative, talented heterosexual women. Clockwise from top: Rechy with Melodie Johnson Howe, a student who became a close friend; Zella Riley, whom Rechy encouraged to study acting; Marsha Kinder, who helped Rechy get his first teaching position.

Howe photo © Tony Korody

John Rechy, circa 1998
Photo by Cynthia Farah

protagonist's instincts tell him that, in the arena of sexual games, there is something to be learned from Neil.

At lunch Neil is again decked out in outlandish leather garb, including a huge studded belt cinched so tightly his considerable girth hangs over it. The image of a paunchy middle aged man wearing exaggerated tough-guy leather drag contrasts absurdly with Neil's fussy movements serving tea—passing cream and chatting in a florid, highfaluting manner. But then Neil turns vicious. When his cat presses up against his boot, purring lovingly, Neil pauses in his tea-party chatter to kick his pet and snarl, "I hate it when he becomes sniveling, affectionate." Neil's leather is a shield for his own vulnerable nature, which he perceives as undesirable. While in costume he especially hates to be reminded of his own soft feelings.

In the *City of Night* arena, the nellies, the sissies, and the queens spend lifetimes suffering ridicule and torment from the stereotypical masculine types. Rechy has always understood how fantasy springs from reality. Many of the men who paid for Rechy and his ilk created sexual fantasies around the villains who had persecuted them because of their homosexuality. As adults these men sexualized their feelings of submission and humiliation to create a dominant fantasy caricature such as a law enforcement or army officer.

Neil lives to lure young men into his extraordinary make believe world—a world that confronts repressed homosexual fantasies. Slowly Neil draws the novel's narrator into this obsession, showing him photographs of young men dressed as cowboys, policemen, pirates, and military officers. He reveals he has equipped his bedroom with two creepy life-sized mannequins, one dressed as a policeman, the other as a motorcyclist. "I had them made especially," Neil explains.

Of course, Rechy was obsessed with his own rough-trade personality. When Neil asks the protagonist if he'd like to be dressed up, the young man can't refuse. Neil ritualistically dresses the young hustler: skintight black denim pants, black leather boots that come to his knees, black leather gloves, a hat arched to one side. (After all, Rechy had once delighted in spicing up his own army uniform.) When the outfit is complete, the protagonist feels excited by this new reflection of himself. "A plantation overseer!" Neil exclaims.

But when Neil tries to entice the protagonist into beating him, the young man leaves, "angered—I moved away from him—leaving him a shattered heap of studs and leather straps sprawled grotesquely on the floor." Throughout his life Rechy enjoyed being the bait, the object of desire. Often he allowed himself to seduce men to the brink of their sexual fantasies, then withdrew angrily before the action started.

The protagonist of *City of Night* is mesmerized by costumes and masks used to explore sexuality. Rechy's own rehearsed demeanor camouflaged his desires and sensitivity just as a cocked leather cap and a studded belt shield Neil's weakness and femininity. Rechy created an alternate identity in order to survive an unfriendly world. Neil, however, adamantly denies any contradiction between his outer and inner selves. When the hustler of *City of Night* refers to his host's exaggerated manner of dressing as "costumes," Neil retorts icily, "Dressing up does not mean wearing costumes."

The paradox did not escape Rechy. On another visit his hustler-narrator sees Neil wearing an apron over Western garb. "Do you find me effeminate?" Neil asks him. The man beneath the tough-guy outfit seems to court pain, cruelty, and humiliation. The image of the policeman or uniformed soldier spoke to the fantasies of many gay men: to be taken by force without sensitivity or tenderness.

In subsequent visits the narrator allows Neil to dress him up as his masturbatory fantasies: a pirate, a cowboy, a Prussian officer. Each masquerade is more sexual and exaggerated than the hustler's own street persona. Or, as Neil puts it, turning the young narcissist to the mirror, "You, as you would like to be!"

Later in *City of Night*, Neil, dressed in tough-guy regalia, wants the young hustler to abuse him with a belt, urinate in his mouth, and grind his boot into his groin. This time, the protagonist allows himself to be seduced into violence.

As the "Masquerade" chapter progresses, Rechy further explores facades when Carl—a large masculine man in his 30s, who is also one of Neil's "dress up" friends—arrives outfitted in motorcycle clothes. The narrator witnesses first-hand the disintegration of Carl's facade. As Carl pours more and more wine down his throat, he drops more and more of his motorcycle persona. Giggling, sucking on his finger, he drops his pose and his voice becomes high-pitched. The protagonist is shocked and disgusted at the transformation:

> All the masculinity has been drained out of him as if by the liquor. His legs are curling one over the other. The once rigidly held shoulders have softened. The hand that had held the wineglass tightly now balanced it delicately with two dainty fingers, the others sticking out gracefully curved. His look liddedly mellowed, and he began to thrust flirtatious glances in my direction.

When Rechy wrote *City of Night* he equated love with femininity and weakness, as when Carl—horribly drunk—blurts out, "I wanna—wanna—lover. Yes! A Lover! And all this—motorcycle drag—it doesn't mean shit to me. I'd wear a woman's silk nightie if it got me a Lover!" Carl unravels, drink by drink, layer by layer, until he is exposed in all his human frailty. Unprotected by his shell, he wobbles like a newly hatched bird, blinking and confused as he regards the world.

In the closing of this chapter, Rechy investigates the depths of eroticism as it relates to pain and humiliation. He looks beyond the masquerades, beyond the roles one perfects and projects, and notes the impossibility of destroying the authentic inner self, a person's own true nature, no matter how many costumes are piled on as camouflage. Neil—a man who serves tea and wears an apron while preparing lunch—so despises his core identity that he seeks to destroy it.

On the protagonist's last visit to him, Neil announces proudly that he has been to "an execution."

"If you had been here you could have witnessed it. My cat—remember the furry one?—he was becoming too weak—constantly simpering whining. I hate weakness. I despise it. I loathe it...so I executed him.... Yes!—I Exterminated him! As all weakness must be Exterminated!... I put that cat out of his sniveling, absurd misery." He went on deliberately: "I put him in a bag and I drowned him in the bathtub." As soon as hes verbalized what hes done, he appears visibly shaken, as if an emotional rubber band had been stretched to the point of snapping.

The reality of the Neil character takes John Rechy further than he would have liked to go. But he dutifully reports his findings in the novel. Rechy's alter ego, the narrator, leaves Neil's apartment for the last time. "Through the open bathroom door I see a water-soaked bag on the floor." In the *City of Night*, the only possible way to manage tenderness is to destroy it.

Rechy's emotional attachments to Bill Regan and Bryce McKoy overwhelmed him at times. The perfect opportunity to escape these involvements came along when Rechy received a letter from Jonathan Herbert (a pseudonym), a wealthy admirer of his "Miss Destiny" story. This was the first time (but not the last) that a reader became so fascinated with Rechy's worlds—as described in Rechy's compassionate voice—that he felt compelled to know the author and sent him the airfare to visit. Rechy fled the suffocating atmosphere of Los Angeles to the mysterious stranger's private island in Chicago. Rechy again took a chance on an adventure—this time on a bigger scale—and found himself in yet another provocative situation he would write about in a later novel. The extreme people and situations of this trip ignited his imagination and Rechy exaggerated them even further in an operatic novel called *The Vampires* in 1971.

"Jonathan, my host, was quite handsome, about 40, but as it turned out he was not gay," Rechy reveals. "He was simply fascinated by the scene." The house was built on an artificial lake a few miles from Mundelein in Illinois. To get to there from the mainland, one had to row in a boat. When he arrived, Rechy was overwhelmed by the opulent house, with its complicated corridors and hidden rooms. "There were two wings to this large house on the island. In one wing I had a bedroom that adjoined his. He had a superb collection of art: an original Miro hung in my bedroom; Giacometti statues decorated the lawn."

Rechy was further intrigued by the mismatched cast of characters staying at the house during his visit. In the opposite wing, Jonathan's 10-year-old son had a bedroom. The rest of the rooms were filled with various women from different periods in his life. "There was his current mistress, a good-looking Israeli woman, and one of his several ex-wives, the heir to a huge American fortune; and then another of his wives arrived, the daughter of a famous American intellectual."

Surprisingly, Rechy got along with all of his housemates, but during dinner once Jonathan accused an ex-wife of being jealous of his other women in the house. "Oh, no," she replied icily. "I'm never jealous of your women. I'm jealous of your men." Actually, other than for sex, Jonathan seemed to have little use for his female lovers. He preferred to spend his days with Rechy. The two men rowed together, sunbathed, or simply conversed. Sometimes in the late afternoon, Rechy joined Jonathan in a large room in the house's lavishly decorated basement. The two lounged on the floor in their bathing trunks, bodies touching, limbs casually crossed over each other, sometimes one using the other as a pillow, as they sipped rum and cokes and listened to Elvis Presley records. On occasion, Jonathan's current mistress joined them, sitting very close by, quietly observing their overt eroticism. When he needed to be alone, Rechy escaped into the extensive library and spent an afternoon reading.

Late at night Jonathan would make love to his mistress then slink into Rechy's adjoining bedroom. The two men lay naked in bed without touching. Instead, in the darkness, Jonathan voiced his resentments over the many women he seemed to retain some strange hold on. "I think he was one of those men who needs women sexually but detested them," Rechy explains. Sometimes Jonathan confessed to Rechy that he wished he was gay, and he'd tell the story about the time he had gone to a party in drag with Jean Genet.

Rechy passed many quiet days on the island. He was content to be there—the peculiar setup, the drama between Jonathan and his women stimulated his imagination. Near the end of the curious summer, the ladies departed and Jonathan told Rechy that he too would be traveling. But he offered to let John stay in the house while he was away. Rechy accepted, but felt spooked alone on the island at night—wandering alone through the art-filled rooms. After sundown he imagined vampires. Jonathan had left his car, so Rechy rowed to the mainland, drove to a near-by city, and rented a room at the YMCA. Eventually he closed the house and moved to Chicago.

Rechy again found himself a stranger with no name in uncharted territory. This new freedom gave him a chance to discover Chicago's version of Times Square. Everywhere Rechy ended up, he found a continuation of the mysterious kingdom in which he ruled, his city of night. He loved the secrecy, the thrill, and there was always the temptation to give in completely to his addictions and live out his life in this world where he was happiest.

But then he'd be jolted by the reminder of what lay in store for the young men who made hustling their lives. In every city he saw the same faces mixed in with the new beauties. Year after year, a little more lined, a little saggier...a little less desirable. Still, they returned to the parks and the bars because it was the only life they knew.

As the months ticked away, Rechy became conscious of the

years elapsing between the time of the book contract he'd signed with Grove and the book being published. He kept postponing the due date. "I was avoiding writing about the street experiences," Rechy says, "but, at the same time, the need to do so was becoming powerful." If he was going to make a mark in the literary world so that he would always have a safe place to escape, he would have to publish a book soon.

Rechy's subject matter was still controversial enough to be groundbreaking. But the literary times, they were a-changing. Contemporary novels grew more daring, particularly on the subject of homosexuality. Grove had already paved the way for more explicit material with Henry Miller's *Tropic of Cancer* and D.H. Lawrence's *Lady Chatterley's Lover*.

By becoming a successful writer, he could protect himself in a way that was impossible for his street contemporaries. Yes, he was selling his body, but he was simultaneously selling his mind to a very different world.

As luck would have it, back in Los Angeles, Bryce had begun to come to terms with the "real" John Rechy—an older, more sophisticated model of the kid he had picked up hitchhiking. In 1962, he contacted Rechy and offered to finance him if he went back to El Paso to finish the novel. This removed any means Rechy could find to distract himself from finishing the book. With Bryce's financial help, he returned to his mother's small house and wrote every day on a rented Underwood typewriter. His mother kept the house quiet while he worked. After dinner, he would translate into Spanish and read to her (she never learned English) certain passages he considered appropriate. "You're writing a very beautiful book, my son," she told him. And these quiet evenings took their place among the most cherished moments of John Rechy's life.

Later some critics criticized Rechy because of what they felt was a lack of structure in his books. Terry Southern, for example, writes in *Contemporary Authors* that Rechy, like John Kerouac, wrote at great speed off the top of his head, which he felt "often leads to an embarrassing amount of overstatement, subjectivity, and a complete lack of craftsmanship."

Southern's assumption, however, is inaccurate. In actuality, Rechy put himself through a very strict regime of writing. To begin with, before sitting down to write, Rechy listened to a specific genre of music to absorb the right mood, whether it was the dark sexuality of rock, the formal structure of classical music, or the ordered dissonance of modern composers. As a result, the sounds of Presley, Chuck Berry, Fats Domino, Beethoven, Tchaikovsky, Strauss, Stravinsky, and Bartok would often be heard blaring from the house in the projects.

Each chapter went through as many as 12 drafts—often paradoxically, to create the feeling of spontaneity that Southern misinterpreted in Rechy's writing. The first four paragraphs that open *City of Night* were edited down from about 20 pages. The first chapter was written last, the last one came first. Although four years elapsed between the time he began the book—with the unsent letter—and the time it was finished, most of it was written during one intense year in El Paso.

While Rechy was revising his sensitive passages about sex and loss and the fear of aging and death, he heard the news of Marilyn Monroe's death. As in childhood, John continued to be very influenced by the movies. From the start of her career in the early 1950s Marilyn Monroe had deeply touched him. So when his brother Robert came home and said simply, "Marilyn Monroe is dead," John was devastated.

"I was more moved by her death than by Kennedy's death the following year," Rechy remembers. Years later, he would channel his feelings for the tragic actress into his novel *Marilyn's Daughter*. But for now, his awareness of mortality and the death of beauty were heightened, and some of those feelings made their way into the manuscript.

By late 1962 three titles had been announced, with published excerpts for the novel in progress: *Storm Heaven and Protest, Hey, World!*, and *It Begins in the Wind*. The intertwining chapters that connect the portraits were called "City of Night" from the start. But for some reason it never struck Rechy as the book's title. He played around with other names that might fit the framework of the book, coming up with *Ash Wednesday*, *Shrove Tuesday*, *The Fabulous Wedding of Miss Destiny*, and *Masquerade*. Nothing seemed exactly right. Finally, he decided *Storm Heaven and Protest*. Then Don Allen suggested the obvious: *City of Night*.

PART THREE

A SCREAMING NEED

Chapter Six

It's one of those books that has a life of its own. It goes on without me.
—John Rechy

CITY OF NIGHT WAS FINISHED. That evening Rechy scampered around the living room with his mother and his oldest brother, Robert. The giddy threesome bumped into each other as they collated copies of the almost 700 page typescript. Rechy had made three or four carbon copies. The next day the manuscript was mailed. When Rechy went to return the rented typewriter, sentimentality took over. He could not bear to part with the special machine and he ended up buying it for $40. Rechy still has the elegant old Underwood, now retired in this age of computers.

When the printer's proofs arrived, Rechy panicked. In print the language struck him as "different—wrong!" He began to change a word here and there, a phrase, a sentence, a paragraph. By the time he had gone through the proofs, the book was virtually rewritten on the margins and on pasted typewritten inserts.*

When Rechy finished the corrections he called Don Allen, then in San Francisco, to prepare him. Allen was startled but agreed to the alterations. Despite the editor's preparations, others at Grove were shocked by the rewritten galleys. Knowing how expensive the resetting would be, Rechy offered to pay for the

---

*These marked galleys are in John Rechy's archives at Boston University.

typesetting out of his royalties. But Barney Rossett made no objection to the changes, and did not charge him for the additional expenses. Grove graciously reset the book and rescheduled publication.

City of Night appeared in 1963. With impressive advance sales, it became a best-seller before the official publication date. And the book inaugurated a new era in gay literature. The shock waves the novel sent through the publishing world would be felt for years to come and would dramatically influence future generations of writers, editors, and publishers. Michael Denneny—who would go on to become one of the most important figures in American gay publishing—was an undergraduate at the University of Chicago at the time. At Chicago, Denneny worked on the university literary journal *Chicago Review,* which planned to publish a first serial of "The Fabulous Wedding of Miss Destiny" from *City of Night*. Reading the book in galleys, Denneny was mesmerized. "Very few books are dangerous," he says. "Very few books are actually threatening to the status quo of society, and *City of Night* was one of them. Which is why it is so important."

Like many men who were affected by *City of Night* in the early '60s, Denneny was heterosexually active but had homosexual fantasies. The novel became part of the respectable academic's private sexualized imagination, which he kept separate from the rest of his life. "It led to many fantasies," Denneny admits. "It was the first time I'd read any gay writing that was sexual. In all the other gay books I'd read up to that time, the eroticism was coded. So it had a powerful impact because the eroticism was neither absent nor veiled, but direct and out there. That made it a very pivotal book."

The University of Chicago, by no means a conservative school, was so scandalized by the proposed excerpts from *City of Night* that the board withdrew its funding from the *Chicago Review.* This caused an uproar on campus. "It had never happened before," Denneny recalls. "There were a lot of First Amendment people as well as radically left people at the university, and they were just horrified that the university withdrew all the funding from the *Chicago Review* merely because we intended to publish an excerpt from *City of Night*. Which says something about the novel's importance."

In New York City, 19-year-old Felice Picano—who would make a name for himself 10 years later with *The Lure*, a book inspired by *City of Night*—was similarly affected by the novel. "I was 19 years old and trying to become a homosexual," Picano recalls. "I didn't even know what there was of the gay world. And *City of Night* was my entry into it. I must say it almost sent me back into the closet because it was not what I wanted to hear." What frightened Picano was the lack of tenderness in *City of Night*. "I was a gay romantic. I wanted to meet the man of my dreams and live happily ever after, and that really wasn't what it showed. It portrayed a lot of show and tell, buy and sell. And loneliness. As I came more and more out I found out that Rechy had in fact tapped in very accurately to a part of the scene. I discovered that even though it wasn't a complete vision of the gay world for me, it was accurate and a little scary, a little attractive."

Rechy felt confident that *City of Night* would be an enormous critical success, but thought it would only sell modestly. Quite the opposite occurred. Before its official publication date the book appeared at number 8 on *The New York Times* best-seller list. As Rechy recalls, "It stayed on all national best-seller lists for almost seven months and was a number 1 best-seller for weeks in New York, San Francisco, and Los Angeles. Many foreign publishers began bidding for it immediately. Eventually it was published in about 20 countries." Yet, as is often the case with new and unusual works, the first critical reaction was severe. Such unapologetic homoeroticism made the literary intelligentsia—particularly homosexuals—distinctly uncomfortable. "The Establishment is not with him, apparently," poet Frank O'Hara wrote of Rechy, "but nevertheless sales have been going well. Good."

Inevitably, early criticism of the book focused on the image of a gay man hustling tricks on the street instead of on the book as a piece of art. Years later Rechy remarked bitterly in *Contemporary Authors*:

> With precious exceptions, its careful structure was virtually ignored. (I believe that self-appointed "important" critics should be licensed to practice—like doctors, so that an artist may sue them for malpractice: the recklessness with which they often assault work they know to be good but which disturbs them for private reasons.)

One notorious review haunted John Rechy and his reputation for many years to come. The vitriolic criticism, which hung like a dark cloud over *City of Night* and set the tone for many articles that followed, was written by Alfred Chester—a notoriously disturbed genius—and published in *The New York Review of Books* under the tasteless heading "Fruit Salad." Few reviews have ever stirred up such controversy or sparked such enduring debate.

Chester began his assessment of *City of Night* by attacking the publishers:

> This is the worst confection yet devised by the masterminds behind the Grove *épater le post office* machine. So fabricated is it that, despite the adorable photograph on the rear of the dust jacket, I can hardly believe there is a real John Rechy—and if there is, he would probably be the first to agree there isn't—for *City of Night* reads like the untrue Confessions of a Male Whore as told to Jean Genet, Djuna Barnes, Truman Capote, Gore Vidal, Thomas Wolfe, Fanny Hurst, and Dr. Franzblau. It is pastiche from the word go.

Thus Chester struck his first blow by casting doubt on whether there really was a John Rechy. In the months to come *The Village Voice* and *The New Republic*—along with scandal magazines and gossip columns—quoted Chester and also questioned the existence of John Rechy. After all, the writing was familiar, but few people had ever met the author.

Rechy felt helpless to rebut the review. It was profoundly unfair and mean spirited, yet this was his first book and he was taken aback that Chester's editors would publish such a diatribe, that a book review of such venom was even allowed. So he did not, then, protest.

More frustrating and painful to Rechy was the fact that Chester was so clever. In a collection of writings by Chester, Gore Vidal described Chester's critical style as "a kind of performance in criticism which is often plainly gratuitously destructive but at the same time a sort of art rarely practiced in bravery's home." Chester tempered his *City of Night* critique by sweetening his venom with well-turned jests. "He wants to be loved and wanted," he wrote of the novel's narrator, "but he doesn't want to love or want—he doesn't, in fact, want to be queer, though this is much too chic a book to admit that, except backhandedly."

Chester also decked out his review with hip phrases and wielded his acerbic wit like a sharp instrument. "Oo-o-o, Mary," he wrote after quoting one passage. "Doesn't it make chills go up and down your spine?"

Rechy sensed the reviewer harbored a secret agenda. He may have been right.

Alfred Chester, an excellent writer in his own right, had by 1963 published his own novel and a collection of short stories, many of them with homosexual themes. Yet today he is most often remembered for his startling appearance. Tragically, a childhood case of scarlet fever robbed him of his hair, including his eyebrows and eyelashes. Short and round—a sort of Brooklyn-born Humpty-Dumpty—the gifted writer was described by an acquaintance as "snarling, growling, barking, rasping, snapping, spitting out his words. He often left me wondering whether his animosity was directed against the topic at hand, himself, me, or the entire world." Because he was popular as a critic, but unsuccessful as a fiction writer, it was with a feeling of loathing toward the literary marketplace that Chester styled many of his reviews.

Today it is obvious that Chester was not honestly writing a review so much as slinging mud. His good friend, the poet Edward Field, said, "Alfred knew nothing like *City of Night* had appeared in America—it killed him that somebody had gotten there before him."

It seems impossible that so astute a homosexual critic could find absolutely nothing of value in *City of Night*. More than anything else, Chester had an issue with "the adorable photo on the rear of the dust jacket." Rechy points out that, as Chester often bought the services of "adorable" hustlers, he probably had difficulty accepting that one could be talented and intelligent.

Alfred Chester seemed to be furious at John Rechy. Furious at him for being younger. Furious because he beat Chester to the punch by producing a brilliant book on Chester's favorite subject, the homosexual subculture. Furious because *City of Night* was destined to become a huge success while Chester's own fiction went unappreciated. But, most of all, furious at John Rechy's beauty.

In spite of two volumes of excellent short stories and a minor masterpiece of a novel *The Exquisite Corpse*, Alfred Chester never had a book that was a popular success. He died a suicide at age 41.

Edward Field, who edited two collections of Chester's writings, goes so far as to say that Chester wasn't the only gay writer who was envious of the young John Rechy. "Even Gore Vidal exhibited a trace of envy when he wrote that Alfred Chester's review of *City of Night* is 'murderously funny, absolutely unfair, and totally true.'"

"Totally true?" Rechy asked Vidal in a 1993 letter. "To the contrary, Chester's review was itself totally fake. I would assume that you, having often been the object of such, would recognize that sort of fakery, the kind that a critic who has been personally assaulted by a book's subject resorts to in order to disguise the fact that he has been disturbed, even wounded by it. Instead of dealing with that, he attacks its quality." Several months later, Vidal sent Rechy what amounted to a letter of apology. "Dear Rechy," he began. "As you know I very much admire *City of Night*, particularly the hustler love scene." Calling Chester "a moral monster" and advising Rechy to "never take these things seriously," Vidal goes on to say, "I had forgotten about him entirely until I reread his totally unfair piece."

Rechy's hurt eventually boiled into outrage. For the next 39 years, Rechy rarely gave an interview without mentioning the Chester review. "That son of a bitch, man," Rechy railed to the *New Times* in 2000, "he wanted a knockout punch. He really wanted to destroy me. I've had to battle this review for years, and each time it appears I become newly enraged, although, clearly, I was the triumphant one in all this."

On October 31, 1996—33 years after Chester's diatribe first appeared—Rechy finally got his say when *The New York Review of Books* agreed to publish Rechy's response to the review. "In May 1963," Rechy wrote to editor Barbara Epstein, "there appeared in your journal a piece of malice posing as a review of my first novel *City of Night*. The 'review' was written by Alfred Chester. You titled it 'Fruit Salad.' I was young, baffled by the personal assault, and I did not protest. I am no longer young and I protest the abuse."

A few months after the Chester piece came out, some excellent reviews appeared. The respected poet Frank O'Hara rallied behind Rechy in his *Kulcher* review titled, "The Sorrows of the Youngman." O'Hara hailed Rechy as a promising new talent:

> In writing this, as well as in reading several of the more vicious reviews *City of Night* has received, I cannot but be convinced that Rechy not only has his own voice but also that it has an almost hypnotic effect on many other writers, which is able to bring out all sorts of bitchy and flatulent attitudes which are otherwise cleverly hidden in conditioned or assumed stylistics. He even manages to get Alfred Chester down to the "Oo-o-o, Mary" level.

O'Hara ended his review by declaring, "The hero is a hustler, but the author is not."

Rechy's friend Christopher Isherwood said, "This novel is not primarily about homosexual prostitution; it's about people. In bringing these people to life, John Rechy shows great and tragic talent. He is a truly gifted novelist, and I am sure his work will continue to be exciting no matter what themes he may choose in the future."

James Baldwin gave a quote for the book's jacket: "Rechy tells the truth and tells it with such passion that we are forced to share in the life he conveys. This is a most humbling and liberating achievement."

The mainstream press also began to recognize the merits of *City of Night*. *The New York Times* praised it as "a remarkable book...Mr. Rechy writes in an authentic jive-like slang; the nightmare existence is explored with a clarity not often clouded by sentimentality and self-pity. The book therefore has the unmistakable ring of candor and truth." *The Washington Post* thought it was a "first novel that must be considered one of the major books published since World War II." And the *Houston Post* noted that "probably no first novel is so complete, so well held together, and so important as *City of Night*."

The novel has become a modern classic—translated into more than a dozen languages and required reading in many creative writing courses. Today *City of Night* still fascinates. Rechy's characters are so keenly observed, so vividly rendered that they still seem familiar today. Generations of readers continue to follow Rechy's nameless drifter from New York's Times Square to Los Angeles's Pershing Square to New Orleans during Mardi Gras. The hustlers and johns and drag queens continue to reach us and make us laugh, forcing us to examine our own loneliness and passions.

"The book was a commercial smash," Rechy says. "No one was more surprised than I was. I was living in El Paso at the time and I refused interviews or to give out photos. Suddenly a woman friend of mine came out to Texas and told me I was the 'new hot writer' back in New York."

Rechy chose not to promote the book himself, realizing that once his face became familiar he would not be able to enter the shadowy world that had become such an important part of his life. He would not go on the talk shows or do the publicity circuit as his predecessors Truman Capote and Gore Vidal had done. Bill Regan observes, "I think that if he'd taken the ball during *City of Night*, he'd be a lot more famous now. If he'd jumped on the bandwagon." In response Rechy says, "I feared becoming a media sensation. I didn't want to lose my life. I always marvel at people who say, 'Once you become famous your life is gone!' They invite it! How can you say that on a talk show? How can you go on television for everybody to see and then lament that your privacy is gone? If you don't want it, you just don't go."

As the controversy surrounding the book raged on, something was bothering Rechy. He knew that the lives of the people he had written about would remain the same or get worse, while he would not only survive but would continue to evolve. Most of the misfits in the homosexual underground could anticipate only alcoholism, homelessness, or suicide. They would never know the role they played in John Rechy's success. In 1979 in an interview with *LA Weekly*, Rechy candidly stated, "I can't tell you how guilty I felt when *City of Night* became a best-seller. All those real people I transformed into characters in my novel—they were still on Main Street and Pershing Square. I felt guilty about leaving them. Of course, I loved the book. The guilt came later. I would often think, *Where the hell is Skipper, or the queen Trudy, who was so cute? I'm a famous writer now but where are they?*"

Some of *City of Night*'s most memorably portrayed New York characters were mirrored by similar individuals Rechy encountered in Los Angeles. His guilt extends to them as well—in this case for leaving them out of the book. He is still haunted by the memory of a Pershing Square hustler "with overtones of Pete...one of the handsomest I'd ever seen; all the buyers wanted him. Then gossip emerged that he was actually gay and he was through, with no place to stay—none of the clients wanted him. Remember, that was in the time and place where hustlers had to be straight. One night I returned to the streets, and he was still hanging around, hadn't made it at all. I felt sorry for him and let him sleep that night in my apartment, although I knew the gossip might spread to me. That night in my garage apartment, where he slept on the floor, he started to talk to me about himself, clearly moving toward telling about his being gay. I pretended to be asleep. I left that out because it had overtones of Pete. But he haunts my memories. Where is he now?" There was also a "poignant man...a sweet, kind man who stirred echoes of tough Mr. King" and who, Rechy wistfully reminisces, "came into town looking for me on the streets when his mother, with whom he lived, was on vacation, and he wanted me to come stay with him—'a paid vacation,' he said—while she was gone. Where now?" These reappearing mirror personas reflect the multiplicity of missed opportunities in a hustler's codified life, and Rechy is acutely aware of his burden.

One eccentric who *was* able to cash in on the success of the book was the fabulous Miss Destiny, who blazed so memorably on the pages of Rechy's short story and then in the novel. She was one of the few characters who recognized herself in Rechy's writing. After the "Miss Destiny" story first came out, she spotted Rechy on Santa Monica Boulevard. When the excited drag queen finally caught up with the writer who had immortalized her, she bowed and exclaimed, "Thank you for making me even more famous!"

With the publication of *City of Night* Miss Destiny successfully extended her 15 minutes by giving an interview to *One*, the underground gay magazine. She showed up for the interview in full *City of Night* regalia: tight capri pants and fluffed out "rair." Sitting, standing, and pacing nervously, she proved to be every bit as entertaining as her literary alter ego, an amusing mixture of intelligence, camp, narcissism, and pathos. The magazine described her as talking in "a hoarse, pseudo-feminine voice, gesturing with her hands in her nervous, exaggeratedly feminine manner." Miss Destiny dished out equal parts gossip and advice. "Every self-respecting homosexual, as soon as he possibly can, should get away from his parents," she said to the amazed and delighted *One* editors. "I prostituted myself from the time when I first discovered that men would keep me," she confided grandly. "Of course I never had the grand wedding that I told John Rechy about. The idea came to me one night. So I made up the story because I thought how nice it was. I have had my marriages, but never anything so fabulous. I have had, on the other hand, as many as 20 tricks in one night."

By that time Miss Destiny had begun to appropriate some of the characteristics Rechy had created for her. For the cover of the magazine she posed in the majestic garb Rechy describes in *City of Night*: a tight strapless gown and opera-length gloves. Of John Rechy, the man who made her "even more famous," Miss Destiny said, "I only had sex with him once, and he didn't disappoint me. But I was a silly girl in those days, and I couldn't stand to do the same one twice. Besides, I could see that he was really a queen." Rechy maintains they never had sex.*

Miss Destiny closed her interview (this was five years before Stonewall) by proclaiming, "The future of the homosexual lies in some kind of unity. We don't seem to be able to band together. We could start by stopping to hate the types that we are not comfortable with. After all, how can any homosexual afford to be intolerant? All adjustments that hurt no one else ought to be accepted and understood—at least by homosexuals."

Miss Destiny is the only character from the hustling and queen bars who stayed in touch with Rechy. She would call him off and on over the years, usually at odd hours. Once she invited John to her birthday party, another time to dinner at a neighborhood restaurant. Rechy didn't go. "I wanted her to continue to

---

*"You know, her implication that I made it with her is wrong," Rechy says. "I never did; the possibility didn't even exist under the circumstances. She was bragging there, God love her."

exist as I remembered her and as I had re-created her," he says. But he enjoyed their phone conversations, especially when she called him to prove to her latest stud that she was indeed the fabulous Miss Destiny from *City of Night*. Loudly slurring her words, Miss Destiny would put her latest "husband" on the phone and Rechy would be treated to the young man's barely literate grunts of admiration.

• • •

In 1964 Rechy didn't know what to do or where to go. It was a strange time in his life. *City of Night* was a success, but he had no money. The royalties hadn't come in yet, and Grove had paid his advance years before. His main objective was to move his mother out of the projects, so he asked Barney Rossett for a $5,000 advance from *City of Night*'s future royalties. Once he made the down payment on a new house for his mother, Rechy was still broke, stuck in El Paso, and driving a 1952 Studebaker his brother Robert had given him. Unrecognized, he hustled a couple of times, but his feelings about the scene in El Paso were ambivalent.

An uncanny chain of events led Rechy to the next chapter of his life. In New York two young men who would later become friends of Rechy's—Floriano Vecchi and his companion Richard Miller—had read *City of Night* and were so excited about the book that they called a friend, a very prominent psychiatrist, Ralph Williamson (a pseudonym), to tell him about it. "We had started to feel the effects of Rechy's writing when he was publishing short pieces in *Evergreen*," Vecchi recalls. "Without having met John Rechy everyone knew who he was. They admired him. They wanted to meet him."

Although Richard Miller tried to share *City of Night* with Dr. Williamson, the doctor declined the offer, stating that he never read fiction and he simply didn't have the time. Ignoring the protests, Vecchi mailed a copy of the book to his friend. Williamson read the novel immediately and was so taken with it that, without telling Miller or Vecchi, he set out to find Rechy. "I think I sent it mostly to shock him a little bit," Vecchi says. "I didn't think he would be so taken with it or that he would be able to contact John Rechy."

Williamson also called Dr. Evelyn Hooker about the remarkable book he had just read. Dr. Hooker, who had interviewed Rechy in 1958 for her study on homosexuality, said she knew the author. She gave Williamson Rechy's address and telephone number in El Paso. Soon the two men were corresponding and eventually conversing on the phone.

Everyone who knew Dr. Ralph Williamson spoke of his genius, his innate dignity, and his sterling reputation in the psychiatric community. Among other impressive achievements, he had served on the panel of interviewers at the Nuremberg trials. But there was another side to Williamson that few people knew about. As one friend puts it, "This man was a very mysterious person."

Williamson told Rechy he found *City of Night* extraordinary. He couldn't stop talking about it. He asked Rechy to send him the reviews of the book. Rechy did and Williamson was furious about the Alfred Chester piece. It prompted him to write a letter blasting the piece to *The New York Review of Books* (a letter the *Review* did not publish). The doctor even offered to go on a literary television program to rebut the critic, but Chester did not accept the challenge.

The correspondence between Rechy and Williamson intensified. "I have known you a thousand years," Williamson wrote. Soon after Williamson mentioned that composer Benjamin Britten's *War Requiem* was going to premier at the Tanglewood Music Center in Lenox, Massachusetts, Rechy received a recording of the *War Requiem* in the mail with a note from Williamson asking for his opinion of the piece. Rechy loved it, and, upon learning this, Williamson invited him to be his guest at the concert in Tanglewood. He suggested they meet at his apartment in Riverdale, N.Y., in order to get acquainted beforehand.

Several years earlier Rechy had taken a chance when he accepted an invitation from a mysterious stranger to spend some time at the stranger's house on a Lake Michigan island. That experience had provided fertile ground for Rechy, who farmed from it a wealth of flamboyant characters and unexpected situations in his fourth novel, *The Vampires*. When the ticket from Williamson arrived Rechy again took a chance and headed to New York. More knowledgeable than before, Rechy knew what might happen with the doctor. Yet he was astute enough to expect nothing.

Rechy took a cab from the airport to Williamson's apartment in Riverdale. Not about to relinquish the image that had captivated so many, he arrived dressed for the part in his signature engineer boots, jeans, and tight T-shirt. When the cab pulled up in front of the swank high-rise the driver took in Rechy's getup and remarked, "Make out, boy—they don't eat hamburgers here, it's filet mignon every day." Undaunted, Rechy took the elevator to the 14th floor penthouse and rang the bell. The door opened to reveal an imposing man in his mid 50s. Behind him was a rendering of Michelangelo's "Creation of Man." Rechy was impressed. He took in Williamson's regal lounging clothes, white hair, and noble features. His resemblance to the God of Michelangelo's masterpiece was uncanny.

"The thing is, I was at a very vulnerable time," Rechy explains. "I didn't have any money and yet all this was happening to me. I had traveled all the way from El Paso to meet this stranger. We introduced ourselves. We talked. He offered me, of all things, a Manhattan. I got a little tipsy. Before I knew it, he was standing in front of me holding two paintings. One was of Bacchus, with horns and the wine spilling all over him. The other one was a drawing of St. Sebastian, naked and looking very beautiful and vulnerable. Dr. Williamson was saying to me, 'These are the choices. Which would you be?' The whole thing was hallucinatory. Beginning with the cab driver. The Michelangelo. God. And here he is, looking like God! And he kept saying, 'These are the choices, who are you?' Jesus Christ, it was unbelievable to me. And I said, 'I'm sure that there are many other choices in between.' Because I believe it."

Rechy was seized by an uncontrollable urge to call his mother. He quickly called Guadalupe and told her he had arrived safely.

Now, stuck between lives, Rechy entered into a most extraordinary kind of relationship with the doctor. Although he had not made a move sexually, Williamson indulged Rechy, giving him a private bedroom while the doctor slept in his own quarters. Soon after, they traveled together to Tanglewood to hear the performance of Britten's *War Requiem*. Williamson was delighted to be in the company of a young man who was as knowledgeable as he was attractive, and was drawn to the aura of excitement, danger, and sexuality that surrounded Rechy.

The first of many obsessives who read *City of Night* were starting to track Rechy down. He was hounded by a priest from Boston, Father Sereno, whom Williamson insisted on inviting for a visit. The priest wanted Rechy to help him start a group called Homosexuals Anonymous. Rechy warned him that this was a "stupid idea." But Father Sereno started the group without Rechy's assistance. In the first few weeks there was a suicide.

One day *City of Night*'s British publisher visited Rechy at Dr. Williamson's to discuss the U.K. edition of the book. The publisher originally asked for 20 deletions from the American edition. Rechy refused. The publisher then produced a list of 10 offending passages he wanted to cut. Rechy held his ground and again refused to alter his book. Eventually he agreed to three cuts: He removed "on the lips" from "kissed me on the lips," he changed "opened the buttons of my fly" to "opened my pants," and, from the opening of the "Jeremy" chapter, he deleted the word "doubly" from "doubly orgasmic thrusts."

With all the upheaval in his world, Rechy had found refuge with the doctor—and so he decided to stay in Riverdale for a while. The doctor's apartment overlooking the Hudson River had a mythical, faraway atmosphere. Once an eagle landed on the balcony and peered in through a glass wall. The number of the Penthouse was 14H; and Rechy wondered if the "H" stood for "heaven or hell or perhaps a little bit of both."

Williamson never discussed his patients, but as Rechy gained his trust the respected psychiatrist began to reveal more of himself, telling Rechy about the time he had briefly treated Marilyn Monroe. Rechy, whose idolization of Monroe would lead to his novel *Marilyn's Daughter* (1988), listened raptly. The doctor confided that, while he had been treating Monroe, he had felt she was being destroyed by her acting teacher, the legendary Lee Strasberg.

Rechy was fascinated by Williamson's many complexities and mysteries. Like Rechy, the doctor seemed to be many different people contained in one body. He drove a Jaguar, he dressed beautifully, yet he also went down to skid row to give money and to volunteer his services at clinics there. The two men grew closer, though the doctor, who was Catholic and regularly went to confession, never talked about being gay. He never spoke of his own desires. "He was a person whom I never talked about sex with," says Floriano Vecchi. "He never spoke about a romantic relationship with either a man or a woman, and I never asked. So I was puzzled that he loved *City of Night* so much. But I know nothing sexual ever happened between him and John Rechy."

Instead, the doctor would sit for hours, talking to Rechy about what he called "The X World," the world of rich men—abusers—who take advantage of young beautiful men who have lost their way. Williamson never understood, as Rechy points out, that "corruption can be mutual."

Rechy eventually discovered that a series of young men had enjoyed a similar arrangement with Dr. Williamson. Some nights, Williamson told Rechy about them. Once Rechy came across a letter from a young ballet dancer the doctor seemed to be courting. Another young man had been invited on a world tour by an older gentleman and called Williamson late at night for advice. Rechy could hear the doctor talking to him in calm, even tones. While looking for an envelope, Rechy came across some photos Williamson had taken of the late-night caller. In the photos the young man was naked except for jockeys, and he was wearing a set of antlers.

The doctor fetishized young corruptible men and, like most fetishists, he surrounded himself with the objects of his fixation. Yet he never allowed even close friends a glimpse of his secret world. He seemed to only want context. One night he had an attractive man in his 40s to dinner. The man had been kept for many years by a wealthy older patron who was now pushing him away. He spent the evening bemoaning his situation and talking about starting a drag show.

Williamson continued to keep Rechy in a "hallucinatory state," leading him through an emotional terrain even Rechy could not understand. That the doctor did not come on to him—did not, in fact, demonstrate any sexual desire whatsoever—unnerved Rechy. "Only later," Rechy says, "did I find out that I was just one of a string of hustler types that he courted and invited and traveled with, but never touched."

Williamson surrounded himself with men accustomed to being desired. Yet he refused to be seduced by them. Once he had his subject under his spell, he withdrew desire and took on a mentoring role. By not treating him as an object of desire and by keeping his own longings hidden, Williamson stripped Rechy of his power, leaving him lost and confused. "Looking back, it was very smart of him," Rechy says. "He had done it with that ballet dancer. He had done it with that kid who kept calling up. Warhol used a somewhat similar technique: Court beauty and then withhold desire. When you're used to being desired, that is brutal. It is a thing that annihilates you."

Rechy says that the doctor's indifference pitched him into one of the most promiscuous periods of his life. "Without the power—the power of sex—I would be someone I would not recognize," Rechy wrote shortly after in an incomplete unpublished sequel to *City of Night*. When the atmosphere at the apartment became too overwhelming, Rechy told the doctor he was going into Manhattan. He needed to prove to himself that he still possessed the power. He did not tell the doctor he was going to be photographed in the nude by a famous physique photographer. Nor did he tell him he was going to Times Square to hustle the very territory where he had been initiated seven years earlier. Rechy turned trick after trick, affirming to himself that he was still desirable.

Soon after Rechy first arrived at his apartment, the doctor had hired a houseboy to care for him—a young man named Alfonso who had on occasion worked as a cook and a caterer. Alfonso, Rechy recalls, was a moody mulatto with amber eyes and who moved like a dancer. "He was golden! Incredible!" Under the silent, watchful eyes of Williamson, the two young men became enthralled with each other. "I always wondered if he hired this houseboy knowing that this would happen."

Alfonso lived in a mental haze that made him extraordinary to Rechy. One time Rechy observed him standing on a ladder to put away some food. Alfonso forgot he was on the ladder, stepped back, and fell to the ground. It was Alfonso who first observed that there were Rechy impersonators making the rounds on the homosexual circuit. One Monday morning he hurried into the apartment to announce, "There are people impersonating you." He explained that over the weekend he had worked a Fire Island party where Rechy was supposedly the guest of honor. Rechy, of course, had been nowhere near Fire Island. He told Alfonso, "I don't want you to tell anyone I'm here."

By now the tawdriness and "show and tell–buy and sell" aspects of *City of Night* became a point of reference for those who inhabited a particular region of the homosexual world. And Rechy's bleak, grand panorama was territory other gay men wanted to explore. Sophisticated men longed to meet Rechy to probe the complex mind of the book's narrator. They wanted to encounter the characters he described, to live what he had lived. Rechy's presence at a social gathering that season would have been any host's crowning achievement. When cult poet Frank O'Hara attended a party that featured campy drag queens and sleek hustlers, he wrote to painter Larry Rivers that it was "just like John Rechy's novel." Felice Picano remembers leaving a get-together and "walking down a Manhattan street in the middle of nowhere when a limousine pulled up alongside of me. The window rolled down and somebody started talking to me, and I said to myself, *This is a scene out of* City of Night."

Despite his notoriety, Rechy remained hidden in Williamson's Riverdale high-rise. When a family emergency called Williamson away to Mexico, Rechy and Alfonso had the run of the vast apartment and began to play psychosexual games with each other. On the doctor's first day away, Alfonso brought Rechy breakfast in his room. Rechy lay in bed naked as the houseboy initiated an incredible seduction. "While he was serving me breakfast he was almost choreographing subservience. Fussing around me," Rechy recalls. "The houseboy was coming on to me in the most elaborately worshipful way. It was staggering."

In the five days Williamson was gone, Rechy and Alfonso forged a weird and highly erotic relationship. Rechy perceived this drama of psychological dominance and submission as an act of vengeance against the doctor. Still enraged that Dr. Williamson had not demonstrated any desire for him, Rechy thought, *I am desecrating his apartment.*

When Williamson returned from Mexico the houseboy was reluctant to end his relationship with Rechy and threatened to tell the doctor about the affair. Rechy's psyche was still in tatters, and he allowed the relationship to continue. The doctor didn't notice, or pretended not to notice, the sexual interplay between the younger men. Nor did he remark on the tension.

One stormy night when Williamson was not at home, Alfonso stood in front of Rechy, making a move to open his robe. "No more!" Rechy shouted. "It's too confusing."

Alfonso screamed back, "You think I'm a devil and you think he's God, don't you? I'll show you whose side you belong to!"

When the atmosphere in the apartment reached a peak of volatility, Williamson whisked Rechy away on a trip to Puerto

Rico. There on a Caribbean beach Rechy read in newspaper gossip columns what Alfonso had already told him—that imitators claiming to be John Rechy were crashing various parties.

Throughout their vacation, Rechy continued to find Williamson at once engaging and infuriating. During the day the doctor indulged his fondness for taking pictures of attractive men, photographing Rechy over and over against various tropical backdrops. But at night he never touched his young companion.

Suspended in this disturbing stasis, one afternoon at the beach Rechy noticed some young men milling about. It wasn't a cruisy beach, but Rechy's radar detected something was afoot. The men would go back and forth, then pause near one place. Rechy walked toward the men. As he got closer, he saw a man who had built himself a thatched shelter against a sand dune. As he squatted in his lean-to, young men stopped by to be blown.

On closer inspection, Rechy noted that the man in the hut was young and reasonably attractive. "When I came by, the man was clearly very interested. I looked back and I couldn't see Dr. Williamson in the distance. Then I did something cunning. You must understand that by then my mind was fucked over with all this stuff—Alfonso, the nude photographs I had taken of me in New York, hustling, and this man withholding desire." In a kind of surrogate sexual act, Rechy led the man in the hut out to the ocean, making sure Williamson could see him. "And then this gentleman came and squatted in the water, camouflaging what was going on. He started blowing me. I looked at Dr. Williamson and waved." John wasn't sure if the doctor was aware of what was going on. In his unpublished manuscript, intended as a sequel to *City of Night*, he writes, "I kept looking at Dr. Williamson, and when I finally came, I came with a thrust that was certainly more than sexual."

Rechy returned to his towel. "Do you feel better?" Williamson asked.

Williamson had his own subtle ways of inflicting an emotional wallop on Rechy's psyche. One day at the beach a young striking red-haired Puerto Rican man appeared and sat on a wall a few yards away from them. The stranger looked over at Rechy, then at Williamson. Then he took his shirt off. The doctor seemed mesmerized. He could not take his eyes off the man. "I was furious," Rechy says. "I wanted to kill that motherfucker on the wall! *So, I thought, So he's got a new kid.* I thought, *Fuck this shit. I'm going to go back to New York now, without saying a fucking word to him.*"

Rechy told the doctor he was going back to the hotel, with every intention of taking off.

"You can even become jealous of someone you're not involved with, because the ego comes into play," Rechy explains. "He didn't come back for a time. I was actually getting ready to leave when he returned. He had been shopping and had bought some presents for me."

There was no further drama until they returned to the apartment in Riverdale. Alfonso sulked in silence. Williamson asked Rechy, "What's wrong with Alfonso?"

Rechy professed to have no idea.

"I have a feeling that he did know about our relationship," Rechy says. "And in some perverse way, he was enjoying it." Rechy had been with the doctor for only a little over two months, but it had begun to feel like years. He was troubled and felt drained by the conflicts in the apartment. Soon after their trip to the Caribbean he decided to return to El Paso.

Williamson continued to correspond with him. A year later, Rechy prepared for another visit. But before Rechy left for New York, Williamson's brother called with the news that the doctor had drowned in the Caribbean. He had gone on a trip to St. Martin with a young man he was putting through school. Williamson was snorkeling when he apparently got a cramp and drowned. When Williamson didn't come back from the water, the young man panicked and went to the police. He was arrested on suspicion of murder and held in jail. Williamson's brother had to bail him out.

Rechy recalls, "This gets so incredible because now I was in touch with the brother, who is overtly gay. He's living with a boyfriend, and he tells me that all these young men are turning up, demanding that they be put through school. Funds were promised for education. The doctor had so many men. We were a string. But he hadn't touched anybody. Yet, for me, Dr. Williamson remains a great man and a great enigma."

Confused and dismayed, Rechy again retreated into the safety of El Paso. Guadalupe had a reception for him in the house he had bought for her. She invited the whole family and made spectacular Mexican food. She then showed him through the house he had bought her with his *City of Night* earnings. Then mother and son linked arms and walked outside for a tour of the breathtaking rose garden Guadalupe had planted. "It was the greatest triumph to result from *City of Night*," Rechy says. The little boy who dreamed of rescuing his mother had finally achieved his goal.

After spending some time with his family Rechy returned to Los Angeles to discover an entirely new atmosphere surrounded him. No longer just a moody and intelligent drifter writing about his experiences, he returned to his old stomping grounds as one of the most celebrated authors of his generation.

CHAPTER SEVEN

Not all intellectuals are as handsome as I am.
—John Rechy

AFTER THE SENSATIONAL DEBUT of *City of Night*, Rechy's personas began to merge in ways that confused him. He had always been able to keep his "selves" perfectly divided. He could go to the streets and forget everything, falling into his macho stance with the sexiest and toughest of street trade. Then he could go home, take a shower, and examine his life through sophisticated eyes, often reading Camus or other intellectual writers.

Every season has a new personality, a new star—the most desired guest at every dinner party. For the rest of 1964 John Rechy filled that role. One of the perks Rechy enjoyed with his newfound fame was an introduction to the literary intelligentsia. Part of the genius of *City of Night*—as potent today as it was nearly 40 years ago—is that it makes readers want to *know* the author. Who was the man behind the nightworld mask? Now that he was in demand, Rechy needed to create a new image to present to a totally different assortment of admirers.

The literary community wanted, first, to know if he was real. Fueled by Alfred Chester's review in *The New York Review of Books*, speculation mixed with idle gossip to form a loose consensus that John Rechy was the pseudonym of some older, more experienced author. Perhaps this Rechy was someone more famously familiar with the homosexual underground—James Baldwin or Tennessee Williams writing in the voice of a younger narrator—or even someone who derived the story from a hustler who shared his experiences.

Someone who knew better than to believe these rumors was Christopher Isherwood. His novel *A Single Man* came out in 1964 and presented a single day in the life of lonely, middle-aged homosexual man whose partner dies. The author of *The Berlin Stories* was delighted to be on friendly terms with the notorious Rechy and continued to invite him to the house he shared with Don Bachardy in Santa Monica Canyon.

The success of *City of Night* enabled Rechy to venture from the dark side of his personality—the realm of the mysterious, moody drifter—into the sparkling social circle of an Isherwood dinner party. Through Isherwood's hospitality Rechy befriended a number of witty, urbane homosexuals, like writer Gavin Lambert, and director James Bridges, who would eventually make *Urban Cowboy*, and Bridge's companion Jack Larson—an actor on the *Superman* television show—who was also a good friend of Montgomery Clift's.

Rechy began a new chapter in his journey toward self-discovery. He had fled his Catholic roots and his family in El Paso to explore his sexuality in the liberated "nightworld" critics called "the homosexual underground." Now he found himself seated at dinner tables with famous gay intellectuals.

But the acceptance of this new world led him to further confusion. What did people want from him? How did he want to be seen? Was he sexual or intellectual? Rechy knew how to act on the streets. His persona there had been perfected years before on the sidewalks of Times Square. He knew well how to become a fantasy figure. His johns wanted him to be dumb, tough, and ready for sex. He also knew how to behave at a dinner table, how to carry on a conversation, and what fork to use. Yet his enigmatic hustler persona was too compelling to give up completely—so he wore it to cocktail parties, along with a fetishistic necklace and a self-designed flesh-tone fitted silk shirt. While his dinner companions appreciated his wit and charm, at the end of the night some wanted him to be dumb, butch, and sexy. They also wanted him in bed. Although Rechy was responsible for this confusion of identities, it became increasingly difficult to draw lines and make distinctions—for himself and for the people around him.

After his visits to Los Angeles, Rechy would return to El Paso where the quiet existence he cherished with his mother would resume.

The life Rechy led while he roamed the country remained something unspoken between them. "I never was very sure if my mother was aware that I was gay," Rechy recalls. "That's one of the enigmas about our relationship. I never mentioned being gay to her. I once overheard my mother talking to one of her sisters who was visiting. I was in my study, and I heard my aunt telling my mother, 'Well, yes, your son may be famous, but do you know what his book is about?' Then my mother said, 'Whatever it's about, my son could go in the front door of places that wouldn't allow you in through the kitchen.' And I settled down. I thought I couldn't have said it better. I guess she had to have known."

With his mother, Rechy tried to live quietly on the book's earnings. Adding to his apprehension about fame, strangers began to show up at his house. In one terrifying experience, a strange young woman appeared, claiming to be the inspiration for the character Barbara from the book. "I was alone," Rechy remembers, "and she pushed in. She couldn't have been over 17, maybe younger...heavily made up...then she proceeded to pull me to her. I was sure that someone would burst in and accuse me of seducing a minor. She wouldn't leave. She kept crying and...throwing herself at me. Then she ran into the bathroom and locked herself in. There was a terrible silence. I didn't know what she was doing. Then she rushed out at me, and I had to carry her out of the house. By then my mother—who'd been out visiting—had returned. Late into the night, I would look out and the girl was still there, parked in her car. Just waiting there."

He also received weird letters from a teenager named Billy Biden (a pseudonym) who decided he was going to live like the drifter in *City of Night*. He somehow got ahold of Rechy's phone number and address and began calling and writing. Rechy told him, "You've misunderstood the book." Eventually Rechy received a letter declaring, "Billy Biden is coming to meet John Rechy." Rechy instantly contacted him and put a stop to it. Billy was later arrested in New York City for hustling.

Because notoriety invited bizarre incidents like these, Rechy became increasingly antisocial in El Paso, retaining only a few close friends—writers and other intellectuals whose company he craved in his domestic isolation. "My friends were almost exclusively heterosexual Jewish intellectuals," Rechy remembers. "Friends like Mollie Shapiro and Frank Oppenheimer. With them I felt entirely at ease because I was viewed as an artist, and we discussed art, politics, and I absorbed many of their left-wing attitudes from them. The evenings at dinner with them remain among the most stimulating memories of that time."

Rechy also enjoyed the time he spent with his mother. "There was a lot of happiness then," he recalls. "I'd take my mother out to lunch to her favorite places—and she'd always be treated like a queen. I'd take her to dinner, to the movies. I hired a woman to do the work in the house."

Sometimes friends like Floriano Vecchi and his partner Richard Miller would visit Rechy in El Paso. They noted the exceptional love he had for his mother. "It was fierce to the point where he adored this woman," Vecchi says. "The image I have of his mother is that every time we went on some kind of a trip, as we left the house she was at the front door giving the sign of the cross, like the Pope giving a benediction. She was a very beautiful woman. She looked very much like him."

Rechy was fascinated by the relationship between Vecchi and Miller. Once, as the three of them drove to New Mexico, Rechy quizzed them about their union. "He was puzzled by the fact that two people had been living together for over 10 years," Vecchi says. "I remember very clearly in my mind, he asked, 'What would happen if one of you died?' My friend Richard looked at me and said, 'At the risk of being selfish, I hope I'm the first one to go.'"

The conversation proved tragically prophetic: Richard Miller died in a car accident not long after their trip.

Rechy remained a loner in El Paso. He would take long drives into the Texas desert or along the banks of the Rio Grande. Often he climbed mountains by himself.

Yet throughout his self-imposed exile, Rechy received hundreds of letters from fans writing about how *City of Night* had affected them. "Young men. Old men. So many," he recalls. "I answered them all. These letters would make an interesting book in themselves. They were profoundly moving but very personal. The University of California at Berkeley had offered to buy them. But I felt that would be a violation of trust. I worried that if something happened to me, these letters would end up in the wrong hands. So I burned them." Although he answered all the letters, Rechy continued to keep the outside world at arm's length.

In late 1964 Rechy began a sequel to *City of Night*. The book, which he called *In the Beginning*, centered around his experiences with Dr. Ralph Williamson and the surreal events that took place in the psychiatrist's Riverdale high-rise and on the Caribbean beaches. "In the book I would write, I would dissect a man who was trying to be a saint," Rechy wrote in unpublished notes. "By writing about him I'd see how saintly he really was."

The manuscript opens with a literal re-creation of Rechy's meeting with Dr. Williamson in Riverdale. As with *City of Night*, Rechy tells the story in the first person. (He also continues his unconventional use of capitalization and punctuation.) Rechy says he dashed off 50 pages a day as he recorded the events as factually as possible. "Each night I kiss myself in the mirror and say I love you," Rechy writes in the manuscript. Today Rechy confirms, "I used to do that. I don't know when it stopped."

In the Beginning exists as a long first draft, recording—perhaps too literally for Rechy's comfort—the events with Dr. Williamson. Along with the manuscript there are copious notes throughout, handwritten in pen and pencil, documenting events to be included, revisions, and stylistic techniques the novel should employ. "It's all a terribly rough first draft," Rechy says, "and I will never revise it." Just as the manuscript reached 1,000 pages, Rechy heard the news of Williamson's death. Rechy says he was too distraught to complete it and feared he might be unfair to the doctor. Fifteen years later a rare-book collector asked Rechy why he never wrote a sequel to *City of Night*. John confessed he had a sequel in manuscript form that was 1,037 pages long—the number of pages in *Gone With the Wind*. The collector immediately offered him $20,000 for the manuscript, a large sum at the time. Rechy refused. To this day only two other people have seen the manuscript.

Eventually Rechy built a gym in his mother's new house. As he entered his mid 30s, he still looked at least a decade younger. Bill Regan, who continued to see Rechy whenever Rechy was in Los Angeles, remembers how important it was for Rechy to be sexually desirable, even after he gained fame as a writer. "He would get furious with me because there were times that I wouldn't give him my full attention," Regan says. "He needed somebody in his life who would say, 'God, you look great!' It wasn't in my nature to be that way, so he would ask me, 'How do I look?' He had to pull it out of me."

Rechy worked out obsessively. His narcissism fueled his bodybuilding just as it had fed his desire to hustle and, later, to write about hustling. The reliable aphrodisiac of youth was gone. He couldn't remain young but he certainly wanted to remain "better." Rechy had to develop something new to take youth's place. In the homosexual community a hard, muscular body is almost as desirable as youth. And that was within Rechy's control. He couldn't stop the clock, but he could reshape his slender, boyish body into a pumped-up, magnificently cut hard-body.

Even with a perfect body he knew pumping iron would not ultimately preserve him. He had to continue writing.

•••

In 1965, Rechy had a comfortable new house in El Paso and a sleek black-and-tan Mustang with a custom steering wheel. He also had a new stereo and shelves full of the books he loved. Contentment was in his grasp. Yet most of the time he remained edgy and would become bored and restless.

Sometimes he fled into the freedom of his sexual identity. Although he claimed in *City of Night* that he would never intermingle his dark side with his life in El Paso, he inevitably gave in to sexual cravings and sporadically picked up men. One day his high school math teacher picked him up, mistaking him for a transient. Rechy recognized his teacher and refused to go with him, reasoning that such an encounter would have been too confusing. Another time he picked up a cruiser and had sex with him. The next day Rechy went to an art show, and the featured artist turned out to be that stranger.

Sex continued to be Rechy's preferred route of escape, a means of distracting himself from past, present, and future. Keeping his fragmented private life from his mother was never a problem for Rechy. In fact, he confessed to friends that he never felt morally wrong about hustling. "I've never looked at the activities that I was involved in as degrading," he says. "Most of the people who look at those kinds of activities as degrading are very much like the people who look at Marilyn Monroe enviously and say, 'Oh, she was trash.'"

The idea of an emotional commitment to another man was unthinkable. Sex was a fleeting thing, a momentary diversion indulged when his reclusive life with his mother became too stifling. It often occurred without any exchange of identity, sometimes without even so much as a word. One mid afternoon in a cruisy desert canyon Rechy "made it" with a "stranger" who—he later realized—was his second cousin.

The underground cruising world in El Paso was small compared to what Rechy was used to, and he longed to compete in more challenging arenas. For brief stints he left the peaceful haven he had created for himself and his mother for sex vacations in Los Angeles. Sometimes Guadalupe accompanied him and stayed with his beloved sister Olga in Torrance. Rechy rented a room in a motel near his sister's home, allowing him the freedom to come and go as he pleased. "I figured I'd catch up sexually," Rechy explains.

With these trips to Los Angeles, Rechy continued to move toward the next phase in his coming out process. Although he still often hustled, his sex life could no longer exclusively revolve around buying and selling. The availability of younger hustlers also made him less desirable on the scene. Rechy began cruising the streets and bars, and more often the parks and woods for quick anonymous encounters. As a cruiser he was still the hottest thing, picking and choosing, and—with his newly improved physique— easily beating out the other men who hunted for free sex. There was always the added bonus of being mistaken for a hustler.

In Los Angeles Rechy soon discovered Griffith Park, a rambling wooded area in Los Feliz that allowed him to continue exploring his sexual identity. Rechy later described his discovery of the park in *This Day's Death*: "As I drove up, I saw men walk from their cars and disappear into a forest of trees to the side of the road...I parked, waited. Then I got out. I entered the green forest. Eyes. Shadows. Sex hunters everywhere."

It was in this wooded playground that Rechy began his uneasy transition from "hustler" to "cruiser." He was cruising—not hustling—in Griffith Park during the daytime. At night he might hustle, but cruising often took precedence then too. For the first time he considered physical attractiveness as a factor in his choice of partners. Payment was no longer the main issue.

During this transitional period, in social situations, Rechy suddenly felt a need to talk about his sexual exploits as part of his identity. One night at a dinner party Rechy chatted with two men who knew he was a writer. Toward the end of the evening both men started to come on to him. Instead of declining politely, Rechy fumbled for an excuse and finally put them off by declaring, "My sexual activities are almost always in Griffith Park now." This, of course, was nobody's business, but it was such a part of Rechy's identity at the time he felt compelled to share it with people. The two men were not amused and one of them retorted irritably, "Well, what about if we go and get a potted plant so you'll feel more on your own turf?"

During his visits to California Rechy's behavior was undeniably compulsive. "It was like going to work," he explains. "I went to Griffith Park every single day." This was Rechy's way to make up for the lost time associated with each day lived quietly in El Paso. He seduced stranger after stranger in a frantic quest to confirm that he was still desirable—and therefore still alive.

In the dense woods of Griffith Park, with its complex winding pathways and hidden roads, Rechy found an ideal way to express his exhibitionism. Like the time he stood on a mound of dirt and rocks in an alcove opposite a main road in the park. As gawking cruisers in cars lined the road, Rechy exhibited himself sensually, stretching his body, looping his fingers over his jeans, opening the top button, flexing—all the while pretending to be oblivious to the onlookers.

"It was a performance," Rechy says, "but it wasn't a vulgar display. I believe exhibitionism should be graceful, not awkward." As the cars lined up, he became bolder. Another button. Another. The branches that stretched over the mound where he stood created a stage, and he was the star performer. "It was entirely exciting to know that everyone in the parked cars desired me. I extended the performance to near-climax, and then I left." These were Rechy's greatest orgasmic moments—better for him than any physical contact.

At 34 Rechy was still an incredibly handsome man. His body was better than it had been when he was a young man and a top hustler. Los Angeles, however, is a city filled with handsome men with painstakingly developed bodies. To remain the center of attention Rechy became more daring. It was he who introduced shirtlessness to the park. Up until the time he started taking off his shirt, guys would cruise the woods in T-shirts and cut-offs. At first Rechy separated himself from the other cruisers by walking around with a denim shirt open to his navel. When some men imitated the look he became more brazen and discarded his shirt altogether. Rechy's body was his power. Soon other buff men cruised shirtless as well. To top the topless, Rechy began opening the top button of his jeans. "He really was something," recalls a fellow cruiser from Griffith Park over 30 years later. Men who didn't identify him as the author of *City of Night* recognized him as a local icon from the park and from Santa Monica Boulevard.

Rechy's next novel, *Numbers*, documented events he experienced during one of his trips to Los Angeles with his mother. On the way to L.A. Rechy and Guadalupe stopped in Arizona for a rest at a luxurious hotel. It was important to Rechy that his success allow him to pamper and protect his mother as she had pampered and protected him. "One of the most beautiful moments in my life occurred that night at the expensive and gaudy motel, when I sat with my mother by the poolside. She asked for a cool soft drink, and I ordered it. She took her sleeping pills. Then she said good night, and I watched her moving away, along the pastel lights of the motel." He adored her and was making up for time he would be leaving her with his sister while he pursued his sexual demons.

Soon after the stopover, with his mother safely tucked away at his sister's house in Torrance, Rechy's long exile in El Paso ended in an explosive sexual odyssey that lasted for 10 days. Obsessed with proving to himself and to those around him that he was still one hot number, Rechy started playing a game with himself. At first he just tried to see how many men he could get to approach him, touch him, suck his cock, as he himself remained perfectly detached from the situation. As the number of men who succumbed to John's magnetism increased, the game became more passionate, more out of control, more dangerous. He set a goal of enticing 30 men to have some sort of sexual contact with him. Rechy not only hit his goal, he made time to visit his old mentor, Bryce, and to attend a couple of dinner parties with the Isherwood crowd.

His experiences during the trip inspired him. Rechy began writing *Numbers* while driving back to El Paso. His mother firmly held a writing pad for him on the console of his Mustang while he steered with his left hand. He drove for hours taking notes, scribbling sentences, and finally full passages. Guadalupe sat quietly beside him. Rechy completed the novel in El Paso after three months of frenzied work. "I conceived *Numbers* as a sexual horror story," he says. "As a result the only writer I read and reread during that period was Poe, a deep influence."

Writing was Rechy's way of mastering experience. *Numbers* is a fictionalized narrative of his behavior on the 10-day trip—a record of his excessive attachment to sex. The main focus of this book was his narcissism and how it fueled his obsessions. "Now Johnny had come three times," Rechy writes, "four people have made it with him and many more have wanted to, one jerked off just watching him. And what does he feel? A screaming need still unfulfilled." As Rechy worked on the new novel, he decided to leave out the mother character. He would explore that relationship in a later book. All the other events in the novel followed his real-life experiences with scrupulous accuracy.

As *Numbers* opens, we see the protagonist speeding in a car from Phoenix to Los Angeles—from the city of the mythical bird rising triumphantly from its own ashes to the city of dark angels. As he drives the protagonist leans into the accelerator, all the while counting insects as they smash against the windshield. The entire book is obsessed with death—though not a single character dies in it. Even the birds are suicidal. Rechy has said that *Numbers* is "as much about dying as it is about sex." The death he describes in this second novel is the death of youth.

With the passing of youth comes the destruction of innocence. Readers see how his experiences have changed Rechy in the four years between his first two novels. The nameless drifter in *City of Night* is brutally sexy—and he certainly exploits that sexiness—but he still has a certain vulnerability. The world of male prostitution, gay bars, and seedy third-run movie theaters is new to him, and he describes his discoveries with a touching wonder that summons readers' sympathy. He delights in the characters he encounters, like a kid at a soda fountain tasting one delicious ice cream flavor after another. Even if he finds his characters repulsive, he sees and dutifully documents their humanity. He is protective of his characters. He loves them. And because of that, we love him.

The man this young hustler has grown into in *Numbers* is now given a name—Johnny Rio. And what a piece of work Johnny Rio is. His main mission here is not to observe others, but rather to see how others react to him—those who knew him in his heyday as a hustler, and the newer, fresher pieces of trade who have moved onto the scene in his absence. This Johnny Rio knows the score.

The curiosity and delight of the young protagonist in *City of Night* gives way to his older *Numbers* alter ego, possessing scorn and contempt and a jaded need to prove himself. He demonstrates his superiority to others by making them want him sexually.

No longer vulnerable, the protagonist is now totally self absorbed. While still fancying himself the sensitive type his actions often seem unforgivably cruel. Sex for him is cold and impersonal. He lures men to touch or blow him, but often leaves them bewildered in the middle of the act. Johnny doesn't want an orgasm; he wants proof of his desirability. After a brief conquest with one man, he immediately sets his sights on someone else. "He feels—he knows he is—more desirable than ever," Rechy writes. "And he feels alive."

In *Numbers* Rechy describes his encounters and himself in the third person. In consequence the book loses the immediacy of the first person narration in *City of Night*. In the earlier book we become aware of the boy's good looks through others' reactions to him. He seldom describes himself. But, flogged by an aging narcissist's insecurity, Johnny Rio in *Numbers* is described at every turn, giving the impression of a handsome man, terrified of aging, looking to a mirror for reassurance. Though readers are given full descriptions of his stunning looks in the opening chapter, there are reminders throughout the entire book that his physique is "lithe and hard" and that he moves his "tightly muscled body" with "panther grace." Johnny Rio never wears underclothes, and he is often described as "a very butch number."

Still unable to accept his homosexuality, Johnny Rio proudly declares, "I have never desired another man. I'm aroused only by what another man does—and not by him; second, I have not reciprocated sexually with another man—nor have I ever let a man come on with me other than with his mouth—and of course his hands—on my body; and third I've done it for money." But Johnny Rio—as written by Rechy—also longs to be desired by women, and the woman he meets at his motel, like everyone else in the book, lusts after him mightily.

No one in the world—even the most beautiful of individuals—is attractive to everyone, but the narcissistic Johnny Rio defies that notion. As we read his story he stares us down defiantly, challenging readers to prove him wrong. Nearly everyone who beholds Johnny finds him deliciously irresistible. Everywhere he goes eyes follow him hungrily. To verify his powers to attract, Rio puts everyone to the test—and he wins almost every time. His only weakness is his fear of aging. It's hard to feel compassion for Johnny Rio. We care about what happens to him, but just barely. He holds our attention by piquing our most morbid curiosities. We become voyeuristic, detached.

To disabuse readers of the idea that Johnny Rio's callousness finds its root in the author's heart, Rechy points out that, although based partially on his own exploits, *Numbers* is not an unalloyed autobiography. Part of the artist's power to transform experiences is the freedom to re-create and re-invent. Although

Johnny Rio is a character Rechy refined out of some of his own poses, the protagonist, he says, does not reflect his own attitudes. Rechy's goal was to invent a memorable character, not to replicate himself.

"It's important to keep in mind," Rechy says, "that Johnny Rio—admittedly sharing most of the experiences I remembered from my own first time in the Park—is only one aspect of me, one of the roles I was playing. His attitudes belong to that role. Many of the attitudes indicated are not ones that I myself would uphold in another context, out of the park, or at another time."

Rechy goes on to explain, "Johnny Rio is a character, and nothing in the world says that a character should be 'loved.' Indeed, among the most memorable characters in literature are those impossible to love, the characters that fascinate. Like Camus's *The Stranger*, another influence on this novel." Ultimately, though, Rechy meant for the character to be tragic—a man caught in his own trap brought on by his addictions. "At the end, Johnny has moved from the excitement of 'numbering' into a state now of numbness," Rechy says. "The title also implies numb-er: that which numbs, and Johnny wants to be numbed to the fact of aging. One of the men who pursues Johnny and seems to become younger and younger as Johnny Rio veers toward hallucination— that man is death. The ending of this sexual horror story is, for me, quite sad. Why is it difficult to feel compassion for the desirable narcissist, whose desirability is rationed by the passing of time? Those who desire can and do move on to new, younger objects of desire. Do I feel compassion for Johnny Rio today? Oh, yes, very much so—and empathy."

What makes *Numbers* successful is Rechy's control of the novel's structure. In the first chapter all the book's themes and symbols are subtly and skillfully introduced, foreshadowing Johnny Rio's dark descent into his mind and into the park that feeds his sexual addiction. Rechy adroitly shapes Johnny's chaotic quest into a tight narrative. The protagonist's passions may be out of control, but the novel never loses its organized intensity.

Unencumbered by the restrictions of political correctness, Rechy chronicles the obsessions of the gay male narcissist and how he views the people around him. Each generation has its own counterparts to the characters in *Numbers*. In the future, readers can turn to this book to see how men cruised, talked, and viewed each other in the urban gay subculture of the mid 1960s. The cartoonish queens, the overblown bodybuilders, and the aging lechers of the day are carefully scrutinized and recorded through Rechy's cold eyes.

Reading *Numbers* is like living in the heart of Boys' Town in West Hollywood, or Chelsea in New York City. By cruising with Johnny Rio, a gay man learns how and why the handsome, muscular man who passes him on the street, sucks in his image, judges him inadequate, and dismisses him—all within a split-second. "I tried to reveal Johnny Rio's rationalizations, self-deceptions—the subterfuges I had once employed," Rechy explains. "In writing about him, I could see through those subterfuges."

Some readers, particularly modern day clones of their generation, will relate to Johnny's subterfuges—and, like his creator, will feel sympathy for the inevitable loneliness that awaits him in old age. On the other hand, Rio's constant posing, preening, and neurotic worrying about how he's stacking up compared to the other studs within view evokes the thrilling, desperate atmosphere of an overcrowded West Hollywood bar on a Saturday night.

As with *City of Night*, much of the critical response to *Numbers* was, as Rechy puts it, "largely hysterical." Again, Rechy was dismayed when critics fussed about the sexual content or misunderstood the structure. Author Gregory Woods summed up many critics' feelings about *Numbers* in *A History of Gay Literature: The Male Tradition*: "The narrative structure consists of little more than a linear ramble from sex act to sex act. For the reader this is a frustrating experience: One is left in the situation of the cruiser deprived of the sex. The experience would be more satisfying if the book was simply pornographic." Other reviewers were astute enough to note the excellent writing and intricate construction. To purchase the book in Germany, readers had to sign a card stipulating they were over the age of 21 and knew of the novel's contents. They also had to promise not to lend it to anyone under 21, nor to anyone 21 or over without informing him or her of its subject matter.

Publisher Michael Denneny agrees with Rechy that most critics had more of an issue with his themes than with the book itself. "I had the impression over the years a number of times that people are criticizing him as a writer because they are heavily influenced by the subject matter," Denneny observes. "I don't think people would be as critical of him as a writer if he weren't writing about the erotic world. I've always taken criticisms against him with a grain of salt. What upsets them is sex, so they dismiss him as not a good writer, where he has clearly been a major force and a major influence on the development of gay literature. Nobody could deny that."

As if to verify the fact that *Numbers* is based on fact and that John Rechy is indeed Johnny Rio, Rechy's photo appeared on the cover of the book. Rechy was still concerned about remaining anonymous in his hustling life, but his vanity won out and in the end he allowed Grove to run his photo—albeit slightly grainy—on the cover. "I'm glad I decided to go with it," Rechy says. "It's a great photograph and it captures Johnny Rio." Grove also thought it was a great marketing strategy to have the sexy author on the cover, rather than on the back, of a novel that so closely mirrored his own provocative exploits.

Rechy did manage to remain anonymous after *Numbers* came out, but the front jacket photo did cause some confusion. Men in Griffith Park recognized him as Johnny Rio, the character in the book, rather than the book's author. "Some writer has written a book about you," a stranger gushed to Rechy when he spotted him cruising in the park.

Rechy was immediately amused and played along with the man. "Who wrote it?" he demanded.

"Oh, I don't know," the stranger responded. "Nobody would write a book like that under his own name."

In Rechy's life, as in his books, fiction mixed easily with biography.

One unexpected result of writing about the next phase of his life, was the reaction of some of the real people behind the novel's characters. Unlike the "nightworld" denizens who drifted through the pages of *City of Night*, some of the characters in *Numbers* were based on literary figures who had eagerly awaited John Rechy's second book. Not all of them were honored to recognize themselves as the inspiration for characters in Rechy's sexual world. Christopher Isherwood, for one, was livid about the character of Sebastian Michaels: "a small, slender, grayish-blond man in his 50s," a famous writer renowned for "fine, serious, often beautiful books." Isherwood's companion, Don Bachardy, appears in the book as artist Tony Lewis: "Once preciously pretty, Tony Lewis in his 30s has become a good-looking man."

Don Bachardy says, "Christopher was fond of John, as I was, but I thought it was reckless of John to identify us—one of the characters was a successful middle-aged writer with a younger friend who was an artist. Who could mistake us? It was also so unnecessary; we're not in any way indigenous to the book. We're just part of the enveloping framework of the book, and I thought it was a kind of gratuitous identification of us without much point."

Bachardy particularly objected to Rechy's fictionalizing a dinner party at Christopher Isherwood's house that was attended by the writer Gavin Lambert (re-created in the character of Paul Blake). In real life the party's guest list included Bachardy, Lambert, and Lambert's lover, an attractive actor named Clinton ("Guy" in the novel) who is described in the novel as "a very handsome dark young man with curly black hair and enormous brooding eyes rimmed with dark lashes." (Rechy disguised the real-life prototype of the character, Clinton, by changing him from a blond.) All the guests at the Isherwood dinner have cameos in *Numbers*, but if anyone had reason to be offended, it was Lambert. Later in the novel, Johnny Rio has a sexual scene in the bushes with the character based on Lambert's lover, and subsequently at a dinner held at Paul Blake's home, Guy and Johnny Rio have the following exchange:

> "We'll have to make it tonight, man, OK? Together—tonight—OK?" And there it was—the tone of urgency that, whatever the source, hints of that deep sense of desolation, of doom, of the despair and desolation which Johnny had intercepted that earlier night.
> "OK," Johnny Rio says.
> "After you say goodbye to Paul, just wait outside for me—OK?"
> "OK," Johnny repeats.
> Returning—and seeing Johnny and Guy standing close together—Paul immediately understands. His face has the look of someone who insists, "This isn't happening"—while he sees it happen.

Yet when Lambert read the account of this actual indiscretion, he took it in stride, understanding that everything in life is fuel for the writer's imagination: "Obviously to people in the know, the characters in *Numbers* were identifiable. Chris (Isherwood) and Don (Bachardy) took great umbrage at this. They felt it was an invasion of privacy, and we were supposed to be his friends. I knew them very well. I don't remember either of them being offended by what was supposed to be the portrayal of them, it was more the action of John invading their privacy. Christopher in particular was very rigid about that, very insistent. I didn't care because I thought, well, first of all, it's all very well for Christopher to get up on his high horse back then, but, as a writer he'd been doing the same thing to people all his life. Secondly, every novelist bases his fiction, to some extent, on in his reality—people he's met, intimacies that occur. Read all through Henry James's notebooks. Everything he writes about started with a dinner anecdote or someone he met at dinner. But *Numbers* never bothered me. I saw exactly what John was up to.

The Johnny Rio character made it with my boyfriend some-where outside, but for him it was just one more number. That was par for the course in the '60s. And I rather liked the book too. After *Numbers* came out, I remember John said he was ter-ribly impressed with my attitude. He said, 'You were the only one who came out civilized about it.' Anyway there was a total break between him and Bachardy and Isherwood, who could get a bit grand at times."

Rechy was incredulous that Isherwood would be angry to find himself the prototype for a character in a novel. After all, as Lambert rightly notes, many of Isherwood's famous literary friends appeared in his novels under different names, including W.H. Auden, Stephen Spender, and Virginia Woolf. In his *Goodbye to Berlin* it was Isherwood who wrote, "I am a camera with its shut-ter open, quite passive, recording, not thinking. Recording the man shaving at the window opposite and the woman in the kimono washing her hair. Some day, all this will have to be devel-oped, carefully printed, fixed." Rechy believed Isherwood should have been willing to face the camera himself, unflinching.

Rechy perhaps mistakenly took Isherwood to heart when Isherwood made his comment, quoted almost verbatim by Rechy in *Numbers*: "One can say anything one wants about a person's morals—describe them as black as black—but never anything dis-paraging about his physical appearance." To keep his character models happy, Rechy lavished compliments on his portraits of Isherwood and Bachardy. Nonetheless, when they read about their fictional counterparts, they were not amused to find themselves in the frame of Rechy's authorial camera.

Over 30 years later, Don Bachardy says, "I thought they were rather trashy characterizations. We deserved a bit better than that from him. He made us sound like very ordinary fags." Bachardy also says he was more upset than Isherwood, but felt that Rechy harmed Isherwood professionally. "He gave the Isherwood character dia-logue in which he put down his screenwriting work," Bachardy says. "First of all, it was completely untrue. Chris never talked in that kind of way about his screenwriting work. He actually enjoyed screenwriting very much, and he always gave it his very best effort."

Rechy had planned attend a dinner at Isherwood's house on a date soon after the couple read *Numbers*. Earlier in the day, however, an unexpected telegram arrived at John's sister Olga's place, where John had been visiting. "You are no longer welcome here," the telegram stated bluntly.

Later, Bachardy tried to get an explanation from Rechy. "I called him on the phone," he remembers. "And he took it personally. He pretended not to see why I was objecting and that I must be objecting because I didn't like him or didn't like his work. He was wounded in a way I thought was unprofessional. I thought, *Well, if he's going to take that attitude, too bad.*"

The *Numbers* incident didn't completely end the friendship. Rechy ran into Isherwood and Bachardy from time to time, and they were always cordial. But the novel, says Bachardy, "created a coolness."

Numbers also severely damaged Rechy's relationship with Bryce McKoy, who had helped out Rechy financially during the completion of *City of Night*. Although Rechy had used bits of Bryce's personality in his first novel in the voice of Jeremy, he had sufficiently camouflaged their conversations enough for his friend not to be offended. In Rechy's second novel, however, Bryce appears as the character Tom, who mirrors the real Bryce much more closely. Tom gives Johnny Rio money for rent, sets up a room in his house for him, and offers to put the Johnny through school. Along with these unmistakable correlations, Rechy reveals intimate details of his relationship with Bryce in passages like this:

Tom asked nothing of him except that he let him make love to his body. Johnny let him: Tom licked every inch of Johnny's body, and Johnny came in his mouth—sometimes several times a day. On weekend mornings Tom would go into "Johnny's room" silently and wake him up by kissing his body lightly all over.

Bryce McKoy was deeply hurt when he read the very thinly disguised version of his relationship with Rechy in *Numbers*. Although Rechy tried to stay in touch with him after the publication, and had even dedicated the book in part to him (along with Bill Regan and another friend), Bryce was decidedly frosty to him in their telephone conversations. "One of the main factors in all this," Rechy explains, "was that Bryce had never thought of my relationship with him as a hustling relationship. Nor, in fact, did I. He was a very generous man who truly enjoyed helping a young man he thought was headed to a dead-end. I think, really, that was the source of disappointment—and, also, that he could no longer be my benefactor since I had become a successful writer."

Rechy remained grateful to Bryce and would sporadically try and contact him for many years to come—until Bryce's number was disconnected.

If Rechy lost a few friends because of *Numbers*, the novel also brought him a few new ones. Liberace, recovering in the hospital from a case of blood poisoning (cleaning fluid used to spruce up one of his gaudy Las Vegas costumes had seeped into his bloodstream) got ahold of a copy of *Numbers*. Reading about Johnny Rio's erotic exploits in the parks and seedy movie theaters of Los Angeles speeded the legendary pianist's recovery. On his release from the hospital Liberace announced to a friend of his who knew the author, "I'm dying to meet John Rechy." When the friend showed Liberace another photo of Rechy, clearer than the grainy image on the *Numbers* cover, Liberace exclaimed, "The sooner the better!"

The friend arranged a dinner party at his Hollywood Hills home. Learning that Liberace attributed his current good health to *Numbers*, Rechy knew what was expected. He dressed that night as Johnny Rio would, in his exquisite, flesh-colored silk shirt that fit like a second skin.

During cocktails outdoors, Liberace hid in a corner standing between his muscular bodyguard and his dresser. The bodyguard was a boyfriend on the way out. The dresser was a handsome man who had come before the bodyguard and who Liberace now generously retained in his paid entourage. When the slightly late Rechy made his grand entrance onto the patio, Liberace unwedged himself to mingle with the other guests.

When the two finally spoke, Liberace hastened to make it clear to Rechy that his bodyguard boyfriend was on the way out. Rechy duly noted this fact.

During dinner Liberace made sure he was seated next to his quarry. Once Rechy realized his sexy outfit was a success and that the flamboyant entertainer desired him, he began to play down his hustler image and play up his literary image. It was important, of course, for Rechy to be desired by the Las Vegas legend. But with that accomplished, he felt free to relish being the successful writer, the intellectual dinner guest. Certainly Rechy was aware he was giving Liberace mixed signals—he often did in mixed company—but he couldn't help himself. That's what his life was all about.

He was talking about literature—with his shirt unbuttoned to the navel—when to his abject horror and delight he felt Liberace's hand on his crotch under the table. Rechy stumbled over his words for a moment and managed to spill only a minimal amount of wine before discreetly removing the gaudily ringed fingers. Meanwhile, Liberace—his ex-lover sitting on the other side of him and his bodyguard one seat over—never dropped his famous smile, and spilled a bit less wine than Rechy.*

Liberace wasn't offended by the rejection. He remained sweetly good-natured throughout the dinner and excused himself soon after dessert, sweeping out grandly with his burly companions in tow. Rechy remained with the other guests.

A little while later Rechy's host received a telephone call from Liberace, who wanted to talk to Rechy. "He said he was

---

*In 1977, John wrote about this encounter in *The Sexual Outlaw,* veiling Liberace's identity by referring to him as "the star": "His fingers dig into my fly. I'm trying to be cool. Not to embarrass anyone. Others at the table are unaware of what's happening under it."

despondent," Rechy recalls. "And so alone. So terrified. It was terrible. Naive after the groping? Sure I was. But he sounded desperate."

So while Rechy understood Liberace's motives, there was always a part of him that responded to loneliness—and it was, after all, Liberace! Under the heady influence of sympathy, curiosity, and alcohol, Rechy agreed to meet with him.

"My friends drove me in their car, so I wouldn't have difficulty finding the place—to his mansion in the Hollywood Hills. As the car pulled up to his driveway on Valley Vista Boulevard, I saw the bodyguard rushing away. It was as if he was spying."

Rechy entered a black and white kitchen where he was greeted by a nervous herd of black and white poodles, each with a contrasting black or white ribbon on the front poof of hair. Then Liberace led him through the black and white dining room, into a black and white living room. It was like walking along the keys of a gigantic piano.

Rechy wondered whether Liberace had just moved into the flash and trash mansion. In *The Sexual Outlaw* he described it as "cluttered like an overbought antique store. Chandeliers like crystal spider webs. Devouring velvet chairs. Figurines and statues battling limply for attention. Plastic corpses of flowers." After some perfunctory conversation, it became apparent that Liberace's demeanor was as artificial as the surroundings.

"Mr. Liberace was not all that despondent," Rechy remembers. "He was just horny. And he charged at me. And I said, 'No, no, no.' See, my identity was confused. I met him as a writer. But now I was a hustler. What was I? See, that happened very often—as it had with Isherwood. I said, 'Look, you said we were going to talk.' He said, 'Yes, we are going to talk...but let's talk over here.' So he led me to a couch and we talked a little bit and he was starting to seem sincere. 'I want to show you my private quarters,' he tells me."

Rechy followed Liberace up the black and white staircase leading to his black and white master bedroom. "I was probably just curious to see it," Rechy says today. "He had a closet as big as most people's apartments, filled with rows and rows of all that gaudy stuff."

Rechy described "the star's" bedroom in *The Sexual Outlaw*: "His bed is on a platform. It's a cross between a throne and a circus tent; drapes held at the top with a golden crown."

Undaunted, Liberace began promising Rechy they would go to Palm Springs to his house there. "And what would you like?" he asked John, letting him know the sky was the limit.

"Now he was really treating me like a hustler on the make," Rechy says, "and I wasn't. I was a successful writer. I didn't need his blandishments. And then he was on me. He was extraordinarily aggressive and I had to push him away. By that point there was nothing, nothing, nothing. I wasn't attracted. No feelings for him. He said, 'I'm so lonely.' I said, 'Bullshit.'"

Rechy realized Liberace knew all along he would be rejected. "Now, having rejected him, I had to get home," Rechy says. "It was the second time I'd done that...with him and with Isherwood. I had to walk all the way down that fucking hill. Back to Sunset Boulevard to hitchhike, again, because I had left my car back where we had dinner! You know, with anyone else it would have been terrible. But Liberace was really, from all I knew of him, a good man. He was a good man. He did take care of them—the guys he brought into his life. But he went after the wrong person every time. And he lamented that he could not find love."

"It was no different," Rechy observes, "from some of the men who wanted street hustlers to love them."

As in his earlier encounter with Isherwood, Rechy had allowed a situation to develop that would inevitably entail sexual overtures. But his need to be desired was too great; he could not stop himself. He encouraged the adoration because it flattered him, even though he knew that in the long run the admiration would not be mutual.

An interlude with the rich and successful Liberace would have been an ideal situation for a hustler. Liberace had a reputation as a good man who was kind to his ex-boyfriends. He made sure they always left with something valuable. On the other hand, he had met Liberace at a dinner party—not on a street corner. As he had in the past when his identities threatened to mesh with each other, Rechy panicked and withdrew.

CHAPTER EIGHT

I have only Me!
—John Rechy, *City of Night*

FLEEING FROM THE INTERVALS of excitement derived from anonymous sex in parks and movie theaters, from literary dinner parties and controversial fame, Rechy always returned to his mother, to El Paso, and to the secluded life he had created in the years following the publication of his first novel.

Once again he longed for the restorative power of the quiet life. But his mother's deteriorating health and an arrest in Griffith Park thwarted his search for emotional tranquility. These situations also supplied the subject matter for his next book.

This Day's Death fictionalizes Rechy's experiences in the two years following his "numbers" period. During this time, he faced two kinds of prison: the metaphorical prison of life in El Paso with his ailing mother, and the possibility of an actual prison term brought on by his arrest.

At 35 Rechy was still a few years away from accepting his homosexuality. He continued to exist behind a camouflage of games, playing numbers to see how many men would approach him, give him a blow job, want him, then move on quietly. If ever something more than a casual encounter developed, he quickly brought it to a halt. "I began more and more to hustle and cruise—whichever occurred first—in El Paso, on a downtown street, in a desert Canyon, in a small park. One such time I met a man I made it with, and then he revealed he knew who I was and told me he had a friend who would be thrilled to meet me. He took me to meet the friend: a very kind, very complex man. That developed into an intensive sexual interlude that escalated because I apparently misread his signals, and the scenes began to veer into a kind of domination. After one such encounter I left, and when I returned he had devised a crude crucifix and posted it on his door as a way of keeping me out. I was horrified. I did come back, and eventually that relationship leveled off into a real friendship, no more sex." This is the man who had taken the famous photo of Rechy that appeared on the cover of *Numbers* (although he refused to be credited for it with his real name). He is also one of the men, along with Bill Regan and Bryce McKoy, to whom *Numbers* is dedicated.

Another man Rechy met in Griffith Park remained in his mind for years to come. "Cruising anonymously keeps me from suicide," the man revealed to Rechy. This desperation was common to many men at that time. For Rechy, sexual satisfaction was still secondary. The "orgasm" for him was in being desired. He still derived his emotional fulfillment from his relationship with his mother—the intense love and loyalty they shared. His sexual forays with men continued to be carefully separate from his home life. Sex with strangers was easy—all sensation *sans* emotion—and any connection with a partner ended the moment he zippered up.

Perhaps if he had been able to go off on his own and break the emotional habits he had cultivated as an isolated little boy, Rechy would have matured into accepting his sexuality much sooner. And he could have had some fulfilling romantic involvements. But Rechy seemed unable to recognize that his attachment to his mother stunted his sexual growth and continued to hold him psychological hostage. Rechy's close friend, Marsha Kinder, has observed, "Narcissism is total commitment to someone who is a reflection of yourself. In many ways that's what happened to John and his mother." He clung fast to the safety of his mother's arms. Another friend observed, "As he got more successful in his life, it made him feel farther away from his mother, so that it was difficult for him to take on possessions that were his own, that didn't have something to do with his mother—to create his own life apart from her. He was always sort of balancing this. He was always walking this fine line about creating his own life and what his life with his mother was."

Yet even today Rechy proclaims, "I blame my mother for nothing." With Guadalupe he felt protected, just as he had as a child when he hid behind her to escape his father's brutality. He refused to accept that his cushion against outsiders was now an old lady.

Rechy had achieved money and fame and respect. More importantly, his father was out of the picture. At last, with his mother's full attention on him, Rechy could feel worthy of the love and affection Guadalupe lavished on him as her favorite. He insists even today that there was nothing oedipal about the relationship, claiming, "Freud was wrong, so wrong. It has nothing to do with sex, incest—only a special love that defines itself." Yet it seems apparent that as a grown man Rechy longed to recover the mother he remembered from his youth—which would, of course, wipe away the mother-son relationship and make them contemporaries.

"I did not realize that my beloved mother, who had waltzed with me in my imagination and then in reality—had grown old," he wrote for *Contemporary Authors*. "I never saw her aging."

Unable to face the horror of his mother's deterioration, Rechy focused instead on her eyes—eyes that had seen so much pain. To him her eyes grew more beautiful, more luminous as the face surrounding them aged. "With the money from my books, I would try to make up for all her years of poverty and sacrifice," he says. He sent her on a lavish vacation to Mexico City with his sister Blanche. In El Paso he entertained her with sumptuous lunches and dinners and demanded that she socialize with friends she hadn't seen in years. He did everything with extreme love and the best of intentions, but what he could not fathom is that his mother, in her 70s, was tired and wanted only to rest. When she couldn't keep up with his pace, John raged at her.

"What do you want me to do—become young?" she finally pleaded. Guadalupe understood, even if her son did not, that this is exactly what he wanted.

In defense, she retreated to her bedroom, which reflected her fragile personality. Her chamber was like a doll's room, with delicate filigree and gentle pastels and gold-fringed ivory drapes. With the drapes drawn the room glowed faintly. Guadalupe hid behind her illness, an illness that was never given a name. "She fainted," Rechy explains. "She was tired after a very difficult life."

His fiercely conflicted dynamic with his mother remained too precarious to confront face-to-face; only through writing fiction could Rechy begin to explore it. *This Day's Death* continues Rechy's fictionalized documentation of his life. In it he attempts to articulate the complicated feelings between himself and his mother, painfully exploring their many-sided relationship. Years after it was written, in his essay for *Contemporary Authors*, Rechy claimed the book "does not understand the situations it attempts to explore, because I did not understand them. I will return to that subject in another book, the subject of a mother and son trapped by love—only love—so powerful it begins killing both." The novel, however, may have more truth in it than Rechy can bear to admit.

"He blames himself, mistakenly, for not doing enough for her and for leaving El Paso on occasions," Marsha Kinder observes. "It's a lot like what Jack Kerouac was feeling with his mother. I mean, how do you 'go on the road' and get away from one life into a totally different one—each having nothing to do with that other realm?"

As it is with most of us, Rechy's feelings for his mother were extremely changeable. One moment he might feel angry with her, the next he might appreciate and love her more than anything. Next he would want her out of his life. But every resentment always gave way to an overpowering love.

"To love is to become a victim," one of Rechy's characters remarks in *The Vampires*. The constant shifting of his emotions tormented Rechy. "I wanted to separate our lives so that both she and I could have our own," Rechy says, "so that they would not be so entangled, painful for both of us. I should have moved out, but I wasn't able to. I didn't want to."

Throughout his career, Rechy's writing reflected the great love he felt for his mother. *This Day's Death*, published in 1969, takes a different look at their relationship.

As mentioned earlier, Rechy's mother—like the mother in *This Day's Death*—was frequently unwell, although it is unclear exactly what was wrong with her. Even as a child, Rechy was aware of her fragility. "I used to listen to my mother's heart when she was sick so often, and I would think that she had died, leaving me alone." *This Day's Death* hints at hypochondria. Although she is bedridden, the doctors can't find anything wrong with the protagonist's aging mother. There are unexplained nosebleeds. She keeps a tank of oxygen by the bed. In the novel it seems clear that the mother uses illness to keep her son chained to her, to prevent him from going off again.

Even more terrifying is the mother's desire to have her son die with her. Rechy says that as a child he imagined himself dying with his mother, and he reinvents this desire in the character Jim from the novel: "Thinking that she wanted to hear it, Jim promised his mother that when she died (except that he said 'if' she died) he would kill himself. She looked at him enigmatically, in silence."

As if to verify the autobiographical aspects of the novel, Rechy interweaves real history throughout the narrative, changing only a location here or a character's heritage there. The deceased father, for example—"sulking, seething, sullen, broody, black, furious, contained"—is French rather than Scottish. But like Rechy's real father, the fictional father *was* born in Mexico. Rechy's father was a failed musician; the father in the book was a failed lawyer.

Rechy re-creates himself in the fictional character of Jim Girard. Like Rechy, Jim lives with his ailing Mexican mother in Texas. He too has a respectable life—working in a law firm with ambitions to become an attorney and pursuing a romance with a local woman (the recurring "Barbara" character). All the while, Jim hides his secret desires—desires he has managed to keep in check most of his life, but that he has just begun to explore: an infatuation with anonymous homosexual encounters.

In his domestic Texas prison—the house Rechy bought for himself and his mother—Rechy's love and rage coexisted uneasily. He is perhaps describing his mother's bedroom when he writes in *This Day's Death*: "It's as if he entered a grave. A heavy twilight darkness. Pale-lavender drapes intercept whatever light Escapes the drawn blind."

The odd emphasis on "escapes" signals Rechy's longing for freedom. The sunlight is kept out of the mother's room while the protagonist is trapped inside. Like Rechy, Jim occasionally escapes to Los Angeles, where he finally indulges his homosexuality in the blazing daylight of Griffith Park, the sprawling sexual playground. This temporary escape from his mother, however, does not go unpunished. His attempted sexual activity in the park eventually attracts the attention of vice cops, who arrest Jim—just as they did Rechy in real life.

Ironically, throughout his *City of Night* experiences as a hustler in New York and Los Angeles, John Rechy was never arrested. He was, however, picked up, interrogated, and fingerprinted many times during his Los Angeles–Pershing Square period. For the hustlers hanging around the park, this was routine. Every so often a new batch of young men would be picked up by the police on charges of loitering or vagrancy. The cops would patrol Pershing Square and, when they'd spot a hustler for the first time, they'd round him up and bring him to the station for an interrogation.

There was one well-known cop at the time whom the queens

called Shirley Temple. (His real name was Sergeant Shirley.) In *City of Night* Rechy mischievously dubs him Sergeant Temple. The burly sergeant would parade into the park like The Grand Emperor. He'd round up a bunch of guys, calling out, "You! You! and *you!*" and haul them in down to the interrogation room, where he'd keep them for several hours. There, he threatened and lectured like a pompous high school principal dressing down a group of rowdy freshmen. The hustlers were sure he always chose the boys he desired most.

At other times the cops swept into Cooper's Doughnuts, a popular hustler hangout downtown. Rechy recalls sitting in Cooper's with the Cowboy—Chuck in *City of Night*—when the cops burst in and demanded everyone's name, except for his and the Cowboy's. Satisfied that everyone had proper ID and that no crimes were being committed, the cops began to leave. But before they reached the door, they turned around and said to the pair, "You two come with us."

"Isn't it against the law to have so many people jumbled into one car?" Rechy wisecracked in the squad car. "And they marched us into the station," he says now. "I remember the women secretaries saying, 'Oh, look at the two cute ones!' " At the station Rechy—always able to switch out of hustler mode—fell easily into his intelligent act. The police thought he might be working undercover and let him go.

Rechy actually escaped being booked many times by implying he was undercover. Once, Rechy was taken in by a cop who claimed he had given him the finger, but the interrogating officer fell for the undercover ruse and ordered the arresting officer to drive Rechy back to where he had been picked up. Instead, Rechy told the cop to drop him off on Main Street—prime hustling turf—so his friends could see. Rechy remembers, "Really, I was very brash at the time; I thought I was untouchable as far as that area went."

But in 1966 Rechy's luck ran out. It started off like any other day in his cruising life. Rechy was prowling the park when he spotted a handsome young man not unlike many handsome young men he had targeted in the past. John instantly wanted him as one of his numbers. And the man wanted John. They did the cruising dance, silently leading each other down a tree-lined path to a place that in *Numbers* Rechy called "The Cave," where dried twigs and vines twist to form a shell that resembles a cave wall. The regulars in the park knew of many hidden places to have sex unnoticed—except by members of their own secret club.

CHAPTER NINE

I had to follow that penetrating glare no matter where it took me.
—John Rechy, *City of Night*

(THE FOLLOWING IS FROM AN INTERVIEW WITH THE AUTHOR.)

And he was about to come on to me. It was that odd period just before someone makes the first move. The pause. The dance. After a while he slid down in front of me. I didn't say a word but I unbuttoned the top of my pants. I just got that far. Before anything happened we heard a noise. There had been no encounter. Nothing was exposed. I said, "Somebody's coming!" And then we saw the cop hurrying toward us with a vengeance. Before he reached us he called out, "You're under arrest!" The other guy tried to run because he had been arrested before. And then another cop came hurrying from a different direction. When he caught up with the guy who tried to flee, he handcuffed him. I said, "What the hell for? Nothing happened!"

It was going to happen, but the cops had interrupted it. So there was no reason to arrest us. It did not happen. Listen, if something had happened, I'd admit it now, all these years later. There's no reason to change, except it adds more irony to the fucking incident.

They took us downtown to the station. We were separated. It's just so awful. They strip-search you. I mean—and you know—they're getting off on it! I remember trying to get back at them, and I flexed for them. I figured, fuck 'em. I knew I looked terrific.

The other guy—his name was Tim—he was put in a tank, and, I suppose because I said I was a writer, they put me in alone—across from a black guy, and we talked back and forth. A friend—knowing I went to the park so often and that it was hot with vice cops—had given me the name of a bondsman. When the bondsman showed up, oh, my God, I was never so happy to see a gay person in my life when I looked across that window— you talk by telephones—and I thought, The bail bondsman is gay...thank God! *[Laughs] I opened my shirt again while we were talking and I went into my routine and he had me out...right away. And I tried to get him to get Tim out too, but he'd gotten somebody else.*

Then the bondsman drove me to the park to get my car. He said, "Listen, you need to relax, you need to relax...you need a drink. Let's go to my house and have a drink." Can you believe that? The bondsman himself started coming on to me! But you know I was so nervous...there was nothing he could do that would arouse me. I mean, my God, I'd been busted! The offense that I was charged with was punishable with up to five years! Imagine that. I had found out that I had been charged with being involved in "oral copulation," which is a felony in public. And it had been about to happen, but it had not happened. But there it was and then began the nightmare.

I knew the park like the back of my hand and I knew the cop didn't see, so it was obvious he made the entire encounter up. You know they lie all the time. Especially in that area. So I got an expensive attorney. I said, "There's no way he could have seen!" And my attorney, who was famous for this kind of case, said, "Let's take movies of the park and get the cameraman to take movies of you as you walk down the same path."

I hired a photographer. I wish I had that film. And because it was going to be shown in court, not to outrage the fucking judge, whoever it would be, I didn't take off my shirt, the way I had that day; instead, I wore a flesh-colored shirt. The one I wore to meet Liberace. It was smashing. It was a silk shirt that had been tailored to me...molded to me. I rolled up the sleeves so my arms would show. And I opened it at the neck. My waist was tiny. Really sensational. So here we are making a movie for court and I wore that shirt. [Laughs] I have to laugh at it myself because the lawyer took me there and the reason the film was being shot was to show it in a court case...but the moment I saw the fucking camera I'm doing my thing, man. Smiling and flexing and doing the whole thing. It's actually quite funny. God, I wish I still had the film!

I also drew maps and brought in galley pages from Numbers to indicate that I had been doing research. But I was sure the film proved my point. I mean, my God, I proved that there was no way the son of a bitch could see. So we go to court for the first time. I was sure the case was going to be thrown out. The lawyer hiked his fee. They didn't look at the film during the first hearing. As it turned out the case wasn't thrown out—it was going to trial. It was a nightmare. So I had to go back and forth from El Paso to court in Los Angeles. The hearings kept getting delayed. I had to bring my mom with me to Los Angeles, to stay with my sister Olga, and neither of them had any idea what was going on. I couldn't tell anybody. That was the sad part. I couldn't tell my sister. The tensions were mounting. I was looking at five years in prison. My main concern was what would happen to my mother. And I never knew when I turned up in court if I would be arrested then. Every time we had a hearing. It continued and continued.

I'd go back to El Paso. My mother started getting sick. It was a nightmare time—one of the worst times of my life—because everything was hanging over me. I made arrangements the best I could for money for my mother to be cared for. So everything would be taken care of if I went to prison. And I kept on driving back and forth.

That thing went on through Christmas because the judge kept postponing it. Tim wouldn't testify because of his prior arrest; so I was the one who testified. And then we showed the movie. Can you believe it? We showed the fucking movie in court. We showed the damn film in court, and there I was smiling at the camera and wearing a tight-fitting flesh-colored shirt—and the judge said, "There's only one thing to do. I want to see the park."

Tim's attorney told him I was deliberately dragging out the trial so I could write about it. And I would have done anything to have ended it. Well, at the moment the judge decided we were going to see the park I thought, We're fucked. Because now we were going to go to one of the heaviest cruising areas in the whole fucking park. We were going to go around noontime, *which is when people got out for lunch...and went to cruise the park. We all knew what sections were most popular at which times, and that section was for people who didn't have too much time. And so it was an incredible congregation. And that's when we were going to go there.*

I got into my Mustang and I went by the freeway.... I sped by the freeway, because they were going to come there...the District Attorney...the lawyers, all of them in their cars. Imagine! Along with the detectives, the two guys who had arrested us. I rushed into the park like a gay Paul Revere—this is incredible to believe, even remembering it—I went in shouting, "There's a trial coming! There's a trial coming!" And people were jumping out of the bushes.

So the fucking judge gets there and guess what he was driving? A Rolls Royce. Then the others arrive. So now we have to locate ourselves...me and Tim in "The Cave" ...and that cop had to go to the area he claimed he spotted us from. See? Because they're so clumsy they never expect to be challenged. He said he was 50 feet away. I had measured with the camera 50 feet away. So he stood a measured 50 feet way. And they couldn't see anything. So he kept changing: "I was here." And they'd move up a few feet, but they couldn't see anything and then he'd take a few steps forward. "No I was here." Getting closer and closer. And Tim and I were standing in that cove where we had been busted. And the one detective who had arrested me kept getting closer and closer until he was right up to us. And then he freaked. He shouted, "I was standing here and this is where you were!" And he put his hand on Tim to push him down to kneel. I was furious! And I hit the cop's hand and I said, "Don't you touch him!" That cop had hideous malice. A really hideous malice. It came out in this encounter when I hit that motherfucker. Obviously he was going to come back at me. He wasn't going to let a faggot hit him. But before anything more could happen the attorneys came over and calmed everyone down. The judge said, "I've seen everything I need to see."

*As we were walking out, two guys were popping out of the bushes. God knows what anyone thought. I was sitting in my car and the District Attorney came over to me and said, "You know, I read your book—*City of Night. *It's really a remarkable book. Congratulations. And yours is a really good case. It's over."*

I had to come back to be sentenced. I was shocked: We were found guilty! Of a lesser charge, a misdemeanor. But still it was my first arrest. I was convicted of prostitution. The charge of prostitution is not a criminal act like the one I was originally charged with. So I was found guilty under the ordinance soliciting for the sake of prostitution. Right after the verdict I went back to El Paso and returned to Los Angeles only to be sentenced. Directly following the sentencing I drove to the park and had sex—an act of defiance—like purging myself.

I was put on probation. The probation officer was a very nice guy. I was put on probation for...I forget...two years? And a big fine. Can you believe that son of a bitch judge fined me twice as much as Tim because he said I made a lot of money. Twice as much! Because he knew who I was all along.

Then when I wrote This Day's Death, *I sent a copy to the judge. And it got returned to me because the motherfucker was dead.*

CHAPTER TEN

A voice had been stilled, a body has disappeared.
And his need of his mother is unchanged.
—John Rechy, *The Fourth Angel*

WEBSTER SCHOTT ENRAGED Rechy with his review of *This Day's Death* in *The New York Times Book Review*, which appeared under the heading "Mother, The Monster Behind It All." In his critique Schott called the mother's love for her son "madness," and blamed her for his "flight" into homosexuality. In 1970 it was still unfathomable to much of the United States that homosexuality was anything other than the result of some early unnatural or perverted affiliation. Schott never considered that a certain kind of relationship might be the result of an individual's sexual orientation. Instead, the critic used his review as an opportunity to voice his particular theories on homosexuality. "Obviously, Mother has been pointing Jim to the park grotto all their lives," Schott asserted. "His [Rechy's] plot is either nonsense or ignorance. In our culture the male doesn't suddenly go homosexual as an act of defiance. The author's failure to link mother, son, and homosexual choice is a cop-out."

Rechy was not about to ignore another unreasonable and unfair review. By then he had come to realize that critics are opinionated people who sometimes let their personal biases— even over something as irrelevant as an author's photo or sexual orientation—sway those opinions and influence their reviews.

Rechy began his letter to the Book Review by remarking, "It is difficult to determine whether Webster Schott's review of my novel is trashier than the headline you chose for it." Then, as if defending himself and his mother—along with the characters he based on them—Rechy writes: "He [Schott] calls Mrs. Girard's love for her son 'madness.' Let me assure this man: That love was intense, yes—as is Jim's for her. Madness, no." Rechy himself felt more compassion for the Mrs. Girard character than for her son. Far from blaming her for Jim's homosexuality, Rechy countered, "My portrait of Jim's mother is a compassionate one of a beautiful woman who loves powerfully...who is herself as much a victim of her son's great love as he of hers. There is no blame."

Unable to leave well enough alone, Schott wrote a rejoinder to Rechy's letter:

> The author may read the book anyway he wants to...most others will see Jim's going gay as coming from sources long since identified by professionals—in disciplines ranging from medicine to anthropology.

This particular critic, apparently, felt completely comfortable in speaking for "most others."

Rechy says, "That was the beginning of another aspect of the battles I wage with reviewers, especially pompous *New York Times* ones—that they don't read what they trash." Seven years after *City of Night*'s publication, Rechy was still trying to rid his literary reputation of the kind of mud Alfred Chester had first slung at it.

Later Rechy told his students, "Always fight, and you will win. A very quiet, subdued demand for dignity and respect will win." Rechy regularly wrote fervent retorts to critics whom he felt had hidden motives. Referring them to pages or passages that contradicted their assertions, he also often cited the errors in critics' pieces. "I can always tell when people make factual mistakes," he said.

It angered Rechy when publishers and editors told him that it simply wasn't proper for a writer to protest bad reviews. "Why do you have to take shit?" Rechy wonders. "My point is: What have I got to lose? Being silent has never been effective for anybody. And I feel writers get maligned that way. We're actually inhibited. Publishers say that they'll mistreat you in the next review. Bullshit! At least be heard. I have to uphold my dignity—that's the whole thrust of the thing. So fuck 'em!"

When *The New York Times Book Review* did not review *The Miraculous Day of Amalia Gómez* or *Our Lady of Babylon*, Rechy wrote angry letters to the editors demanding to know why he was being ignored. Eventually reviews did appear for the two novels— both negative. "But they appeared in response to my letters," Rechy says. "This outraged my then publisher at Arcade, Richard Seaver; he told me I had been blacklisted at *The New York Times* for writing those letters. Although I doubt that I am blacklisted in any official way, I know there is deep hostility there, from way back when *City of Night* appeared." When no review of *The Coming of the Night* appeared, Rechy wrote a letter to *Book Review* editor Charles "Chip" McGrath asking why not. McGrath telephoned Rechy ("seriously interrupting my workout," Rechy says) to tell him that the reason they had not reviewed the novel was because a reviewer would not be able to find "a single page that might be quoted" because of its extremely graphic descriptions.* Rechy was so taken aback that all he could say was, "Oh?"

For years Rechy has protested to the editor of *The Nation*, Ivan Navasky, that the magazine for which he wrote many lead articles (for the great editor Carey McWilliams) doesn't even mention him now in their roster of past contributors. After one of their donors— Rechy's friend Molly Shapiro—protested Rechy's omission, Navasky wrote Rechy that he would "explain or apologize"—and chose to

---

*McGrath offered to reconsider the matter of a review. But when none appeared, Rechy sent a second letter, which ended, "But, finally, Mr. McGrath, reviews and reviewers don't matter. They are remembered, if at all, in derisive footnotes about their mistakes."

apologize. "Obviously," remarks Rechy, "I would have preferred an explanation, although I already know the reason. It's part of a strange token liberalism that amounts to highly selective homophobia. It afflicts *The New York Times* also, and quite strongly." Rechy remains banished from the roster.

In the case of *This Day's Death*, Rechy was mollified by some of the excellent reviews that followed Schott's piece. "*This Day's Death* is about intense internal pain," wrote the *Los Angeles Times* reviewer, "and it most successfully gets the reader to share some of that pain." *Publishers Weekly* stated simply, "*This Day's Death* has dignity and depth."

By the time the reviews for *This Day's Death* began to appear, Guadalupe's illness had taken a turn for the worse, adding to Rechy's anguish.

While he remained in El Paso, caring for his mother, Rechy's college girlfriend Julie Williams came back to the city. She was still beautiful, Rechy says, and their friendship was immediately rekindled. One day when Rechy's mother was in bed recovering from one of her fainting spells, Julie walked into her room and whispered something to her. Guadalupe sat up and smiled. Julie signaled for Rechy to leave the room, which he did. A few minutes later, Rechy returned to witness Julie (who was an expert ballet dancer and performer) doing graceful tai chi movements. Guadalupe was imitating her. It was a sight Rechy never forgot.

Still, Guadalupe's health continued to decline. "My mother stumbled and broke her hip," he recalls. "At the hospital, I kept a constant vigil—leaving only to get something to eat occasionally—until she was out of the operating room. I littered her room with flowers, visited her every day while she recovered and was taught how to walk again. We even laughed in her hospital room as she took small steps. When she returned home—I hired two women to work in shifts caring for her and the house—it was obvious that she wouldn't be able to walk again without a walker—except one time, a miraculous time. I was in my study writing and she sent one of the women who worked for us to call me. I opened the door, and there she stood, with her radiant smile and green eyes, without a walker. 'Look!' she said. And she took a few steps without the walker. I went to her and held her, and we were both crying. I knew she was trying with all her heart to get well for me. I opened a bottle of champagne to celebrate her progress. But, from there on, it was a steady decline. Only a few months were left."

Despite his mother's deterioration, Rechy continued to write. By 1970 he was readying a new novel for publication. *The Vampires* is a book that he says sometimes baffles him. Poe again heavily influenced him, but Rechy also cites classic comic strips like *Terry and the Pirates* as sources of inspiration. His fourth novel proves Rechy refused to repeat himself, would not duplicate the formula of *City of Night*. "He's never been afraid to take chances," notes his agent, Georges Borchardt. "He's never done it the easy way, always writing the same book over and over again, which some authors do and can do quite successfully."

In *The Vampires* Rechy daringly experiments with formats and styles. It was written, he says, in "Technicolor," employing filmic techniques in prose. "Again, as in all my work, I was experimenting with new forms, adapting the equivalent of a close-up—panning shots, replicated in sentences that moved from one character to another without a break."

He based the story on a visit to a private island near Chicago where—not long before the publication of *City of Night*—he socialized with Jonathan Herbert, Herbert's mistress, and Herbert's ex-wives. Opulent decay and corruption take center stage as the guests play out a pageant of confession and judgment.

The novel displays Rechy's characteristic flair for description. And if his characters sometimes come across as overwrought, Rechy makes no apologies. "It's an operatic novel," he explains, "and I used a lush prose to evoke the lush setting, and the atmosphere of a hellish paradise, or a paradisiacal hell. I was allowing the full range of ambiguity, of mystery, that I would come to nurture increasingly in my work."

In *The Vampires*, evil, frailty, beauty, sexuality, youth, lust, and cruelty take the form of his provocative players, who taunt and judge each other throughout the narrative.

Although *The Vampires* remains one of Rechy's personal favorites, when it finally came out in 1971 it was virtually ignored. Rechy blames the situation on his publisher at Grove, who was going through financial straits at the time and didn't have the money to promote the book. Only one ad appeared, featuring a new novel by Hubert Selby Jr., a new novel by William Burroughs, and a "new novel by John Rechy." Without any PR or even advance review copies, Rechy says the book was completely overlooked by critics. He watched helplessly as his novel quickly vanished without a ripple.

On October 9, 1970, while the fictionalized relationship between herself and her son was still being discussed in reviews of *This Day's Death*, Guadalupe Flores Rechy lay dying in a hospital bed. She managed to come out of a coma just long enough to say things that had remained unspoken in all the years she and her son had spent together. "I understand," she murmured to John. "We love each other so much, my son, that we hurt because of it."

Rechy clasped his mother's hand and told her he knew that too and that she had to live.

As Rechy well knew, there would always be opportunities for momentary excitement in the woods and other cruising zones, but his mother had always been his true passion. Throughout his life—in spite of all his anonymous encounters, his fleeting moments of extreme pleasure followed by absolute emptiness, his artistic triumphs and disappointments, his worries of aging and fading, and of not connecting with anything permanent—there had always been his mother. Since the day he was born, Guadalupe had been his primary relationship, a fortress to protect him when he felt the rest of the world moving in too close. No matter where his wanderings led him, his mother had always been within reach—a friend, a comfort, a longing, a welcoming light. His home. Life without her was incomprehensible.

Rechy did what he could for her. He wanted to be near her, to comfort her, and to help her cross over. To say, "Don't be afraid." He made her passing as comfortable as possible. He even had her transferred from a room he considered ugly to one with a large window that faced out to the Cristo Rey mountains. The sun was just setting as she began to die. Guadalupe could just make out the huge Indian Jesus that beckoned from the top of a distant hill. Jesus had always been very important to her. Rechy wanted his mother's death to be peaceful for her—like passing from one set of familiar arms into another. But in unpublished notes, Rechy wrote that just before dying, Guadalupe let out a piercing scream. Horrified, Rechy tried to stop the death shriek with a kiss; and while his lips were on his mother's mouth, he tasted blood.

Rechy remembered, "There was a brilliant Texas sunset before it all became night." For him, there was no passing into peace. His reaction to the loss of his mother was immediate and violent. He vividly recounts the moment in his next novel, *The Fourth Angel*:

> A scream ripped from his throat, he ran insanely along the hospital corridor to dash himself against the windows as if within the windy darkness outside he would find her.

Now he found his mother only in his memory, the honored place she would inhabit for the rest of his life. Rechy has said many times—in his life and in his body of work—that death exists only for the living. Abandoning his boyhood vow to follow his mother to the grave, the adult Rechy realized what was inevitable; he would have to go on living. He was now 40—and had no idea where to go or what to do. One thing was certain, however: A new companion had taken the place of his beloved Guadalupe. From that day forward Rechy would be living with Death.

PART FOUR

SEXUAL INTELLECTUAL

Chapter Eleven

Why not compassion for the desirable narcissist?
—John Rechy

RECHY ALWAYS KNEW HE couldn't deal well with separation from his mother. Even so, he was totally unprepared for the despair he experienced when she died. He spent the first night after her death outside the funeral home, keeping vigil in front of the closed mortuary where her body would be viewed. When the mortuary opened the next morning Rechy continued his vigil inside, trying to keep everyone else out until the evening service. He wanted to be alone with her. His desire to take care of her, to be a part of her, extended into the rituals of death. While Rechy stood watch, Guadalupe lay in the coffin, dressed elegantly—as she had always dressed—with a beautiful coat with a wide collar lined in mink, a coat Rechy had bought for her. Near the end of the funeral, seconds before the coffin was closed, John placed a flower in her hands and bent to kiss her.

Before Guadalupe's funeral a family member called Rechy's friend, Floriano Vecchi, to ask him to come to El Paso to be with John. Vecchi found his old friend in a wretched state. "He was out of his mind," he remembers. "Weeping hysterically. Screaming. Then suddenly he would calm down. I was frightened to death because he was taking a lot of medication. There was an open casket, and after the service John came to see me in my hotel room. He said, 'It isn't true! She's not dead! I was there and I heard her breathing!'" It was some time before Vecchi could convince Rechy that his mother was truly gone.

Still, accepting her death did not blunt the edge of Rechy's grief. "I had done horrors," he admits, remembering his macabre actions following her death. "I locked her room, I left it intact." For a time he didn't think he would survive her loss. He had known unhappiness, and had certainly lived through depressions—his bouts of melancholia and loneliness when he first started hustling in New York. But this was different: a constant annihilating feeling of loss.

In many ways, the concerned mother who comforted him on the porch of the family home when he was a child and who made clothes for him when he was a college student had continued to nurture and comfort Rechy in his adulthood. With her as his surrogate relationship, Rechy's world always had a foundation. Without that foundation his world crumbled.

At 41 Rechy was still not in a committed romantic relationship. In fact, he had never had one. Moreover, he was not tied to the kind of profession that demanded the discipline of a strict schedule, and so he stopped working.

Rechy found it difficult to do much of anything. He couldn't stand being with anyone and yet he couldn't bear being alone. He wandered around the house like a zombie.

He desperately wanted to stop the pain, but he didn't know how. Sick with grief, he turned to a new group of friends for distraction. They were a cruel, self-centered set of people—qualities Rechy now wanted for himself. "I starting hanging around with this very wealthy woman and her gaunt, wasted husband. Sometimes they stayed in my home. My sorrow about my mother's death was deepening progressively. I wanted any escape. There was plenty of sex and orgies and drugs and anything else I felt I wanted. I was doing cocaine and heroin—especially LSD, which almost destroyed me. I had a monstrous drug reaction and was brought to the brink of suicide."

Rechy's use of sex and drugs as a way of escaping pain was not unusual. But his neglect of his appearance—he stopped eating and exercising—was. When friends ran into him they were shaken by his ghostly pallor and gauntness. Shockingly, the lifelong narcissist didn't seem to notice.

The drugs he took only intensified his despair. "I had been driving around the city locating the right place for suicide, where I might crash the car without harming anyone other than myself." Luckily, some good friends—Molly Shapiro and Frank Oppenheimer—managed to talk him into seeing a psychiatrist. "I don't believe in psychiatrists," Rechy says, "but this particular man was so terrific. So it was him I contacted when I was on the brink—bumming out on acid, friends, and hash. I called him up, and he said, 'Get a cab right away, and come over here.' By then, every bit of reality was gone and I thought he was conspiring to do something to me. It was horrible. But he sat with me in his home, and then he called one of my older friends, Frank Oppenheimer, and he came for me. Frank turned very harshly on the people I had been hanging around with and opened my eyes to the damage they were doing."

By then, Rechy was visiting his mother's grave daily. Gradually, the psychiatrist persuaded him to stop. In 1972, trying to put an end to his downward spiral, Rechy tentatively began a new novel. He has said that his fifth book, *The Fourth Angel*, "is really my experiences after my mom died." He never shied away from self-exploration; even through his unshakable grief, Rechy's gift, his perceptive eye, took in everything. He explored his involvement with these new acquaintances, how his friendship with them was related to the torture he went through after his mother's death. Rather than write about this jaded group as the adults they were, Rechy allowed his feelings of helplessness and vulnerability to transform the characters in the new book into teenagers—even the protagonist, his proxy.

This was a shrewd move. By having children enact the malicious exploits portrayed in the book, the characters become more sympathetic, more vulnerable, and therefore more forgivable. Their tender ages soften their personalities—which need softening, for they talk in a slangy street language, share a delight in tormenting strangers, and even display a considerable degree of malice toward each other. In the opening we meet the first three characters: 16-year-olds who call themselves "angels." Each angel has been knocked around by life (sexual abuse, absent parents, latent homosexuality) and as a result has developed a tough external mask for protection. No angel ever sees another without this disguise.

The female of the group, Shell, is the coldest of the three and (in an odd reversal) the leader of the two boys, Cob and Manny. When one of Shell's friends mentions that the girl's real name is Michelle, she insists, "Just Shell—like something hard." Shell cooks up the cruel mind games the angels play on strangers to fill up their time. Determined to feel nothing, their major concern is obliterating the boredom each new day brings. Their favorite game is to sexually lure someone to a secluded place, then terrorize him by "getting into" his head—discovering what makes him tick in a sadistic interview ritual. The purpose of this pastime is to discover where peoples' weaknesses lie, as if smashing the carapace of others to pick through their fleshy vulnerabilities will strengthen one's own exterior. The angels seem driven to make themselves impervious to the knives life throws at them from every direction. "To survive you've got to learn not to feel, even if you have to teach yourself," Shell concludes.

It is Shell who decides to recruit Jerry (Rechy's alter ego) as "the fourth angel" when she spots him crying on a park bench. Jerry is also 16 and is, like his real-life counterpart, in utter anguish over the recent death of his mother. As in his previous works Rechy manages to unload a barrage of his own feelings through his fictional spokesperson: "A portion of his life rushed after her into death...Death a constant presence every moment of his existence, she dies from him each brutal day."

Shell, of course, views Jerry's suffering as a weakness and is initially attracted to him as a specimen for one of her experiments. She believes that if she can convert Jerry into one of the unfeeling "angels," then her own transformation is real and complete. No matter what kind of pain a person endures, one can always turn into stone to be cured and made whole.

The angels also shield themselves from a hostile world by (like Rechy at the time) taking massive quantities of drugs. Jerry eagerly falls into the drug scene, finding that at least he can find some moments of relief there.

Reviews of *The Fourth Angel* when it appeared in 1973 were mixed. Tom Curtis dismissed the book in an initial review for the *Houston Chronicle*, but after an outbreak of adolescent violence in Texas in August of that year, he revisited his initial critique of the "ugly and unpleasant" novel. On a second reading he found it "more insightful and important than I gave it credit for when I read it a month ago." Curtis observes that while the teenagers in the book do not kill, Rechy "makes us understand how and why they might do so far better than newspaper accounts let us understand how and why these kinds of atrocities happen."

Meanwhile, Rechy continued with his therapy. At the time, narcissism was still considered a psychosis, but Rechy's psychiatrist told him that in his case it probably helped him. "I was still looking terrible," Rechy says. "I could see my friends reeling back in shock from the sight of me. So I gradually started working out again." Although he was again building up his body, emotionally he continued to walk a tightrope. But a safety net appeared when a friend, Dick Trexler—with whom Rechy had been involved in demonstrations against the war in Vietnam—suggested out of the blue, "Maybe we could get you to teach."

Rechy was willing to try anything to alleviate his current depression. Trexler encouraged him to contact his friend Marsha Kinder, who was teaching at Occidental College in Los Angeles.

He thought Rechy and Kinder would hit it off and that Kinder might help him get a job teaching there. So, without selling his home in El Paso ("It had some sort of hold on me. I always thought I would return"), Rechy headed for Los Angeles. "I left— and that was the decision to go on living," he says.

Neither Rechy nor Marsha Kinder knew what to expect. Kinder had read *City of Night* 10 years earlier when her then-husband brought it to her attention. "I was struck by what an amazing book it was, in the sense of discovering a whole world that I knew nothing about," she says. "It was very lush and romantic but it also had an incredible balance of humor." Kinder and Rechy were nervous about meeting each other. She feared Rechy would play the role of a famous writer: impossible and arrogant. On the other hand, Rechy worried that a teacher from Occidental would turn out to be stodgy, "with glasses on a chain and her hair in a bun." So when a young, attractive woman answered the door, Rechy thought, *Oh, my God, please don't let this be her daughter.* Kinder was, like most people, first struck by Rechy's physicality. "He was incredibly handsome, a bodybuilder, with a really wonderful smile," she remembers. (Many friends from this period remember Rechy's smile.) Rechy and Kinder were both delighted to discover they were "two regular people" who felt an immediate emotional connection.

They went to dinner and fell into a long, easy conversation that eventually turned serious. Rechy talked of his great suffering over the death of his mother. Kinder had recently divorced and, during the same period, her father had died. She and Rechy connected through their shared sense of loss. "He had a quality of being very nervous," Kinder recalls. "He had a combination of being very vulnerable, very smart, focused in certain areas. John had incredible strength, and then in other areas, not. And that's what I was very struck with."

Kinder was the first of a group of young, strong, creative, attractive, heterosexual women Rechy would become close to in the

1970s. These relationships were based on intimacy without sexuality, although Rechy often came close to sexualizing the friendships. In unpublished notes for his story "Love in the Backrooms" (originally intended as an excerpt from his incomplete *Autobiography: A Novel*), which he published in *Forum* and later in *Men on Men 4*, John Rechy describes his relationship with Marsha Kinder, whom he calls "Rachel":

> One night on a Malibu beach she and I got close. Close. I had told her about the scream that had preceded my mother's dying, about how I tried to stop it with my lips on her mouth, how I tasted her blood. Rachel and I held hands that night on the beach, we kissed, our bodies drew together. That was all. That night I cruised into morning.

Kinder recommended Rechy for a position teaching creative writing at Occidental. It seemed Rechy would be a natural for teaching. After all, he had been a student of literature most of his life and would bring a wealth of knowledge to his classroom. But because of his notoriety as the author of *City of Night*, there was some concern at the college that parents would object to Rechy's teaching there. "Occidental was a very interesting place because it's a small liberal arts college," Kinder explains. "Very protected. It's on a hill. It's a very safe place. The faculty is actually very leftist, but we didn't know what people would say about John."

As it turned out, nobody said anything. There wasn't a word of objection. "We used laugh about it all the time," Kinder says today. "The school was so isolated and hermetically sealed; John used to call them the Sugar Children, as if all the kids who went to Occidental were sprinkled by this sugar and therefore nothing bad in life ever touched them."

In truth, Rechy was nervous at first, as were his students. But these hermetically sealed, sugar-coated children soon enthralled by the dashing and provocative Mr. Rechy.

There were other gay teachers in the English department at Occidental, but at the time they were not out. Professors didn't exactly hide their orientation, but they didn't discuss it either. Rechy, on the other hand, was always up front. Many of the young men in his classes—gay, straight, or bi—felt extremely intimidated by him. When heterosexual male students became fond of Rechy, they inevitably experienced some confusion. The affection they felt for a handsome, muscular man made them feel threatened. His relationship with female students was easier. Rechy was fond of pretty girls, but there was never any confusion about him wanting them sexually.

Rechy appeared so confident that most people who knew him during this period had no idea that his vulnerability and separation anxiety were so extreme that he was expressing them through strange rituals. Rechy had always been ritualistic, but his current practices—brought on by an overwhelming feeling of guilt about abandoning anything—were excessive. A friend from this period recalls one of his more bizarre ceremonies: "When cooking for himself, every time he opened a can, he felt compelled to say goodbye to it—otherwise he could not throw it away. He would talk to the can as if it were a living, breathing being with feelings that could be hurt."

Rechy's friend Melodie Johnson Howe remembers him taking pictures of his mother from his wallet to show her. He would kiss the photo right in front of her. "His voice would become small, like a child's voice," Melodie remembers. Other friends recall him audibly gasping, speechless at the mere mention of his mother.

As in the past when feeling particularly defenseless, Rechy turned to hustling. On street corners he felt strong and in control. It had been years since he stood on sidewalks and solicited. Of course, he had hustled frequently in Los Angeles years before—but his experiences there in the recent past had been primarily pick-up sex in parks. Once again Rechy's need to affirm his value, to challenge time, would take him back to the streets.

• • •

I felt like Norma Desmond. This wasn't a comeback. It was a return!
—John Rechy

"When I went back to hustling after all those years it was ter-rifying," Rechy recalls. "First of all, when I left the streets after *City of Night* I was a very cute kid. Sexy. A hoody-looking kid. When I came back it was 1973, for God's sake, and I was going to go back to Selma." (From the 1960s to the 1980s, Selma Street was the popular Hollywood hangout for hustlers).

In order to test himself under the best possible circumstances, Rechy waited till evening before returning to his favorite street. But his vanity wouldn't allow him to wait for the complete dark-ness of night. He carefully chose an in-between twilight, which would be kinder yet still allow an element of honesty. He wore what would become his costume throughout much of the '70s: jeans and an open denim shirt, sleeves rolled up.

As he arrived on Selma, the 42-year-old Rechy's blood pumped with the familiar rush that overtook him every time he hustled. But when he settled into his favorite spot in front of the Baptist Church he took in the scene with alarm. A lot had changed since the late 1950s. "Kids!" he says. "Not only kids—but some of them were very fem. Pretty, fem kids. It was an extremely strange scene. Sure, there were some masculine hustlers. But now there was a mixture, whereas when I knew the turf we were the so-called studs. Never mind that we were all posturing. Now here was an arena with everything—including these very effeminate kids, and I thought, *Who's going to pick them up?* Was I in for a surprise! Who was going to pick them up? They were stopping traffic! Everyone wanted to pick them up!"

Rechy's surprise at the new species of male hustler that had flourished during his absence was so profound it quickly turned to terror. If cars were lining up to pick up these effeminate kids, who would want him? He felt so out of place that, in panic, his body went on automatic pilot and before he could stop himself, he was running—literally running away from what he couldn't understand. Could the types who were once doing the buying now be doing the selling?

"Then what happened was one of those incredible things of my life," Rechy remembers. "Would I ever put it in a book? No. But it really happened! I literally bumped into a man who was getting out of his car—he was coming toward me and I bumped into him! He said, 'I haven't seen one of you around in a long time.' And then he smiled. Oh, I knew I was back and everything was OK. I went with him." To his great relief, Rechy found out that his tough-guy posturing held a nostalgic quality that would never go out of style. He was still marketable, and his life as a hustler—still vitally important to him—would continue.

With a promising career as a professor of writing, as well as any number of good prospects ahead of him, there certainly was no financial reason for Rechy to return to hustling. Yet since that first day in Times Square, Rechy had felt a constant call to the streets. "I have a ferocious need to hustle," he explained in the 1970s to an interviewer. "There's no rush in my life like it." Rechy pursued bodybuilding with even greater avidity. "If you have a muscular body and are very masculine, you can extend your attractiveness," he liked to say to reporters, who always noted his appearance. He confessed to a journalist at the time that his daily workout was just as important to him as his daily writing regimen. "I am convinced that I will never age; I want to become better all the time. I have friends who think I've overdone it, that I spend too much time on my body. Then I point out that I spend many hours writing a book or an artist spends many hours painting a picture. And then you want it to be the best; you want as many people to accept and love it as possible. I don't find that different from spending hours on my body and then showing it off and wanting and accepting that kind of admiration."

No matter how determined he was to be admired, Rechy's reentry into hustling was by no means smooth sailing. In this business where youth is the most marketable asset, there were times that his despair at the unstoppable reality of aging horrified him. Decades later in *The Coming of the Night*, Rechy wrote about this fear. "Growing old was kind of like dying, maybe worse because you were aware of growing old—making out less and less until you couldn't make out any more." In that book he also confronted his secret fears about how he was viewed by the younger set on the streets. He created a younger character, Nick, who observes an older colleague:

> Oh, fuck, that hustler over there—an older guy—still standing waiting to be picked up. He'd been there for hours. Must've been real good looking when he was young, Nick bet, still was but you could tell he was way up in his 20s. Some of the hustlers who bragged the most about how much money they always made—you'd still see them hanging around real late, looking scared. Fuck, what would that guy across the street do next year, and the next? Nick looked away from him, touching his own body.

The cruelty of younger homosexuals toward the older set— something Rechy had understood as far back as his *City of Night* days in the late '50s—was for the first time directed at him. People are often hostile toward the things they desire, and Rechy's age gave his admirers the ammunition they needed. After tricking with one persnickety older client, the client turned to Rechy and said, "You know, you're not exactly in the bloom of your youth. How many years do you think you have ahead of you?" Comments like these really hurt Rechy—hit him right where he lived. But he also believed there were hidden motives behind them. "As cruel as the world is," he reasoned, "I think comments like that were rehearsed. Remarks designed to hurt me because of the impudence of me to still be getting paid for sex. I got that a lot. I think that by that time a lot of people knew who I was and they were outraged."

He found proof of his theory from time to time when certain men later confessed they had been incensed to find him still on the streets. "You don't remember me?" a reporter once asked Rechy. When Rechy admitted he didn't, the journalist revealed he had insulted John on the street several months earlier. "You just looked better than I could have imagined, and I wanted to bring you down," he owned up. When his interview appeared in print several weeks later, the journalist reported that Rechy was "enjoying the peak of his masculinity."

At times Rechy's need to hear compliments combined with his paranoia worked disastrously against him. Once he was sunbathing at a small cruisy park, wearing only a brief bikini. A man paused, looked down, and Rechy heard him say, "You have a great body." As was his custom when praised, Rechy contrived to hear the words again. "What did you say?" he asked. The man repeated his remark, this time somewhat hesitantly, then moved away. The panic of the extreme narcissist struck, and Rechy thought, *Did that son of a bitch say I have a gray body?* Rechy was overwhelmed by the idea. He stood up and followed the hapless cruiser to ask him to repeat his words once again. By then, of course, the man was running away.

Regardless of his paranoia, Rechy was not ready to give up the streets. Sometimes his students drove by and saw him on a darkened street corner and waved. "Hello, Mr. Rechy." For many of them, seeing their teacher out on the streets of Hollywood alongside rough trade was unsettling. Several found the image of this sex object hustling among ruffians and transvestites difficult to reconcile with the man they so respected from their writing classes.

His students could not miss Rechy's blatant narcissism, but he combined it with such humor they began to view the situation as funny. "When I get a compliment," he confided to his students during a class, "I always say, 'What did you say?' because I want to hear it again. The day is spent saying, 'What did you say?' to the mirror." Once a student happened upon Rechy at 3 A.M. on Santa Monica Boulevard wearing only tight jeans, boots, and a layer of oil. "Good evening, Professor Rechy," the student said dryly. "Out for an evening stroll?" Rechy often repeats that story. One of his students observes, "That's one of the strange things about him, that he could separate and divide himself that way. We could laugh. He had a sense of humor about it. He had extraordinary dichotomies in his life. Paradoxes."

Just as his academic life sometimes confronted him on the streets, there were times when Rechy presented his professional colleagues with his street persona. When Rechy's agent, Georges Borchardt, met him for the first time, Borchardt remembers being "quite fascinated with his shirt because it seemed three sizes too small. I kept wondering at what point in our conversation the buttons would pop open, but they didn't." Marsha Kinder recalls going to a Halloween party with him on Occidental's campus, and Rechy wore what he was going to go cruising in later on. Dressed as himself, he won first prize.

Besides his reputable daytime career, another change from Rechy's earlier days on the Los Angeles streets was that now some of the street people began to recognize him. Men driving by immediately knew who Rechy was. Shirtless and splendid, his arrogance set him apart from hustlers several decades younger. If his hustling companions did not know his actual identity, they understood that he was someone with a reputation outside the hustling world. Word got out among younger male prostitutes on Santa Monica Boulevard that the older, handsome hustler who kept to himself was famous. A mystique developed around the attractive and well-preserved middle-aged man. "I heard about you," a kid announced to Rechy on the street one late afternoon. "I know who you are."

"Oh, yeah?" Rechy asked, bemused.

"You were a famous model," the young man said. Obviously the story of John Rechy had gone through many incarnations on the streets. The young hustler recognized that Rechy was someone special and, in his comprehension, a body model was the highest goal one could possibly hope to achieve.

Rechy continued to notice changes in the hustling world. It was now more aggressive, more brutal, and more dangerous. On slow evenings, with 10 hustlers to every client, the atmosphere became angry and hostile. Hustlers of all types hassled people, spitting and throwing bottles at the men who drove by too many times without picking up anybody.

Gay liberation had banished the myth that all hustlers were straight. No longer were all hustlers the aloof tough guys with slicked hair, cigarette packs rolled up into their T-shirt sleeves, leaning nonchalantly against buildings and street signs waiting to be approached. The '70s had given way to a freewheeling sexuality. A new breed of hustlers took over—effeminate, androgynous. Gender-bending hustlers—with all the flamboyance of Miss Destiny—camped on corners and openly signaled to cars as they drove by.

As always, though, Rechy kept one foot out of the street and safely grounded in his other reputable life. Rescue was always just a phone call away. "I was arrested the second time while hustling on Selma," Rechy says. "A man offered me money; I accepted. On a side street off Selma the passenger door was opened, and another cop pulled me back and handcuffed me, arrested me for prostitution. That night there had been a roundup of hustlers on Selma, and when I was brought into jail there was a sense of camaraderie, hustlers greeting each other as we were brought in. I called an expensive attorney, and I was out in no time—and immediately I felt hugely guilty. The others remained in jail. I asked them as I left whether they wanted me to call anyone for them—but they had no one. The guilt I felt was compounded when, a few days later, I turned up at court with my attorney; he had made an arrangement with the court. I would go first, be given a small fine, and that would be it. Responding to his instructions, I turned up in a suit. Some of the other hustlers I had been arrested with were in the same courtroom, without attorneys, waiting to be called. I avoided their eyes."

Rechy's return to the streets of Hollywood, as both a hustler and a cruiser, had sparked the inspiration for his next book. He was amazed and outraged that, because of the continuing prejudice of heterosexual society, every homosexual encounter rendered him a criminal. As a result, many homosexuals continued to take to the streets in order to have some semblance of a sex life. Rechy viewed with admiration these men who dared to defy the law in expressing their sexuality in public places. To him it was a way of breaking down taboos—another step in the sexual outlaw's journey toward acceptance.

CHAPTER TWELVE

You are what you appear to be at any particular moment.
—John Rechy

AS A HUSTLER, RECHY DID NOT change with the times, preferring instead to continue with his old image. But his other life had changed tremendously. He finally sold the house he had shared with his mother in El Paso, and he began to put down roots. He moved into an apartment in the Los Feliz section of Los Angeles, and began furnishing it. There was a new maturity and self-acceptance in the older John Rechy. He told a reporter, "With all my muscles, I'm not afraid of my femininity."

He hung three huge Hollywood glamour portraits in his dining room—two black-and-white images of Greta Garbo and one of Joan Crawford, both women frozen at the height of their youth and beauty. Rechy oversaw the construction of these four-foot portraits himself. He designed the tight cropping of each face to exaggerate the flawless features of the star. This backdrop appeared in publicity photos taken of Rechy over the next 25 years.

When "the hustler" John brought a client home, he invariably said that he was apartment-sitting for a friend. The stylish surroundings, complete with contemporary artwork, crystal bric-a-brac, movie star portraits, and earth-tone area rugs did not fit his image of a street tough. In *The Coming of the Night*, a macho character who masquerades as a mechanic responds to a compliment on his fashionable apartment:

> "Thanks. A friend decorated it for me." That was a lie, too, not that his place was all that, but, even so, he didn't want Andy to think he was an interior decorator and not a mechanic. He knew a scene could be blown away with less than that.

Rechy now had a solid footing in the world of teaching. His stint at Occidental was very successful and as a result he was invited to be a guest lecturer at UCLA, where he eventually became a professor. He also started giving private workshops at his apartment. Rechy demanded a high degree of talent and limited the class to between eight and 12 students. One student recalls "a tough screening process." As a result there was often a waiting list for admittance. Although he often said, "I don't consider myself a teacher; I consider myself a guide," Rechy's reputation as an outstanding instructor continued to grow.

Michael Denneny, a top editor in the publishing world, has crossed paths with virtually every successful contemporary writer. "I have been hearing for 25 years what a good teacher of writing Rechy is," he says. "From straight writers as well as gay writers. I also know that he is very supportive afterwards in helping students get published." Rechy's goal was to make his students' paths easier by sharing his own experiences with them. Indeed, Rechy often used all of his literary connections to help a student he believed in get published. "It's gruesome out there," Rechy would tell his class. "But there's no greater reward than a creative one. It's worth all the battles—if you survive them. Become the best you can, so that you can indeed wage that battle."

Helping his students become the best they could be, both physically and mentally, was Rechy's goal. "Most of us live as supporting players, and we must be the stars of our own lives," he is fond of saying.

By this time, Rechy was considered a legend in the literary world. Almost everyone who attended his classes had read *City of Night* and had been affected by it in some way. Melodie Johnson Howe, a young actress who had been taking writing classes for years, decided to sign up for Rechy's UCLA extension class after reading *City of Night*. Being familiar with his work, Melodie was somewhat prepared for what the man behind that novel would look like. "I didn't expect anyone with a tweed jacket and a pipe," she explains, "but what I didn't expect was to see this utterly charming man, dressed in jeans and an open tight shirt—and carrying it off with great style and class."

If anyone was intimidated by Rechy's reputation, he immediately put him or her at ease with his humor and warmth. Putting his performance skills to good use, Rechy's sessions became a sort of one-man show, with the students acting as captive audience— and they continue today. "I am legendary!" he'd declare at the beginning of the first class. "If you don't believe it, I will show you proof. And, ladies and gentleman, don't fuck with a legend." Rechy's teaching technique alternates between flashy showmanship and astute critical analysis. He banned a teacher's evaluation form because "those forms don't include physical presentation, musculature, and glamour." One student, Matthew Kennedy, was so captivated by Rechy's teaching style that he took scrupulous notes, which he used in an article for *Genre* magazine, incorporating in the piece many of Rechy's best quotes from the class.

"Rechy's class is not just about writing," says Paula Shtrum. "You learn about life, philosophy, and viewing the world—how we should dress and where to eat lunch and dinner."

Between analyzing manuscripts Rechy would comment on his students' clothes and hair styles. "He compliments the women and insults the men," says Henry Turner, a current student of Rechy's. "And it's funny. He likes to exercise his sense of timing." Once a female student contradicted him and Rechy scolded, "I'm just crazy about you and you're looking prettier every day. Now hush."

"He gives his jokes just enough room without letting them get out of hand—they're a relief from intensity," says Nichole Morgan, another of Rechy's students. "He's very perceptive of people's thresholds. He has a sense of who he can jab and who he can't."

But when it was time to get down to work, Rechy was all professionalism. It was clear that he read each student's work with extreme care. Russell Barnard, who took Rechy's class in the '70s, says, "Frankly from the time I walked in the classroom, John just blew me away. He has such an incredible sensitivity, which is also what makes him such a fine novelist. He hears. He listens. He reads between the lines." Rechy was also proud of the fact that he didn't teach his students to write in his style, recognizing the individuality of each voice.

"He didn't talk about his own work, he really taught," Melodie Johnson Howe observes. "He was a thorough critiquer, to some people's dismay, yet he knew how to praise you enough to keep you going so you didn't go slit your wrists. He knows how to get the best out of you, to not let you fall. If he thought that you had talent, he didn't let go of you, and he thought I had talent and he didn't let go of me. To this day I give him major credit for me being a writer." Other writers who have studied with Rechy include Kate Braverman (*Small Craft Warnings*), Sandra Tsing Loh (*Depth Takes a Holiday*), Gina Nahai (*Moonlight on the Avenue of Faith*) and Pulitzer Prize-winning author Michael Cunningham* (*The Hours*).

Like Marsha Kinder, Melodie Johnson Howe became part of a tight circle of talented and beautiful young women Rechy chose to surround himself with during this period of his life—"beautiful" being the operative word. Rechy understood beauty, its powers and its vulnerabilities, which he continued to possess in its male incarnation. "I love beautiful women," he confided to a reporter at the time. "And it's beautiful to be with them." Rechy and Howe

*Cunningham worked on his first published novel, *Golden States,* in Rechy's class.

became fast friends. "He and I would walk into a room and heads would spin around on their necks," she remembers with a laugh. But Rechy always looked for other qualities in his female friends. Beyond her beauty, Rechy related to Howe's wicked sense of irony and humor. She was also an excellent writer. Rechy often talked about his attraction to creative women, an attraction he now ties to feelings toward his mother.

Around 1973, Rechy began spending time with Wendy Elliot Hyland. The ultra-sophisticated, ultra-petite, ultra-chic Hyland was at the time writing, running a literary agency, and was also interested in producing films. "I went to a dinner party where John was present," she says, "and although I had read *City of Night* a couple of times, I didn't connect him with the book. We had this wonderful rapport because of his charm and his big smile. We giggled and laughed and carried on and I had no idea who he was."

Rechy remembers that someone offered to give Hyland a massage, and she lay prone on the floor for awhile. After Rechy had gone, Hyland's friends told her that "John" was John Rechy, the author of *City of Night*. As she remembers it, Rechy called her the following day inviting her to the movies. "I said, 'John who?' and he hung up!"

Eventually it dawned on Hyland that it was Rechy who had called and she got in touch with him and the two began hanging out three or four times a week. Rechy would visit her in the penthouse suite at the hotel where she lived, and she would make meatballs and serve ice-cold pitchers of martinis before the two ventured out into the Los Angeles nightlife. "There was a long hallway entrance into my suite," Hyland says, "and I had a large mirror at the end of it. John would saunter in with his dark hair, low slung jeans with a comb in the back pocket—he'd walk up to the mirror look at himself and exclaim, 'I can't stand it—I'm so fabulous!' And the marvelous thing about it is that it was true."

Wendy began escorting John to dinner parties and events she thought he might find titillating. It was Wendy who brought John to the White Party, he writes about in *The Sexual Outlaw*, where everyone had to wear white to enter the host's rustic home.

Wendy soon became interested in producing a film version of *City of Night* and Rechy took her on a tour of locations from the book. It was only a decade after the novel was published and many of the places—or similar places—still existed. He started the excursion downtown, proving to her that these were not figments of his imagination. These places were the real McCoy. He showed Wendy what she calls "the city behind the city." The back lanes, dark tunnels, and seedy alleyways—where drug deals were made and cruisers cruised and hustlers hustled, while the rest of the world drove by unaware only a few yards away. "It was extraordinary," Wendy recalls. "He showed me back doors in restaurants that led to an entirely different world." Rechy ended the tour with the rambling cruising landscape of Griffith Park, the setting of so much of *Numbers*.* "I'd wake up in the morning and say, 'I can't believe where I was,'" Wendy recalls. "It was like picking up a rock and seeing the colony of ants that exists underneath." Later Rechy would take other women friends on similar tours.

Eventually Rechy wrote a screenplay Wendy liked, then another one in which he updated the events in the novel to the 1970s, which she didn't. The film was never made because Rechy's agent at the time saw many problems with the contract. Since then he has done a complete revision, setting it in its original time period, and the film rights continue to be solicited by top directors.

Rechy also became close to a sultry 21-year-old brunette named Zella Riley whom he had known briefly in El Paso. In his 40s Rechy retained a magnetism that drew women to him as strongly as he was pulled to them. His look was still informal and tough, but even his casualness was planned and put together. "He was fastidious in his grooming, which resulted in a masculine allure that many found irresistible," Zella Riley says. "I had never seen anything like him before in my life, except I guess in the movies. I

---

*Rechy remembers driving the urbane Wendy through the park and mentioning "existentialism" and Wendy exclaiming, "Dahling! Isn't that wonderful? I'm an existentialist too."

thought, *He's the most glamorous thing I've ever seen.* I was intensely interested and infatuated with him.*"*

When Zella called to let John know she was moving to Los Angeles to take a teaching position, she thought he would be dismissive. But he surprised her and immediately welcomed her into his life. "He took me under his wing," she remembers. "He ended up being my only friend for a year or so." They began seeing each other regularly—he introduced her to the world of classic movies and they often went to revival houses, where they huddled together in the dark.

The two became so close that Riley became convinced Rechy could "look into my heart and read my soul." Though she had never said a word about her secret ambitions, Rechy announced to her one day, "You want to be an actress, Zella." When she admitted that had always been her dream, Rechy sprung into action, coaxing her into acting classes, pushing her to take it seriously. "He fished it out and gave it credibility," she says. "He seemed to think that it was a viable possibility, which stunned me."

Sometimes Rechy sat in the back of Zella's workshops and classes to watch her progress. He was extremely sensitive to people's creative yearnings and he always encouraged people in that direction. He sincerely wanted to see her succeed. "Soon after her decision to be an actress," Rechy remembers today, "Zella landed a part in a Charles Gorgon play. When she entered, there was a gasp from the audience. She looked gorgeous, and I felt very, very proud."

Zella Riley felt his pride. "He talked to me so supportively and intimately in a way no other male had ever done," she says. "He probably knows me better than anyone in the world. But he never would tell me his age. I could never get it out of him. I tried not to think about it. I just thought he was really cute."

Rechy, in return, revealed his feelings for his women friends when describing the main character in his novel *Rushes*. "Endore himself has close friendships with women," Rechy writes, "perhaps closer than with men—he has been accused of preferring the company of women." In one sense these women made him feel closer to his mother. He believed that Guadalupe, in another time and without the oppression his father imposed on her, would have been an innovative and independent woman. He had always admired her because, even though she had little formal education, she was very smart and artistic.

These women were Rechy's way of re-creating his mother, of bringing her back in different forms. Rechy lavished attention on his women friends, pushing them artistically in a way he could never do for his mother.

Several years after Guadalupe's death, Rechy began to try to free himself from her psychological hold. During her lifetime Guadalupe did not allow the men in the family to cook. It was women's work and she shooed her sons out of the kitchen, shaking her head ominously when she heard about men cooking, especially in reference to Rechy and his brothers. Finally venturing beyond her influence in this area, Rechy began to experiment in the kitchen. Soon he became a skilled cook. He was particularly fond of his braised ribs. To demonstrate his talent, Rechy invited Melodie Johnson Howe over for lunch, telling her he would cook ribs. The night before, however, Rechy had an intense dream. In it his sister Olga was saying to their mother, "Can you believe that Johnny is cooking? Not only that, but he's cooking for a woman!" In the dream Rechy's mother was aghast. The following day Rechy worked out while the ribs were braising. As he pumped iron, he could smell the delicious aroma. But soon the scent began to nauseate him. When Howe arrived, Rechy walked out carrying the ribs in a plastic bag, then threw them into the garbage. The two went out to lunch instead.

Unfazed by Rechy's quirks, most of his women friends developed an infatuation with him. He often says that these are the women he would have been romantically involved with had he been straight. Wendy Elliot Hyland describes Rechy as a "homosexual womanizer." "My mother fell madly in love with him," she says with a laugh. "We were all attracted to him in a million different ways," Zella Riley adds. He was as intelligent and articulate as any man, and certainly strong, yet he was terrifically sensitive and warm—with a wry sense of humor he often gamely turned on himself. At the same time he projected an intense masculinity. The combination of all these characteristics made him irresistible. The women knew, of course, that Rechy was gay—there was never any deception surrounding that—but he never discouraged a woman friend's feelings from becoming more intense, although he was skillful at drawing lines.

"I used to try to get him to smoke pot," Zella Riley admits. "I thought I would be more likely to get him to flirt with me or be more responsive to whatever I put out. I could never quite figure out how he could be gay. Actually, there was always this fantasy that he wasn't gay. I guess because I was so attracted to him. But it never went into anything unacceptable. He was perfect at keeping a balance. If ever it would tip a certain way, he would do something that would set it right without turning me off."

Paula Shtrum—one of Rechy's current students—says, "We always say that, next to our husbands, John is the most important man in our lives. Of course John always replies, 'What do you mean, next to your husbands?'"

In his private workshops, as at Occidental, Rechy's strong looks and personality sometimes brought confused emotions to the surface. Most of the students were there to work, so the fact that he was a hustler didn't mean much. If they disagreed with what he did on the streets, it didn't matter because it was all about the writing.

Once the classes began, Rechy's technique was to have a very personal interaction with each student. Wiser students took advantage of this personal connection. But sometimes the student-teacher relationship could be taken the wrong way—particularly by homosexual male students who took the course in order to seduce the legendary hustler of *City of Night* and *Numbers*.

"If there were problems with a male," one of Rechy's female

students observes, "it usually stemmed from the fact that he entered John's class with unreal expectations of what John would be like and what their relationship might be. When you're a fascinating looking person it brings all kinds of things out in people and what they expect from you." Indeed, some of the men found complicated, hidden meanings in Rechy's observations. Once when John was making a critique of a student's prose the young man yelled out, "Well, that takes your dedication off my novel!"

"I would rather be excluded from a good book than included in a bad one," Rechy replied dryly.

Rechy also recalls uncomfortable incidents, like the time an attractive, muscular student stopped by his Los Feliz apartment to do some extra work on a story he was working on in class. They sat at Rechy's now legendary dining room table, and as Rechy went over the manuscript he felt the young man's leg press up against his own. Rechy was not about to cross boundaries of the student-teacher relationship. He had the student move to the other side of the table.

Not surprisingly, one of Rechy's best student friends was a heterosexual man. Russell Barnard, a successful businessman with a background in journalism, had read *City of Night* in the mid 1970s. When Barnard decided to branch out into fiction, he discovered Rechy's workshop. "We connected right off as both friends and student and teacher," Barnard says. Both men had ample ego. But between them there would not be the sexual signals, the posing, the game-playing, or the competition likely to develop in a friendship between Rechy and another attractive homosexual man. Although the two had very different life experiences, each had grown up with a keen awareness of his own talent, as well as of his isolation. In adulthood each had developed skills the other admired. Rechy had an artistic nature, Barnard a flair for business. "Neither of us was afraid to take chances, since we are both so confident in who we are," Barnard says. "So it allowed us at an early stage to have some very interesting and deep conversations."

A few years later, Barnard coproduced a play based on one of Rechy's novels.

One reason some of his young gay students may have felt confused about Rechy was that, although he acted very differently in each of his worlds, his physical appearance remained unchanged. He still wore jeans, often with a tight T-shirt and motorcycle boots. He never wore a jacket or tie. He could not, in fact, go to restaurants where a dress code was enforced. Rechy developed his own style, often turning up at exclusive restaurants clad in Levi's and boots, set off with an expensive shirt and tie. "Ultimately, I got into every restaurant," he says.

Dress codes aside, Rechy was full of contradictions that ultimately caused people to misread him. In spite of his rough appearance, he had impeccable manners. To his writing students, Rechy would offer tips on wine drinking in restaurants—how to properly check the cork, etc. "I don't want you embarrassing yourselves in public," he'd explain.

Some people who fancied themselves as part of the "underground" assumed that Rechy was interested in everything wanton. But he wasn't. He kept his sexuality part of his private life—his other life.

Marsha Kinder observed that Rechy had very funny attitudes about women and sexuality. "He likes elegance," she says. "He'd joke about it. He didn't think ladies should have sex. It was a joke, but it was very amusing, as to what he allowed on one hand and didn't allow on the other hand." Melodie Johnson Howe concurs. "In his own way John was a gentlemen with elaborate sets of rules and his own rules of decorum. At heart he's a romantic."

"It was a curious thing," Kinder continues. "Part of John would have socialist values, and then there was another part that was incredibly elitist. He won't go to any restaurant that he thinks might not be clean. He has gone to Mexico, but he's always terrified of getting food poisoning. He's obsessive about cleanliness in regards to safety, which has probably helped him with not getting AIDS."

For years only his closest friends realized that Rechy created the persona of the street hustler as protection for a highly sensitive nature—though he always preferred to look that part, there was an entirely different and separate person underneath.

"Now he embraces that as part of the legend," Kinder explains. "The fact that he very conscientiously designed this persona. And of course, being a hustler is one of the things he was in tune to, responsive to what someone's fantasy is and then working that fantasy. It worked in the literary world too."

At readings and speaking engagements people expected to see "the legend." And Rechy did not disappoint. "The notion of being oneself is a scary thing, and it's easier to put on than take off," Rechy's friend, the writer Michael Kearns, observes. "I think it served him personally and professionally, but it became an identity that overrode him. When that identity becomes larger than life, it becomes very difficult to let go of, especially when it's sexually identified. Those things are not easy to give up."

Not everyone was enthralled when confronted with Rechy's image. A young actor and longtime fan of Rechy remembers meeting his idol at an OutWrite conference in San Francisco. The actor, however, was less than thrilled with Rechy's physical presentation. "He wore a skin-tight T-shirt and jeans," he remembers. "I thought, *Such poetry and dreams out of this?* It reminded me about how everything among gay men is reductive to sex and the way you look."

At a chic luncheon in San Francisco, Beat poet Allen Ginsberg stopped the highbrow chitchat dead when he bluntly and loudly asked Rechy, "So, you still don't get fucked?"(A *Vogue* photographer, Rechy's editor, and Michael McClure were among the guests looking on.) Later, Ginsberg invited Rechy to visit him at Lawrence Ferlinghetti's apartment, where Ginsberg was staying. Rechy went, but Ferlinghetti was not there. Ginsberg was, and he promptly asked Rechy to undress so he could see his "famous body" (cunning words as Rechy is so susceptible to flattery). This time, however, Rechy managed to keep his clothes on.

Undismayed, Ginsberg picked up a guitar-like instrument and, strumming it, sang William Blake's "Songs of Innocence."*

Others, threatened by Rechy's swagger, blatantly challenged him. "You think you're really hot shit," someone would ask after a few drinks at a party. "You think you're such a stud? How about taking me on?" Rechy would try to calm him down with humor. "Oh, no," he'd quip, "these muscles are just for show." Once at a San Francisco speaking engagement with Ginsberg, Peter Orlovsky (Ginsberg's lover) accosted Rechy and demanded to know how much he could bench press. "Look," Rechy replied coolly, "I don't care how strong I am. It's that I *look* the stronger man."

Usually, though, the reactions he got to his appearance delighted Rechy. In 1976, while he was working on *The Sexual Outlaw*, Marsha Kinder invited Susan Sontag to speak to her film class. (Sontag had directed a short experimental film.) She and Kinder didn't hit it off. Both were strong, intelligent women, and Sontag was intrigued by Kinder's close friendship with John Rechy. Kinder told Sontag that Rechy would be attending the screening of her movie. Rechy did attend, with Melodie Johnson Howe and their friend Roy Walford. After the screening of Sontag's film, the unimpressed Howe praised the merits of William Wyler. At a reception for Sontag, Rechy wore a favorite body-fitting red shirt and the typical jeans and boots. Rechy had also wanted to meet Sontag, and the two writers had a long talk, after which she asked him what he was working on. Rechy explained that he was working on a book titled *The Sexual Outlaw*.

"Oh," Sontag said, intrigued. "What is the thesis?"

Rechy explained that its thesis was that the homosexual minority remained the most hounded of all minorities.

Sontag looked around the room at the serious, doughy-looking film students. With a wicked but charming smile, she said,

---

*"I liked Alan," Rechy says, "and often found him very funny when he wasn't playing exalted guru poet. Or, maybe, even funnier then."

"Yet of all the people here you look the least hounded."

Without a doubt, Rechy's appearance continued to have a big impact on people. "There would be a lot of projection on to John," Marsha Kinder says. "A lot of conservative people would look at John and see their own fantasy of what they wanted an underground figure to be. John would surprise them because then he would turn around and he'd want to be elegant. Or he didn't like it when they were too explicit in their language. They couldn't fathom that contradiction about him."

By 1977 Rechy was making himself more available to reporters, and they couldn't help noting the contrasts between his appearance and behavior. At another reading in San Francisco, a journalist from *The Advocate* waited for Rechy as he checked into the modest hotel Rechy's hosts had picked for him. The reporter entered the room with Rechy, who immediately dubbed the green-walled room "ghastly." In no time Rechy was on the telephone calling the desk. With the reporter trailing him, Rechy went to two other rooms until he was somewhat satisfied with what turned out to be the bridal suite. Rechy apologized to the reporter and then the two settled for the interview. The printed interview, when it appeared, opened, "The Sexual Outlaw is displeased with the decor of his room."

Because Rechy's career was bringing in money again, Melodie Johnson Howe and her affluent husband, record producer Bones Howe, arranged for him to meet their conservative Wells Fargo banker at the Friars Club in Los Angeles. Rechy walked in with his sleeves rolled up, wearing tight jeans and boots. "And with John it's the deception," Johnson Howe says. "You see this hustler-looking guy, but he opens his mouth and out comes very bright, intelligent conversation." The banker—dressed in his pinstripe suit and tie—was intrigued by Rechy's look, and began the meeting by asking Rechy about his writing. "I'm writing about a revolution," Rechy declared. "A coming revolution!"

The conservative banker almost fell off of his chair. "A coming revolution?!"

But Rechy had no wish to incite violence. "I'm not talking about the revolution of shooting people with bullets, but of shooting come." Of course, Rechy was talking about a sexual revolution, and *The Sexual Outlaw* was his most daring work since *City of Night*. The controversy surrounding this new book would be even more intense than that which had surrounded his groundbreaking first.

• • •

The Sexual Outlaw opens with a description of "Jim" (Rechy's double) preparing for a night of cruising:

> He prepares his body for the hunt. A dancer at the bar. A boxer in the ring. Prepares ritualistically for the next three days of outlaw sex. The arena will be streets, parks, alleys, tunnels, garages, movie arcades, bathhouses, beaches movie back rows, tree sheltered avenues, late night orgy rooms, backyards.

Friends noted this ritualistic preparation, but in a less romantic light. Melodie Johnson Howe says that, "He was like a man going to war at night. Think of the streets! Think of what you're putting yourself through! For what? To get attention? It's a tormented thing to do, and there was a torment that was driving him."

Rechy himself was aware of the strand of torment entwined about his obsession with street life, calling that life alternately "the most exciting experience in the world" and "a stark vision of hell." He was like a drug addict forced to choose between the exquisite high with its subsequent despair and a more conventional life. Rechy decided to continue with his addiction.

During a discussion of *The Sexual Outlaw*, Rechy told an

interviewer, "You know whatever rituals homosexuals perform, whether we're destructive or not, we're alive. There's more life in one evening in a homosexual bar than most people experience in half a lifetime."

Rechy described his new book as "the literary equivalent of a film documentary—influenced by Robbe-Grillet's theories on the new novel. Plotless, black-and-white, it is a minute by minute accounting of three days and three nights of anonymous sex as Jim roams the sexual underground of Los Angeles. Many characters appear, only briefly, as their lives intersect with Jim's. All are 'pastless.' I wanted all the characters, including Jim, to be defined only through their sexual journeys." Interspersed throughout the account of this night odyssey are voice-over essays, multimedia splices of commentary. It is a brooding documentary of a misunderstood world."

To help explain that world—and as if to say "this is what you forced us into and this is how we've transformed it"—Rechy takes his readers cruising with him, in and out of gay bars, dark alleys, dank underpasses, shadowy parks, and badly lit streets, transporting them into his own physical and psychological geography. He challenges homosexual complacency in the era after Stonewall and just before AIDS. Homosexuals are viewed by society as sinners, law-breakers, outcasts, jokes, or perverts. They are persecuted by cops, beaten by fag-bashers, and ridiculed in show business circles. "In this context," Rechy writes, "the sexual outlaw flourishes. The pressures produce him, create his defiance. Knowing that each second his freedom might be ripped away arbitrarily, he lives fully at the brink. Promiscuity is his righteous form of revolution."

With *The Sexual Outlaw* Rechy portrayed the undisclosed life of homosexuals who seek sexual gratification in a world that condemns them for their desire and forces them into the shadows. As Rechy puts it, "Every male homosexual lives under the constant threat of arbitrary arrest and a wrecked life."

As in his previous works he uses chunks of his real life for material. But this time he is not writing under the guise of fiction.

More comfortable than ever before with his own dichotomies, in 1977 *The Sexual Outlaw* would be billed as "a documentary." In the beginning of the book he identifies the protagonist thusly: "Jim— he calls himself that sometimes, sometimes Jerry, sometimes John." Rechy mixes names he had given his fictitious protagonists from previous books with his real-life identity, making clear the place his real-life experiences have in all of his novels.

Despite its sexual explicitness, *The Sexual Outlaw* debuted with some excellent reviews. "It rips aside the curtain concealing a subculture few of us even know exists," the *Los Angeles Times* said. "*The Sexual Outlaw* is at once an intensely personal and courageous document of one man's psyche and beliefs and a revolutionary manifesto of defiance to the heterosexual world. It is a book written out of rage, unnerving, thought-provoking, a polemic against heterosexual injustice to a portion of our population."

But the book quickly fell from the best-seller lists when some bookstores refused to carry it and major newspapers and television stations declined to advertise it. John Lack, the general manager at WCBS radio in New York, turned down advertisements for the book, writing to a Grove Press editor: "I read the book. We can't promote this sort of thing. It has no redeeming social value. If it was just about regular homosexuals, OK, but what he [Rechy] describes is unnecessary. People don't want to know about that.... If it were Henry Miller, well, OK, but this is worse than dirty." The difference was that Henry Miller wrote about heterosexual exploits. The manager's attitude confirmed Rechy's thesis.

"I really had no idea when I finished it how controversial it would be," Rechy says. "After all, this was my life. I sometimes marvel at how deep-rooted prejudice can be."

As with *City of Night*, some of the most hypocritical criticism came from homosexual men. Rechy recalls picking up a stranger in an alley and bringing him back to his apartment. Afterward the guy said, "You know there's this dreadful book out called *The Sexual Outlaw*. The gay scene the author describes in the book doesn't really exist, and all it's doing is giving us a bad image."

Obviously, one of the consequences of oppression is a defensive blindness to especially painful truths.

The reviewer for the *Los Angeles Times* declared that *The Sexual Outlaw* confronts the reader with prose that is "shattering, jarring, passionate, astonishing, serious, jolting, revolutionary, unnerving, thought-provoking, revelatory, and resonant." As Rechy's editor said at the time, "No wonder some people are afraid."

The Sexual Outlaw brought Rechy back to the forefront of the literary world. His sex life on the streets continued, but Rechy's emotional life was increasingly lonely. He had never expressed a desire for a long-term romantic connection and to this day says it's not something he ever wanted. But he does admit that there were "desperate Judy Garland times—lots of applause and then you're alone." Times when he had sex with 10 people in the park and then went home alone. If it was still early, he'd call some friends, but by that time they'd already gone out or had plans. Rechy felt terrible anguish at times, yet steadfastly told people he did not want a committed relationship. "I filled any loneliness with sex and so I never felt lonely," Rechy explains. "Despair, yes. I've always felt that. I never felt lonely. I only felt lonely for more friends."

Some of Rechy's friends viewed his situation differently: "We would have dinner at night, I would go home, and he would go hustle," a female friend from the period recalls. "It seemed sad that he couldn't feel content. He couldn't spend an entire evening with a friend just talking...or just go home, put his feet up, and watch television."

Survival had always been important to Rechy. He lived as if he were an emotional island, deliberately self-contained. However, he began to feel a need to disclose his other life, his dark side, to his female friends. "To share with them, to bring those worlds together in their views of me."

Late one afternoon he actually took Zella Riley to the cruisy section of Griffith Park. "Now remember I didn't know about gay behavior," Zella says. "And I didn't know anything about street life. I was very innocent. But I wanted to understand him. He was such a mystery. He seemed so heterosexual. He responded to me in so many ways. I couldn't picture him in those other situations. Going with him was a way for me to try and understand it."

Rechy led Riley through his shadowy cruising areas and pointed to the men popping out of the bushes. "Did you see them?" he would exclaim, as if seeing the illicit activity through her fresh eyes. He also took the young actress to gay bars where she'd stare shocked at naked male dancers and explicit films showing on television screens above the bar. Sometimes he would drive her around Santa Monica Boulevard, pointing out his favorite hustling spots. "See that guy," John would say, calling some young man to Zella's attention. "He's hustling."

Riley was disturbed by what she saw. "It was surreal to me," she says. "I could never see all of that as part of John's life."

Melodie Johnson Howe also recalls driving with Rechy down the streets he hustled. "He was showing me a side of life I would never know, and all the while I'm hearing him talk about it from an intellectual point of view, with the moon shining in through the window. I'd sit there quietly clutching on to his arm trying to put it all together."

Some people close to him began to see the 46-year-old Rechy's hustling excursions as the desperate acts of a desperate man. "For as long as it lasted," says one friend, "my response to it was never judgmental. It just made him more vulnerable in my eyes. The vulnerability stemmed from the fact that he was holding on for dear life to something that was clearly going to get the best of him." His self-confidence now, more than ever, was wrapped up in reaffirming that he was still desirable and could still hustle. Even with thousands of successful nights under his belt, Rechy was realistic enough to accept that there might be some nights when he would make no connections. He may have looked no different from the night before, but sometimes the chemistry was simply not right. Despite his years, he still held his own—but he grew ever more fearful with each passing birthday. Rechy's longtime friend Bill Regan remembers that "birthdays were severely depressing to him."

"He never talked about aging directly, but everybody knew this was a really big issue for him," Zella Riley says. "He would never admit that aging was a possibility or anything that would happen to him. Yet he always wanted reassurance of how he looked. And he fought really hard to hang on to what he had."

A hustler's most horrifying nightmare was rejection by clients for being too old. "Aging," Rechy would say, is, "the monster figure of the gay world."

The monster was catching up with him. Rechy was devastated when one afternoon a tough-looking guy pulled up on a motorcycle and asked him the usual: "How much do you go for?" When Rechy told him the going rate at the time—about $30—the motorcycle guy looked at him askance and said, "Jesus Christ! You must be over 50!" Then he revved up and pulled away.

Yet Rechy would not—could not—consider leaving the streets. One acquaintance says, "Whatever it was that was inside of him—that rebellion—however he took homosexuality, however he saw it and had to live it out in order to appease whatever was haunting him, hustling is how he dealt with it. And it was painful for him. It was not an easy thing to do."

Even in middle age Rechy still resembled the alter ego he had created nearly 20 years before in *City of Night*. He still presented the hard, impassive exterior while fiercely guarding the sensitive, impassioned inner life he shared through his writing. There were still many encounters. But they were fleeting and worthless when it came to comfort and security. There were his brothers and sisters, but they now had families. They knew of John's street life peripherally, through his writing, but it was not something they acknowledged in their dealings with him.

A romantic relationship might have smoothed the transition from youth to maturity. But Rechy was terrified at the prospect, and he intentionally made it difficult for any man to get close to him. Submitting to a relationship meant acknowledging need. Offering trust meant surrendering autonomy—something Rechy was not ready to do. Instead, he made sure each budding relationship was terminated before anything could truly blossom. There were sex partners—men Rechy met while cruising who later became friends—but once they became friends, they no longer had sex with each other.

Rechy explored only the very peripheries of what are called "relationships." These forays were brief interludes with men in situations of mutual attraction, not in a hustling context. "There was a young man I met in the park cruising," Rechy says. "He came into town several times and even stayed over in my apartment. After a long, long affair of about two days, I decided to let him know who I was—since I had been playing the street-role throughout that time. I showed him my books—at the time there were only five. He seemed very disturbed. 'Joe,' I asked, 'What's the matter?' He seemed to be struggling to answer. Finally he said, 'Most people you meet have written *one* book.'"

These brief flirtations were his first tentative steps toward something more. "There was another guy who had been a dancer, a bodybuilder type. I saw him a couple of times," Rechy says. "Oh, yeah, and then there was that kid who had been in one of my classes at UCLA, that I drove around with but we never had sex. He was also a bodybuilder and it was very competitive...very, very competitive." (Friends remember their rapport as two men showing off their muscles to each other.) "Then there was this Chicano from El Paso, very handsome," Rechy remembers. "He stayed over a couple of nights and then I asked him to leave."

Marsha Kinder explains why she thinks it was so difficult for men to get close to Rechy. "John had these elaborate sets of rules when dating," Kinder says. "I mean, you can do this, but you can't do that, and you can say that, but you can't say this. They'd make your head spin, his rules. It took so much patience to get through to him. It took someone very, very confident, who was so confident with himself that he was not threatened by this. Someone who could say, 'Oh, well, this is just one of John's quirks, and it's not really me. I know that ultimately he's a wonderful person and I'm going to stick with him.'"

In 1977, Rechy did meet a young man who would be instrumental in his emotional growth. Rechy had gone to New York with Melodie Johnson Howe, and was spending his days cruising the Hudson River piers, which at the time was the main meeting place in Manhattan for anonymous homosexual encounters. It was at the decaying piers that Rechy met a young man named Bobby, whose mixture of innocence, beauty, and sensitivity would inspire Rechy's story "Love in the Back Rooms."

Bobby silently observed Rechy cruising the piers, doing his "numbers routine," going from partner to partner throughout the day. Finally, as Rechy recounts in "Love in the Back Rooms," Bobby approached him and asked, "Why did you let just anybody do that to you? All afternoon, flexing your muscles, showing off. Why?" At first, Rechy was angry, but then he recognized that the kid was only about 18. He saw the boy's fear, the tears in his eyes, and Rechy was touched.

"You shouldn't stay here if you don't like what happens," Rechy told him, gently.

"My brother told me guys come here to meet guys and make out, I mean, my brother was bragging the other day about how him and his friends come here and beat up on queers, so I knew this is where I'd find someone, people like me..."

"Jesus," Rechy said, steering Bobby to the cleanest part of the piers. And there they had "a very mild, very sweet, encounter," Rechy says. He also told Bobby that he was staying at the Gramercy Hotel. Later Bobby stood out front of the hotel waiting for Rechy to emerge. At last he spotted Rechy coming out of the hotel. "I knew if I kept hanging around Gramercy, I'd see you," Bobby told him. "I've been back and forth all day for two days." But Rechy was leaving for the theater with Melodie, so he told Bobby to call him later. He did.

Later that night Rechy met Bobby in the Village and they

walked around in the cold for awhile. Bobby revealed his plans to join Rechy in Los Angeles. He would get a job in a gas station and the two would build a life together.

"I love you," he blurted to Rechy.

To burst the boy's fantasy bubble, Rechy told him he was married and had a young son. Rechy writes:

> The lie hurts me, but I told him what I think will release him most quickly and with the least pain from his shaping obsession. When he looks up, he's still smiling, as if the smile has not yet had time to be assaulted. Then there's anger. "I thought you were the greatest, the most beautiful person I ever met, but you're fucked up, like my goddam brother! Fuck you!" he shouts at me. Shoulders defiantly straight, he walks away from me along the cold, windy street.

Memories of his brief encounter with Bobby haunted Rechy from then on, and the young man's character would appear not only in "Love in the Back Rooms," but also in Rechy's next novel, *Rushes*. But more importantly, Bobby's tender earnestness and gentle desire to love and be loved had pierced Rechy, ultimately opening the door for a future relationship with another young man named Michael.

By the late '70s it was obvious that Rechy couldn't go on hustling for much longer. He still looked wonderful for his age, and there were still cruisers who preferred older men or the rare tough-guy image Rechy projected—but it remained a world where youth ruled. Friends were beginning to worry about him; it was difficult not to wonder how Rechy might end up. His image of himself was so entangled with the need to be desirable, a hot number, it was clear he wouldn't enter his maturity gracefully. The older characters in his books were sad, wasted creatures, while the younger ones merited tenderness and admiration. What would happen when the rejections became more frequent for Rechy himself?

Russell Barnard, who saw a lot of Rechy during this time, began to consider "this whole issue of the loss of beauty and whether John Rechy the novelist could stand it or not. Very early on in our relationship, the first couple of years, I had very serious concerns about whether John was beating himself down an irretrievable, unchangeable path toward suicide. That he couldn't allow himself to get old because he wouldn't be as beautiful in his own eyes as he had been."

Barnard, who cared deeply for Rechy and considered him family, began thinking about different paths John could follow that would take him from his addiction to the streets. "Should I talk about his beauty within," Barnard wondered at the time. "I was very, very concerned about how this would all turn out."

Some acquaintances thought suicide was inevitable. But others—close friends like Melodie Johnson Howe—knew that "John endures." But, she adds, "I think—if not for Michael—it would have been a very unhappy John enduring." Michael would change Rechy's life and be—in many of Rechy's friends' eyes—his salvation. As Marsha Kinder puts it, "Michael is somebody quite extraordinary. The only one who had the patience to stick it out."

• • •

Rechy met the extraordinary young man who would change his life on an ordinary evening in 1979. Rechy was hustling on a corner, although the area wasn't exclusively hustling turf. Rechy describes it as "a limbo of hustling, cruising, and everything else."

Michael Snyder was a 21-year-old actor who had recently arrived in Los Angeles to study and try to advance his career. While exploring the city he had driven to this limbo district to check out the cruising scene. Rechy glimpsed him parking his car and immediately experienced one of those rare, frightening moments that combines a feverish and wild chemistry with the thrill of spotting a gorgeous someone; a moment when emotions spin out of control, elevating ordinary desire to extraordinary heights.

"He looked like an angel to me—a cross between an angel and Tom Sawyer," Rechy says. "Even in the dim light his reddish-blond hair glowed."

Rechy immediately tried to signal to Michael without giving off any indication of hustling. "I didn't want to drive him away," he explains. A man approached Rechy to offer him money, but Rechy quickly brushed him off. The unimaginable was happening. John Rechy was passing up a score. "For the first time ever I had the feeling of truly wanting someone," Rechy says. The two eventually hooked up and went back to Rechy's apartment. Still playing his street persona (though not playing the hustler, as that would have sent Michael away), John gave barely literate answers to Michael's questions and explained his elegant apartment with his standard line about apartment-sitting for a friend.

After the encounter, John gave Michael his phone number. But ironically, for the first time in his long career, Rechy's street demeanor was working against him. Michael thought John wasn't smart enough for him. "That's how good I was at my role," Rechy says, "and I was trapped in it."

A few weeks passed and Rechy began to wonder if Michael was even going to call. Actually, Michael had told his sister, "I met a guy I like but he's much too dumb for me. Where could it go with somebody that dumb?" Finally, Michael decided to give the dumb guy another chance and he called John.

Michael had just seen a film by Luis Buñuel called *That Obscure Object of Desire*. When they got together again in Rechy's apartment* Michael told him how terrible he thought the film was. "I don't know how this guy is a well-known director," he complained. "You can take all his movies and dump them."

---

*Rechy asked the author specifically not to call the encounter a date. "I hate that word 'date'—it is so sophomorically hetero!" he says.

Rechy could no longer keep masquerading as an illiterate. Buñuel happened to be a favorite of his. "You throw away his films," he retorted, "and you throw away a large part of classic film history."

John's sudden outburst startled Michael. "He looked at me," Rechy recalls, "I suppose with pleasure. And then I became very angry—mostly with myself. I said, 'Do you know who I am?' I marched him into my study and I said, 'See all those books? I wrote them!' And Michael was really astonished. He said, 'You wrote *Numbers*?' That's the book he had read."

From that moment, Rechy dropped all pretenses, creating the possibility of a relationship with the young actor. It was turbulent, but Rechy hesitantly allowed it to develop. The two men began seeing each other, casually at first. But soon Rechy realized this young man was different from the others. Michael was intelligent and affectionate, but he knew enough to back off when Rechy began to feel stifled. They went to the movies together, shared their favorite music, and slept in the same bed all night, which was rare for Rechy. Then Rechy would suddenly back off, reluctant to take the relationship to a deeper level. Michael made himself scarce for days at a time.

"I thought he was much too young to get into a kind of involvement," Rechy says. John was also terrified that a serious commitment with Michael would mean an end to the kind of life that had sustained him. "I treasured my freedom for myself and for him. I was very honest in saying that I was not going to stop my street life." Cruising, for Rechy, was a flight from death. Giving that up would force him to face his own mortality. There was also the fear of loving someone completely—and then losing him. "This," he says, "was my first experience with mutual desire."

Rechy remained determined not to surrender his life to what he called "the imprisoning concept of fidelity," which he equated with ownership. But he was also safeguarding against the possibility of pain. He feared loving another man was a sign of weakness that would ultimately lead to loss. In lighter moments he told his writing class, "Marriage! That's for ninnies of either sex."

Confused, Rechy discussed his conflicting feelings with friends. The writer Felice Picano was living in Los Angeles at the time, and he and Rechy had become friendly. When Picano's partner was visiting from New York, he introduced him to Rechy. Afterward John told Felice, "He's really nice. I guess this sort of a thing can work out OK."

Picano agreed. "It's really wonderful having somebody right there you can share things with, and you could have fun together—it's not just bourgeois."

Rechy listened intently and explained, "I'm seeing this guy Michael. He wants to take it further and I'm not sure what to do."

Picano encouraged Rechy to give it a try. "I had two thoughts," Picano remembers. "One was he was getting older and he couldn't be on the streets much longer. I would still see him in front of Circus of Books, which is a very cruisy bookstore in West Hollywood, with his shirt off, and I thought, *This can't last—you don't want to do this forever.* Then I met Michael and I really liked him. John was wavering. He said to me, 'I don't want a textbook gay romance.' And I told him, 'Figure out your own way. You're two adults, you don't have to follow anything.'"

Frankly, Rechy wanted the best of both worlds. Years later in *The Coming of the Night*, he fictionalized what he had in mind for his relationship with Michael:

Their unique "arrangement" had begun during their very first year together. Paul wanted to be "faithful," and Stanley wanted an "open relationship." "No reason why we can't both have our choices," Stanley had said.

Yet something in Rechy was changing. One night while hustling on Santa Monica Boulevard, a man pulled up, lowered the window and made the usual arrangements. Rechy got in the car, but as he looked out the window he saw Michael coming down the street. Their eyes met through the car window.

"Oh, God, something's happened," Rechy told the startled man. "I can't go with you." The man was bewildered, but he stopped the car and Rechy opened the door and ran after Michael. "I caught up with him and said, 'What's the matter?' And he had tears streaming down his face. I couldn't stand that. I couldn't stand for him to be hurt." John told Michael that his life didn't have to change, that Michael would always come first. He had just proved it by leaving the potential client for Michael. Rechy knew it was an unconventional relationship, but the two men continued to see a lot of each other. Sometimes Michael would show up at one of Rechy's cruising spots and pretend he'd just happened to find him. John would always leave with Michael.

Friends observing John and Michael together noticed that Michael had a gentle side, but also a strength that seemed built right into him. His unconstrained spirit was one of the things that had drawn Rechy to him in the first place.

One day Michael accompanied John to the grocery store. The simple action of two men shopping together suddenly panicked Rechy. Just the thought of pushing the cart together traumatized him. "You go get your cart and I'll get mine," he blurted, "and we'll meet at the checkout line."

Michael immediately understood the implication and snapped, "You'd better be careful. Not too many people would put up with you."

Rechy began to understand his own limits. He began to draw Michael closer, impressed with the fact that Michael was sometimes willing to acquiesce to his idiosyncrasies, yet remained firm about setting boundaries and making sure his own dignity remained intact.

Rechy confided his unease about his growing attachment to Michael to friends like Melodie Johnson Howe. "But his doubts were in a caring way for Michael," she says, "because he wasn't sure his lifestyle would be fair to Michael. I could tell from the way John talked about him that his deep concern was for Michael.

That no matter what John thought or did, it was out of his control at that point. It was Michael."

Rechy's fear of commitment began to sneak into his comments in newspaper interviews. He seemed to be trying to talk himself out of monogamy. He told one reporter, "A beautiful relationship need not be destroyed simply because at one particular time a partner desires someone else of another physical type."

Eventually Michael gave Rechy a taste of his own medicine. Showing up on the street late one night, he told John he had gone off with somebody. Rechy was furious. It was OK for Rechy to desire someone else, but he couldn't stand the thought of Michael wanting anyone else. He pretended it wasn't Michael's indiscretion that bothered him. The two argued on the street, and suddenly Michael sprang away from Rechy.

"I don't know what happened," Rechy recalls, "but he got away from me. I started chasing him through an alley." They quarreled some more about it, but finally made up.

Still, Rechy began to wonder if Michael was too young for him after all. "I'd seen young people come under the influence of people who are older and are somewhat famous," Rechy says. "I've seen what happens to them. I didn't want Michael to be thought of as John Rechy's boyfriend. He was much too much himself for that."*

Rechy decided it might be best if they spent time away from each other. Through some friends, he helped Michael get an assistant teaching position at the Actors Studio in New York.

Sending Michael off to New York was also Rechy's way of testing him. "I suppose, in a way, I didn't think he'd take it," he recalls. "But he was excited about it! He said, 'Oh, God, yes, yes, I'll take it!' I remember looking out the window to see this gorgeous young man who was very excited about going to New York and leaving me. I was sad, but I was triumphant at the same time. I looked at him and I thought, *Jesus Christ, I don't know this guy. He wants to leave me. But I made it possible.*"

*For that reason, Rechy seldom uses Michael's name in interviews.

Thoughts of Michael now influenced Rechy's writing. A new tenderness appeared in his descriptions of male characters. The main character in Rechy's next novel, *Rushes*, wistfully describes a lost boyfriend named Michael: "He remembers the blond head nestled under his chin. The reddish-blond hair. The beautiful face fresh even on awakening. And the laughter—unscarred; his laughter was unscarred."

With Michael away, Rechy would sit talking with friends like Marsha Kinder over dinner. He always felt better after talking to Marsha, particularly about relationships. "He was very despondent about Michael heading for New York," Kinder says, "because all through his life John had found that when people left, they left for good."

But Rechy told Zella Riley that he wanted Michael to go off for his career. "He was very concerned about holding Michael back from any career or life situations," Riley says.

Rechy says, "I blamed myself for his absence. On the other hand, I was very proud of myself. Because I didn't want him to be, and I still don't want him to be, ever, John Rechy's boyfriend."

CHAPTER THIRTEEN

I don't mind saying this: I know what's what. I'm one of the best writers
of our time, best of my generation. I certainly rank with Norman Mailer.
I certainly outshine Philip Roth. Same with Gore Vidal. I know I rank
with them, and that's my rightful place. And not as a gay writer, not as
an ex-hustler, not as a sexual outlaw.

—John Rechy

WHILE MICHAEL WAS AWAY, Rechy kept himself busy with writing, working out, and continuing with his active anonymous sex life. In the late 1970s the S/M scene was dominating many homosexual clubs and bars. At first Rechy observed this growing phenomenon with fascination. But his interest eventually turned to apprehension. Was the S/M scene something gay men could enjoy and make their own, or was it an expression of self-hatred and loss of dignity? Rechy felt strongly that it was the latter. He became obsessed with the subject and discussed it often with his friend Russell Barnard. Finally Barnard said to him, "John, this means so much to you. You're so fascinated. Write it!"

In 1979, Rechy came out with *Rushes*, whose subject matter combines the S/M scene, his burgeoning emotions for Michael, and his determination to persist with the cruising and promiscuity that had been part of his life for over 20 years.

Rechy describes *Rushes* as a realistic and symbolic account of one night in a sadomasochistic leather bar and orgy room. He was still struggling to preserve the personal freedom that allowed him to explore such bars, even as he felt pulled toward committing to a dedicated union with a compatible other. As a reflection of his brooding over that choice, Rechy created one scene in the novel where a group of men in a sex bar talk about the possibility of having just one lover. "We even claim to have lovers when we don't, as if alone we're incomplete," one character says. "That's sad—and unnatural—whether you're homosexual or not. And I was talking about the selfish possession of bodies we call 'faithful love.'"

Rechy still seems compelled to expose his secret sexual hunting grounds to readers unfamiliar with modern homosexual subcultures, just as he still liked to introduce some of his female friends to his private cruising life by taking them on excursions to his favorite parks and street corners. *Rushes* begins and ends by taking the reader on a tour of the most notorious homosexual cruising spots in New York* during the 1970s—areas Rechy himself had roamed. He depicts the decaying Hudson River piers and the nearby streets of the meatpacking district, which fill with dozens of men cruising for sex in the dark. Also prowling these streets are the fag-bashers—young men whose smoldering anger propels them to do violence to the various embodiments of their own frustrated desire. The bashers lure unsuspecting men into the shadows where they beat and rob them.

Most of the book is set in a bar called Rushes, which Rechy based on the notorious S/M bar Mineshaft, where a doorman judges who can and cannot enter bases on a man's attire, age, and desirability. The type of boots a man wears or the way he tilts his fatigue cap can determine whether he is deemed sexually desirable and admitted to the bar. One man is instantly dismissed for wearing cologne.

In the book Rechy continues to explore his fascination with masquerades, the different uniforms homosexual men of the era

---

*Although the city is deliberately not named, it is clear that Rechy is using New York as his model.

needed in order to feel masculine. The sexual revolution of the
'70s permitted gay men to live out their role-playing fantasies in
the course of their routine social life. Images of these fantasies
cropped up in popular culture with groups like the Village
People. The novel reflects the trend of homosexual men who
caricature heterosexual masculinity. In Rushes almost everyone
who makes it past the doorman wears a macho uniform—a
motorcyclist, a construction worker, a cowboy. These are costumes Rechy first introduces in the "Neil" chapter of *City of
Night*. Regarding *Rushes*, Rechy said that for heterosexuals, "I
intend it to be a vision of a world they created with their pressures. The pain that comes out of *Rushes* is very important,
because it's been inflicted by heterosexuals."

Rushes does not have much plot. Rechy finds the novel's drama
in the conversations and emotions of a group of friends of varying
ages and types who meet at the bar. Their interactions are lively,
but each man keeps one eye on the constant parade of men, trying to decide whom he will end up with at the end of the night.
There is Chas, 27, the leatherman: cocky, preening, fastidiously
attired. Chas is obsessed with being viewed as a "top man," and
wears his keys, handkerchief, and earring on the left side to project his preference for taking the dominant position. Bill is 23,
blond, slender, dressed in tailored western garb, and longing for a
lost love. Don is the older, undesirable man who gets into Rushes
on the coattails of his more desirable friends. He hides his pain
and discomfort by drinking too much. Although he is a successful
lawyer, in Rushes Don's intelligence and wealth mean nothing. He
is merely pitied for his lack of looks.

The main character in *Rushes* is Endore. For once not given a
name with the first initial J, the protagonist seems to be an amal-
gam of Johnny Rio from *Numbers* and the nameless drifter from
City of Night. Endore, like Johnny Rio, is desired by almost everyone, but in *Rushes* the character is in his upper 30s. And he has
grown more complicated—still extremely vain, but somewhat less
compulsive about competing, and much more sensitive to the men

around him. Unlike the earlier protagonists, Endore does not have any perception of being sexually attracted to women. Rechy writes, "There are women he loves—without posing at desire or bisexuality: he considers that a subterfuge, disdains it."

Endore is a writer, a "popular columnist" grappling with the idea of committed love. He has a sometimes-boyfriend named Michael.*

As noted earlier, the period in which Rechy wrote *Rushes* brought with it the first possibility of romantic love. That possibility kept his emotions in upheaval. Toward the end of the book, Endore and Michael run into each other at the bar after a long separation. They talk about the time Michael said, "I love you," to Endore.

"I did feel it—" Michael says, "but you told me there was no such thing."

To which Endore replies, "No no! I said, let's not brand it, just experience it."

Endore longs for what he had with Michael, but he is also attracted by the heady violence of macho sex he finds at places like Rushes. He is fascinated by its "balletic rites." Endore is tender with Michael, but he hungers for the hunt. These conflicting impulses compete for dominance. "You'll always need the Rushes," Michael tells him sadly. They separate, and once more Endore heads out into the dark and dangerous world of late night–early morning cruising.

Many critics would note Rechy's meticulous attention to structure and detail in *Rushes*, but few picked up on the fact that the author had carefully based the leather bar and orgy room scenes on a Catholic Mass. Rechy presented blatant clues by titling each chapter with quotes from the Mass. The first chapter is headed "I will go into the altar of God," and follows with the opening line, "As often as he comes to the Rushes, Endore still feels a clash of excitement and dread in anticipation of the sights, sounds, odors he knows will assault him."

Rushes is dedicated to Michael Snyder and to the memory of Rechy's mother.

Rechy explains: "The sleazy bar finds careful parallels in the structure of a church, the pornographic drawings on the walls evoke the Stations of the Cross. The contemporary dialogue at times paraphrases sections from the Mass. Realistic incidents involving people that would frequent such a bar find equivalents in the rituals of baptism, initiation, sacrifice, even possible purgation. There is even a credo that follows the religious Catholic credo. 'I believe in the Rushes,' a character says, speaking about the bar he loves. Also included in the novel are two crucifixions, one symbolic in the orgy room, one real—a brutal murder outside the bar, perpetrated by gay-bashers."

As with his earlier works, some critics were put off by the narcissism in the nocturnal world Rechy re-created. The *Los Angeles Times* complained that "the shallowness and vicariousness of Rechy's characters make all of his meticulous rendering of their thought processes ultimately dull reading. Would you drink five minutes with some chopper cutie who's preoccupied with whether the young man in leather looked at him?" But the reviewer also called *Rushes* "a tour de force...like peering into the gates of hell." A reviewer in *People* magazine wrote: "Excruciatingly specific. In his best book since the classic *City of Night*, Rechy aims both high and deep."

By now most readers were able to look beyond the controversial subject matter to recognize in *Rushes*, the work of a superb craftsman and the keen insights of a "moral navigator" and "street philosopher."

With its imagery of blood—blood from the meat in the streets of the meatpacking district, blood from the victims of violent fag-bashing, and blood exchanged in rough sex acts—*Rushes* foreshadows the coming AIDS epidemic. It also anticipates some of the themes in Rechy's retrospective novel about AIDS, *The Coming of the Night*, published in 1999.

By the time *Rushes* came out, Rechy was not only a gay icon, his influence was apparent across a wide swath of mainstream popular culture. Rock stars like David Bowie, Mick Jagger, and

Jim Morrison (who intoned the words "city of night" in his song "L.A. Woman") all expressed their appreciation for Rechy. Bob Dylan called Rechy to tell him how much he admired *City of Night*. Rechy even had an influence on fashion. "I walked through downtown Los Angeles in a genuine motorcycle leather jacket—I still have it—and no shirt," Rechy says. "Oh, wow! was that startling." He invented the "scoop shirt," a T-shirt with a stretched down neckline. When *Cruising* came out in 1980, William Friedkin acknowledged Rechy's influence in the controversial film by inviting him to a special screening, which Rechy attended with Marsha Kinder. "When we saw Al Pacino on the screen," Kinder observes, "it was clear that he was dressed like John. It was a costume that John really constructed and eventually over the years got imitated. It became accepted. And the movie had scenes that were right out of John's *Rushes*." David Hockney gave *City of Night* partial credit for his move to Los Angeles and painted a representation of Pershing Square that was purportedly inspired by certain sections of the novel. When making *My Own Private Idaho*—the 1991 film about drifting hustlers—Gus Van Sant told both River Phoenix and Keanu Reeves to read *City of Night* before they started shooting. Reeves was so taken with it he went on to read more of Rechy's work.

In *Bodies and Souls*, Rechy's next book, eroticism mixes freely with movie trivia and melodrama. The novel, published in 1983, is an apocalyptic view of contemporary Los Angeles, which Rechy imagines as a modern paradise lost for rebel angels. A young woman and two young men are Rechy's lost angels—whose actions yield a catastrophic ending.

Some critics complain that Rechy's middle works are too melodramatic, filled with florid dialogue, overheated conflict, and cliffhanger cutaways. But Rechy's use of these devices is intentional. Throughout *Bodies and Souls*, he uses scenes from old movies, including a modern re-creation of the endings of *White Heat* and *Duel in the Sun*. The Book of Revelation also figures prominently, especially in its end-of-the-world rages. "It's a novel in which I was commenting on violence in America," Rechy explains, "on the unreal romance of old movies. I used a variety of styles, consistent with the intended epic scope of the book."

Bodies and Souls is also his first book in his opus that doesn't feature a Rechy-based protagonist at its core. Instead the novel tells many stories—as with the character portraits in *City of Night*—but without a narrator's intervention. However, several of the characters are imbued with various "Rechy" characteristics, including the female porn star, the male stripper, the butch hustler, and the titled bodybuilder. But Rechy's spirit is mostly detected in the character called "The Lecturer." In this section of the novel, the unnamed Lecturer espouses Rechy's own dark philosophy, and he informs readers that he has been described as "raging in intellectual and sexual promiscuity." The young man who questions the character's nihilism at the end of the lecture represents Michael. Rechy then allows the expression of hope the young man is demanding.

Bodies and Souls is also Rechy's love letter to the seamier side of Los Angeles, which continued to be a muse. Although the novel highlights characters from all social circles, Rechy shows a special compassion for a gallery of rebels: angry runaway kids who sleep in abandoned buildings, fuck freely, and carve themselves up for kicks. Less charitably, he reveals the hypocrisy of classes, documenting the same hungers and sins in the affluent homes of Beverly Hills, Bel Air, and Encino. Here characters include a Supreme Court judge and the wealthy guru of a bodybuilding empire. There is also a successful anchorwoman, a famous female television evangelist, her brother, and her gothic family.

In Rechy's Los Angeles, the outcasts of the city—the runaways, porn stars, strippers, derelicts, and homeless—display the greatest dignity. These antiestablishment characters possess physical magnificence, sometimes hidden at first. But their complicated beauty always reveals itself. Rechy brings them to life through sensual detail—the taste of ice cream melting in a young girl's mouth, the feeling of a hot wind blowing a white silk dress between a woman's thighs, the look of a boy's lustrous black hair gleaming in darkness. It is the conventional inhabitants of the decadent city—the characters representing the mundane, ordinary citizens—who are hefty and unattractive. Rechy equates fleshiness with vacuity. Lines in the face signal decline. Although this may sound cruel, Rechy honestly captures an attitude that prevails in Hollywood to this day, particularly in the gay scene.

Some contemporary writers like Gary Indiana criticize Rechy's post–*City of Night* work because his characters "have hardly any dimension, being mainly defined by their physical appearances—indescribably 'beautiful' if they're young, distinguishable only by height, hair color, muscle density and the exact nature of their sexual wishes. If they're old, fat, or plain, they're 'trolls.' Both types lack the kind of interiority a fictional character needs for the reader to care about his or her fate."

But these are simply the social realities of the worlds Rechy inhabits. In the tough, cruising terrain of *Numbers*, or the more contemporary narcissistic Los Angeles of *Bodies and Souls*, "fat" would be the only thing most of the beautiful rebels could think to say about unattractive people. Rechy's are politically incorrect characters who judge others by the way they look, how much they work out, and how old they are. If someone isn't sexually desirable, he is dismissed with a few abrupt adjectives, words Rechy spied on the doors of gay bath houses keeping out "fats, fems, and over 35s." The same sentiments are rampant in personal ads and internet dating profiles today. It is cruel and at times maddening, but the inhabitants of these worlds are aware of their brutality.

Of characters some reviewers want to wish away, Rechy says, "Stereotypes are a source of great strength. Sissies, drag queens, bull dykes—these are our heroes. They are the ones who step out into the world and say, 'We are here.' I disagree with banishing the stereotypes."

There were also enthusiastic reviews of *Bodies and Souls*. *The New York Times* borrowed Rechy's description of Los Angeles and called the novel "a scarred beauty," while the *Los Angeles Times* lauded it as a "memorable feast."

Meanwhile, during his two years in New York, Michael had excelled at the Actors Studio. Eventually he went on to work with all the major names in the New York theater scene: players like Lee Strasberg, Stella Adler, and Joseph Papp. Rechy was very proud of his progress. The couple spoke on the phone every day, each keeping tabs on the other's career moves. Rechy visited Michael in Manhattan and Michael spent long periods in Los Angeles. "For the first time in my life," Rechy admits, "I was able to combine desire and love, with Michael. I discovered the specialness of mutual desire, mutual love, mutual fulfillment."

When he was alone in Los Angeles, Rechy continued his promiscuous sex life, though he was cruising more than he was hustling. Yet he regularly felt the need to hustle and returned often to the streets. During the day, he cruised Griffith Park, accumulating sexual conquests. He was arrested again, entrapped by a cop. People gathered as he was led out of the area in handcuffs. A park attendant drove by, paused, and the cop said to him, "You mind if I set fire to this area so I can burn all these faggots?" Rechy told the attorney who represented him to fight the entrapment. The attorney called the District Attorney, who asserted that no one would believe that an "officer said such a thing." This time, it was Marsha Kinder whom Rechy called to bail him out.

Rechy told Michael about the arrest and Michael returned from New York to be with him during the sentencing. Rechy was grateful to have Michael at his side, especially when he was found guilty, though it was of a much lesser offense that merely carried a fine. "Our love had only been strengthened," Rechy says. "When he returned to New York to continue to explore theatrical opportunities—with my encouragement—I felt more certain about our love, although I still retained my view of the finality of separations. The telephone calls increased between us. Then Michael returned to live in Los Angeles, as he had always intended."

Michael stayed with Rechy for a while before moving into his own small apartment nearby. Soon Michael got a job as a production assistant. Then one of the producers he worked with hired him as his own assistant, and he quickly rose in the ranks. Today Michael is a Hollywood producer of top-grossing movies.

Even with Michael back in Los Angeles, Rechy was still hitting the streets. He was unconvinced that a committed love affair with another man would be enough to sustain him. He still needed the risks, dangers, and games—to gamble and win with his sexuality— to feel alive and worthwhile. And that identity was entwined in his body of work, his image as a literary figure. It seemed he would never be able to give it up completely.

But now things were different. In the early 1980s AIDS drastically changed the life of every gay man. "Like everyone else," Rechy explains, "I resisted believing what was becoming apparent—that the illness was contracted among gay men through sexual contact. I was one of the first to write a warning article about it, in *The Advocate*. I wrote a letter protesting what I considered an exploitative article about it in *The New York Review of Books*." The letter was featured prominently in *The Advocate*'s "Letters to the Editor" column.

"My own life changed radically about the same time everyone else's did," Rechy told the *New York Native* in 1986. Rechy realized that many of the previous decade's attitudes about open sex might be associated with him. "I would love to say to people, don't associate me with promiscuity, S/M, and gay sex, but it wouldn't be honest. I believe that when I die I'm going to be exhumed so that people can ask me once again about those subjects—hustling included—and I will never be allowed to rest."

He went on to say that AIDS "has shattered many myths about society. Symbolically, it unraveled so much that many of us from a certain generation believed in. Some thought that when we all came out, there would be overwhelming decency toward us. AIDS has proven that wrong. That's part of the sadness. AIDS has revealed how deep the prejudice is."

While Rechy says he admired the courage of Larry Kramer and

the ACT UP group, he disapproved of the gay activists who used outing as part of their campaign. "Outing for acceptance is a damn myth," he said wisely. "Wishful thinking. Certain people in power should not come out until they can hold on to their power or they become nothing more than a headline in *The National Enquirer*."

Michael Snyder and John Rechy attended an exhibition in West Hollywood of a large portion of the AIDS quilt. "Seeing it," Rechy remembers, "so resplendent, each object somebody's memory of someone beloved gone, I thought, *It's our colorful graveyard, beautiful, glittery, and tragic*." As they roamed amongst the various panels, the two men saw names of people they had known, but had not known were now dead. "I knew that gay men of a certain generation would now possess a graveyard of memories—as I do—remembering frequently someone encountered briefly, intimately. Now where? Would a new generation remember our own holocaust?"

Even if the AIDS epidemic had not occurred, Rechy was now well past 50. There was no way hustling could remain an option for him. But giving up that life was not going to be easy. "He had to learn how to let go of some of his life in order to let Michael in," a friend says. "I think it has saved John. I have no doubt about it."

Fortunately, Rechy slowly disentangled himself from his complicated ties to his life on the streets and found sanctuary in his relationship with Michael. "The beauty of John," Melodie Johnson Howe observes, "is in his ability to endure and reshape his life, restyle himself, and to allow somebody to come into his life at that point. I never thought he would allow anybody in his life in that sense."

Michael Kearns observes, "Once he allowed Michael in, he was finally able to shed some of that armor."

That the relationship with Michael had lasted and seemed to be on solid ground made Rechy less fearful of a committed relationship and allowed him to gradually let go of the only thing he had been able to rely on throughout his life: the assurance of his sexual desirability. His advancing age and his feelings for Michael enabled Rechy, step by step, to give up his street life without tragic results. Rechy remembers a momentous event: "The last time I hustled was around 1981, the dawn of AIDS. I was in Griffith Park, cruising. Griffith Park was not a hustling turf—there were a lot of attractive men going with each other. Yes, I had at one time or another met someone there who would take me out to dinner, etc.—but that was not, technically, hustling. One afternoon in Griffith Park I was hanging around, and a man—perhaps younger than me!—asked me if I was hustling. So I thought, *What the hell,* and said yes. I forget what the price was then—that wasn't important to me—but he offered it. He wanted to go into the bushes behind us and have sex. So we went. By then I had begun to suspect that he knew who I was—the writer—and that he was probably indulging a longtime fantasy.

"When he started to come on to me, I became quite certain he knew, and so I couldn't get aroused, despite the offer of money, which always would assure my arousal. So we broke it off. He gave me the money, and he walked ahead of me, disappointed. As he was about to get into his car, I called him back, and I gave him back the money. 'It was just an act,' I said. He stared at me, I think in disbelief, but, I hope, with some kind of admiration too. I pressed the money into his hand, and—I remember this so clearly—we smiled at each other."

Rechy surprised himself by allowing the relationship with Michael to deepen. "The richness, the fulfillment, the depth of...sustained love and desire and all that, I couldn't begin to compare it to fleeting encounters. It's a different activity for me. I never looked for a relationship; that's what makes it so wonderful that I found it. Obviously if I had a choice, would I choose promiscuity over this? The answer is no, of course not. But most people don't have that choice."

Friends noticed a mellowing in Rechy, a peacefulness they had not seen before. There was no longer a tragic air lingering around him, the aura of inevitable doom they had worried about. "As his relationship with Michael developed and as he became older and more mature, I no longer had concerns about how he would end up," Russell Barnard says. "It's fun to talk about sometimes, but there's way too much in John's life now. He's much more than the novelist and teacher. He's a fully rounded person and Michael has helped him be that."

The two men worked together on projects, which brought them even closer. "He continues to be the person I trust to read my manuscripts," Rechy says. "He offers the best criticism— which I, of course, reject angrily and then accept, apologizing for my initial 'artist reaction.' Our relationship extended into the creative realm, enriching it further."

Rechy adapted *The Fourth Angel* into a play. The first reading was cast with top actors, including Joan Allen in the role of Shell. Michael read the part of Jerry, and Rechy says, "He's the only one who has played Jerry who has, in my mind, done it right. He was beautiful in it, moving." Eventually the play was successfully produced in Los Angeles, starring a young Sarah Jessica Parker. Michael was the director.

John and Michael decided to take the play to New York in 1986 under the name *Tiger's Wild*. The production had a new cast, with Michael again directing and Rechy's former student, businessman Russell Barnard, coproducing. *Tiger's Wild* had a limited, unsuccessful run off-Broadway. Rechy blamed the critics who he felt were predisposed to dislike it. "We opened without previewing it in the traditional way," he says, "because we didn't want critics and so-called dramaturges to interfere. It was a superb production at Playhouse 91. But we were upstarts, invaders in New York, not having tried out the play, not having let anyone see it. But the harpies, the so-called critics, had been waiting, sharpening their talons." The play closed after 10 performances.

Michael moved back to Los Angeles; and once he and Rechy were officially together, they never separated. Neither pressured the other to make an exclusive commitment; they just fell into it naturally. "There were never any demands," Rechy says, "and there still are none. I'm with him because I choose to be with him. I'm happier now than I have ever been—with Michael. It is no exaggeration to say that he saved my life—he deserves credit for all that I've accomplished since I met him, every book I've written. That's why I dedicate all my books to him. When I met him I was still on the streets, and I was heading toward a dead end. I resisted the change, yes, but increasingly my love for him allowed us to create a new life together, and it was *that* that very possibly saved me from suicide."

Rechy felt grateful to have someone like Michael so devoted to him. He proudly told friends about the time he had a serious knee operation: Michael stayed with him in the hospital room day and night. (The doctor was a friend of Rechy's and arranged it without a problem.) One evening a gruff male nurse burst into the room while Rechy was still somewhat sedated, shouting, "Wake up!"

Michael instantly sat up and furiously berated the nurse, who quickly retreated. "Don't ever yell at him like that!"

Rechy was touched by this display of protectiveness. As turbulent as the relationship had been in its initial years, he says without hesitation today, "This is the most peaceful I've felt in my life. And perhaps the only time I've felt peaceful."

In a relationship and moving beyond using hustling and cruising experiences as his primary sources of inspiration, Rechy's fiction began to take on more diverse subject matter. His first two novels after *Bodies and Souls* were *Marilyn's Daughter* (1988) and *The Miraculous Day of Amalia Gómez* (1991). Although there are gay characters, each book sidelines the narcissistic protagonist to bring a vulnerable female character to center stage. "My female characters are the ones I generally feel a lot of compassion for," Rechy told *Frontiers* magazine in 1990. "The characters I have modeled after me do not move me because I know they will go on."

Marilyn's Daughter pays homage to Hollywood and all its mysteries. Rechy focused the novel on a young woman named

Normalyn who is led to believe that she is the daughter of Marilyn Monroe and Robert Kennedy. The story of the movie star and the politician is revealed through a series of cleverly constructed flashbacks. For Rechy, it is a novel about the power of legend over truth. He set out to write a myth of his own, using as a catalyst the legendary Monroe, whom he considers "a masterpiece of modern art." Rechy explains, "I wanted the book's structure constantly to call attention to its falseness—that it was all invention, the way Marilyn Monroe has come to be."

Monroe died in 1962. Rechy sets the novel in 1980. Normalyn is a combination of Norma Jean (Marilyn Monroe's real first name) and Marilyn. Thus, Rechy's 18-year-old heroine possesses elements of the icon's fragile true self and her glamorous public persona. In the flashback sequences, Rechy creates for Monroe a fictitious best friend, Enid Morgan, who grew up in orphanages with the young Norma Jean and who remains faithfully in the shadows when Norma Jean transforms herself into Marilyn Monroe. Normalyn is born shortly before Monroe's death and is raised by Enid, who flees to Texas with the child.

Eighteen years later, when Enid commits suicide, she leaves a note for Normalyn that states simply: "Marilyn Monroe is your real mother and she loved you and wanted you with all her heart." This sets up the mystery that propels *Marilyn's Daughter* and sends Normalyn on a journey to adulthood. She sets out to discover her real parents and learn the secret of her true identity. Is she the daughter of Enid Morgan or Marilyn Monroe?

At the beginning of the novel, the innocent Normalyn leaves Texas for Los Angeles, just as John Rechy left El Paso to discover his own true character. Normalyn encounters a Hollywood version of the world Rechy discovered during his own youthful odysseys to Los Angeles—including encounters with intriguing bit players, perilous adventures, sex, danger, and excitement.

In telling Normalyn's quest, Rechy interweaves his own extensive knowledge of Hollywood history with the movie star fantasies that have influenced him since childhood. He concocts a colorful array of show business has-beens, watchers, and wannabes who, bit by bit, divulge disturbing secrets about the departed cinema goddess. There's a kind-hearted, if scatter-brained, former confidante to the great stars, as well as an aging, bitchy gossip columnist, and a Pulitzer Prize-winning journalist. He mixes these characters with historical personalities like Joan Crawford and Lee Strasberg, who play a part in the fictitious history Rechy creates for Monroe. Further blending fantasy and reality, Rechy gives bit parts to fictitious movie characters like Norma Desmond from *Sunset Boulevard* and Eve Harrington from *All About Eve*.

In the most intriguing segment of the book, young Normalyn falls in with a bizarre gang of angry teenagers called The Dead Movie Stars, who are attracted to the dream quality in Hollywood's star-studded past. The group's leader, Lady Star, presides over the assemblage of deeply troubled youths who prefer unreality to truth and cover up their own teenage angst and despair by impersonating glamorous stars from Hollywood's history.

Among The Dead Movie Stars there are a teenage Rita Hayworth, Tyrone Power, James Dean, and Veronica Lake. The group manages to attract some media attention, and consequently a variety of frantic youths long to be a part of the gang. Aspiring Dead Movie Stars must audition to become a favorite star from Hollywood's golden age. "There is a passage I'm particularly proud of," Rechy says. "Lady Star gives a speech to those who are auditioning for roles as dead stars, and I paraphrase Hamlet's advice to the players, syllable by syllable."

Rechy had long been touched by the tragic life of Marilyn Monroe, and he bestowed the character Normalyn with all the qualities the young John Rechy shared with the famous icon: a lonely childhood, a love of books, a strong will, a fierce need to persevere, and—of course—physical beauty. Ultimately, Normalyn is the love child of Marilyn Monroe and John Rechy. He even announced on publication, "I love Normalyn. Normalyn is my daughter. I adore her."

Most reviewers heaped praise on *Marilyn's Daughter*, especially Richard Hall of the *San Francisco Chronicle*, who called it "a masterpiece of narrative engineering," referring to its intricate structure of flashbacks within flashbacks, and who called Rechy "a major American novelist."

The Village Voice found in the book "the innocent trashiness, the vulnerable screw-loose fascination of Monroe herself."

Years later, Rechy still felt protective of Monroe. When in April of 2000 Joyce Carol Oates re-created Marilyn Monroe in, according to Rechy, a "dour" and "degrading" novel called *Blonde*, Rechy was one of the few critics not cowed by Oates's revered reputation. Reviewing *Blonde* for the *Los Angeles Times Book Review*, Rechy wrote:

Oates demeans Marilyn's genuine sensuality, strips her dignity, reduces her strengths... But no one finally can diminish Norma Jean's grand triumph, the creation of the most astonishing figure in Hollywood's history, the masterpiece called Marilyn Monroe.

Rechy also cited "pages of loose writing, resulting frequently in unintended humor" and "murky observations straining for profundity." To his private class, he was even less charitable. "I will spread the word," Rechy said. "That woman can't write."

In Rechy's next book, *The Miraculous Day of Amalia Gómez*, a middle-aged Mexican-American woman experiences a series of degradations over the course of one day. Each hits her like a blow, but ultimately her trials lead her to a miraculous moment of self-awareness.

Rechy recounts the novel's origins: "This is how the novel came about. I was sunbathing in the park, and I looked up at the sky and saw a ghostly cross made by clouds. I thought, then, some people would convert that into a sign. I thought of the Mexican women I had seen in the projects in El Paso; they would see a sign there, I knew. I rushed home and wrote a short story in one draft, called 'The Miraculous Day.' That night I read it to Michael. He loved it and insisted I should write a novel. I did, and Amalia is a favorite character of mine."

Amalia's life is filled with tragedy, but she clings to the Catholic religion, hiding the pain of her own realities. She longs for tenderness. She has been raped, beaten, abandoned, and betrayed by every man she's had any sexual contact with throughout her life. Amalia is forced to marry her first husband when she becomes pregnant after he rapes her in an alleyway. Her obsessively religious mother, rigidly holding on to the laws of the Church, can only view her daughter as a lustful tramp and refuses to give her compassion or love. "Never ask God for anything," she tells Amalia contemptuously. "Be grateful that He's even permitted you to live."

If tenderness, empathy, and kindness are in short supply among the characters of *The Miraculous Day of Amalia Gómez*, there is an abundance of pent-up rage, bitterness, and hostility. The men are especially cruel, using women sexually and then discarding them. Amalia, as needy as she is, refuses to accept her own reduced emotional capacity. She cannot, for example, accept the truth about the way her oldest son died in prison after falling in with L.A.'s gang culture. Nor can she bring herself to explore the reasons for the hostility in her two younger children, a teenage boy and girl. She distracts herself with their physical beauty rather than dig for reasons for their anger or deal with the dangers brought on by their budding sexuality.

Amalia also blinds herself to the lewd appetites of her common-law husband. And she can't even admit her own sins to herself. She uses her belief in God's understanding and forgiveness to avoid facing the pain of her tragic realities. She has been sinned against—and for that reason she creates justification for her own shortcomings as a spouse, mother, and woman.

Unrealistic about everything, even her own fading beauty, Amalia wanders the streets of Hollywood on a blistering Sunday, seeking comfort and distraction in friendship, trinkets, food, and, most of all, religion. But each attempt only thrusts her deeper into the reality of her despair. As the reader journeys along with Amalia, the novel makes a powerful statement against the indignities and prejudices Mexican-Americans continue to suffer in contemporary America. They are looked down on by the Anglos and harassed by the police. "Fuckin' Mexican bitch!" a group of angry white men yell as Amalia sits at a bus stop. They fling greasy chicken bones in her face as their car races by.

As she wanders around this hellish Los Angeles, Amalia has no real destination—except that of her own destiny. She finally demands, and ultimately receives, a miracle from God acknowledging her existence. For the first time she feels accepted for the living, breathing human being she is, even including the reality of her living, breathing flaws.

While *The New York Times* dismissed this book as ultimately "not so miraculous," *The Miraculous Day of Amalia Gómez* was praised by almost every other publication. *The Washington Post* informed its readers that Rechy had written "a novel with more truth in it than a carload of best-sellers." *Newsday* called the novel, "A triumph, a sad, beautiful and loving book...Amalia comes to stunning and heartbreaking life." Since its publication, *The Miraculous Day of Amalia Gómez* has gone on to become a staple of many Chicano literature classes.

The original idea for Rechy's 11th novel, *Our Lady of Babylon*, came to him during his USC graduate course "Literature and Writing the Novel." Required reading included the Book of Revelation. When the class was studying the passage describing the Whore of Babylon, one of Rechy's students marveled at her and asked who she might be. That question stayed with Rechy. Who was the mysterious woman branded "mother of all abominations"? In *Our Lady of Babylon*, Rechy seeks to provide an answer. He roams through the history of blamed women to find the accused Mother of Abominations.

In this novel Rechy gives voice to each blamed woman, writing in the first person for the first time since *City of Night*. He asks and answers questions posed by the lives of epic female characters, starting with Eve, who, Rechy says, "took the rap for the fall from grace," and continuing with Helen of Troy ("Was her beauty really the cause of the Trojan War? Or was it Paris's small cock?") and Medea ("Was she really the monster that legend describes?") Rechy makes the reader aware of another side to every classic story of women's guilt. *Our Lady of Babylon* does have some gay material—most controversially, a steamy encounter between Christ and his betrayer, Judas. "Finally, though," Rechy says, "I deliberately pitched everything into ambiguity at the end, when, dangerously, the real Whore of Babylon is revealed. It's a favorite novel of mine, and I'm sure that if it had come from another writer not associated as 'gay author,' it would have gotten the attention it deserved—and will, I'm sure, eventually get, when people see beyond *City of Night!*"

Throughout the publication of these later books, Rechy felt himself trying to emerge from the shadows of *City of Night*. "That seems strange, to overcome one's own novel that is now often called a classic, translated into about 20 languages, has not ever been out of print. But I do feel that people were so affected by *City of Night* that they don't even want to consider my latter work, which to me is much, much better. With the 'nongay' books—although all my books have gay characters—I lost much of my gay audience, and I did not gain among the mainstream readers. Yes, I feel often that I have to battle the reputation of *City of Night* to draw attention to my other novels, where I've experimented with form, pushed content much further each time. My work has developed, and I try to make every sentence as perfect as possible. Structure continues to be a major aspect of my work."

Yet people still approach him and say, "I loved your book." His heart invariably sinks—even though he still asks each time, "Which one?"—because he knows they can only mean *City of Night*. "And sometimes," Rechy says with chagrin, "I want to shout at them, 'Yes, damn it, thanks a lot, but have you bothered to read any more of my work?' "

Rechy feels much of his work has been overlooked, not just because of the *City of Night*'s long shadow. "I do want you to remember that I know I am as good a writer as any my time has produced," he declares. "And I'm sure it is not generally acknowledged the way it will be, not only because I am gay, but because I hustled, and because I don't look like they think a writer should look, and because I am so fucking arrogant. But I'm arrogant because I look the way I look and I'm arrogant because I know that I am a superb writer."

Chapter Fourteen

You never feel like you're a legendary figure when you
wake up, you're disgruntled, and you need a cup of coffee.
—John Rechy

THE 1990S FINALLY BROUGHT RECHY some overdue recognition and well-deserved honors for his long writing career. In 1997 Rechy was the recipient of the PEN Center USA–West's prestigious lifetime achievement award. He was the first novelist to be so honored.* When the letter arrived informing him that he would be the 1997 honoree, he assumed the announcement was intended for somebody else. "Here was a beautiful letter announcing this extraordinary honor," he said. "I had to turn it over and make sure it was for me. And, oh, my, yes...it was!"

The *Los Angeles Times* ran a story about Rechy under the headline "Credit Where It's Overdue." But Rechy was simply grateful that his time had finally arrived. "This is so tremendous," he said to the *Times* reporter. "Such an affirmation from a group of professional writers, that I have to say that right now I feel nothing but joy." Victory became even sweeter when *The New York Review of Books*, which had published Alfred Chester's vicious review of *City of Night* years before, reported Rechy's award under the head-

---

*Neil Simon, Betty Friedan, and Billy Wilder were the only others to have received the award.

line "Congratulations!" "An exclamation point," Rechy observes today. "They never use exclamation points. And they did it for me! Can you imagine? For me! And I received *two* standing ovations while I was there—with Michael and my sister Blanche and my brother Robert looking on."

In 1999 Rechy was finally able to sort through his complicated feelings about the origin of AIDS and its devastating consequences on the world in general and the homosexual community in particular. In his novel *The Coming of the Night*, Rechy follows an ensemble cast of mainly gay characters over the course of one day in 1981 in Los Angeles, just before the AIDS crisis began to unfold.

Rechy based the novel on something he witnessed in 1981, an event that has haunted him ever since. "A very beautiful 21-year-old kid in the park at 3:00 in the morning took off all his clothes and pasted his body against the tool shed, and people proceeded to line up and fuck him. It was almost like a crucifixion and it haunted me. After witnessing that, I ran into a friend who I asked if it was true what I had heard about a new gay illness."

By now Rechy, nearing 70, was familiar with the cruelties and obsessions of the gay scene. He used all his years of experience and observation to document his discoveries through a multitude of personalities. Each character in *The Coming of the Night* is framed by a chapter that exposes his desires, fantasies, and insecurities—scrutinized according to his age, weight, color, masculinity, dick size, or effeminate mannerisms. Among the menagerie are a short bodybuilder obsessed with his small penis ("Did most bodybuilders have small dicks? Muscles didn't shrink your cock, right?"), an insecure African-American, a brooding priest in search of a parishioner's son, a hustler with a tattoo of a naked Christ on his back (an image also used in *Bodies and Souls*), an aging alcoholic, and a young man with a philandering lover. Their common goal is finding the ultimate erotic experience. The scorching Santa Ana wind propels each of them on his individual odyssey.

Rechy's portrayal of the gay scene is blistering and ultimately dead-on. As in *The Sexual Outlaw*, the characters in *The Coming of the Night* are without histories. "I wanted to create the impression that they appear just as they would appear in a cruising arena," he explains, "defined by your physical presence, by how you sex-hunt. The novel is saturated with graphic sexual scenes to convey that time when sex was everywhere."

As in all Rechy's novels, physical beauty is the only virtue anyone cares to possess. All else is unimportant. Of an older character, Rechy writes: "Certainly, he had other friends, men, women, cultured friends who had him over for dinner, or he would have them, or they went out to the opera, the ballet. All were unattractive." Another character says bluntly, "the three curses of the gay world—unattractive, old, and fat. I've been spared the fourth curse, the curse of a small dick, but that's not a blessing for me because no one notices."

Defending the pathetic lives he often gives his older characters, Rechy says, "I decry ageism, but I always point out that it's there. And certainly ageism lends itself to our preoccupation with physicality."

Jesse, the protagonist in *The Coming of the Night*, is young, sexy, snotty, shallow, and obsessed with sex—an accurate portrait of a number of young gay men living in America in that era and of attitudes which continue today. Rechy sums up Jesse's judgmental outlook in one short passage:

> On the street now an old man passed by, paused, looked him up and down, and stopped. Ugh! Jesse discarded him with a look of disgust. He felt insulted when old guys thought they had a chance with him. One guy had offered him money. Well, he wasn't a whore like those guys on the boulevard. Why did people let themselves grow old? He sure wouldn't.

Young Jesse, in the days just before the AIDS epidemic became public, subconsciously chooses to kill himself with sex rather than face the loss of desirability that comes with aging. At the opening of the novel, Jesse is determined to experience the most sexual day of his life to celebrate turning 22. He also wants to celebrate "one glorious year of being gay." Jesse does not mince words when he explains to Dave, a hot biker, what he has in mind:

"It's a special day for me—like a celebration. I want to keep just getting hotter and hotter and sexier and sexier until it's real late at night. Then I'll have lots and lots of sex, hot sex, with lots of hot guys, really hot, not go home to do it, either—stay in one place, because I don't want to waste time, not even come till the last, and that'll be the hottest, and it all has to be the wildest. Really wild."

Jesse and the biker start setting up the evening, inviting various studs to meet them in the park late that night. The Santa Ana winds and the whims of fate direct all the characters to the park, where they witness or participate in the sacrificial and increasingly violent gang bang of the possessed Jesse. Rechy's apocalyptic scene provides space to accommodate the reader's sympathy for the ravaged protagonist.

The Coming of the Night was eagerly anticipated, and word of mouth was excellent. In a prepublication profile of Rechy for the *Los Angeles Times*, Pamela Warrick described *The Coming of the Night* "as exciting as it is chilling." Rechy was especially enraged when Gary Indiana's less flattering review later appeared in the book section of the *Times*, but he does admit he was very pleased with the drawing of him which appeared on its cover.

Indiana praises Rechy in the beginning of the piece: "He often writes beautiful sentences—a rare skill—and can make objects, rooms, and landscapes vibrate with life." But he goes on to compare *The Coming of the Night* unfavorably to a Jackie Collins novel, complaining that "Rechy may be more shocking to the still-shockable, but Collins is a lot more fun."

The Coming of the Night was favorably received elsewhere. The reviewer for *Salon* magazine said, "Rechy very nearly touches greatness...feeling his way toward that place within each of us where the ecstatic teeters on the edge of a psychic abyss." The book became his most successful in years, reaching number 2 on the *Los Angeles Times* best-seller list. Nevertheless, Rechy, still infuriated by the Indiana review, immediately went on the defensive. He gave a long interview to Scott Timberg of the *New Times*, during which he seethed over the *Los Angeles Times* book review. He lumped Indiana—whose name he sometimes pretended to forget (calling him Gary Indian)—with Alfred Chester, theorizing that their criticism sprang from "penis envy."

"Look," Rechy says, "Gary Indiana is not an attractive gentleman. Alfred Chester was a monster. Which is irrelevant. Except, what I represent is a kind of envy to them. It is a curious thing—it finds its parallel in the straight world—that the desirer and the desired are different entities. The desirer is intelligent, perhaps rich. The desired is just physically attractive. And when the desired becomes identified as being intelligent, then you have transgressed. It's the *Blue Angel* syndrome in heterosexual terms—the blond bimbo."

In his Monday evening class Rechy was less philosophical, telling his students, "If you see Gary Indiana on his Web site and then see me on mine, you'll see what it's all about. And I would bet he has a very small penis. Very tiny!"

In April 1999 Rechy received his second acknowledgement of lifetime achievement, the William Whitehead Lifetime Achievement Award from Publishing Triangle—an association of lesbians and gay men in publishing—at the New School in New York. The award announcement quoted Edmund White's description of Rechy as "one of the most heroic figures of contemporary American life," and "a touchstone of moral integrity and artistic innovation."

That evening, editor Michael Denneny encountered Rechy, and the two spoke at length. Rechy told the publishing giant the award had special meaning for him because it came from the gay world. "It seemed to matter him that it was gay people that were honoring him," Denneny says. "I found it pretty astounding that it was his first because he played an important part in a huge number of gay writers' lives. Certainly in the history of gay writing, the liberation of the gay imagination, he was extraordinarily important. Especially for talents who are famous for the more current gay outlaw novel, like Dennis Cooper or Alan Bowne, who wrote *Forty-Deuce*."

Others present echoed Denneny's words. In his introduction at the presentation, author and critic Michael Bronski said, "[Rechy] super-radically and forever altered how mainstream American culture wrote about, saw, experienced, and conceptualized homosexuality. What he has given us for the past 30 years is a wonderful and terrifying gift." That evening Rechy received another standing ovation.

In 1999, Michael obtained the rights to two of Rechy's books that were going out of print: *Bodies and Souls* and *The Miraculous Day of Amalia Gómez*. Michael approached Grove Press about republishing them, and in 2001 the two books appeared in splendid new editions. A rave review appeared in the *Los Angeles Times*, proclaiming "The Mastery and Genius of John Rechy."

Through the years Rechy's family members remained important anchors for him. But he kept each of them away from certain areas of his life—areas that, since he was in his 20s, had belonged to him alone. It was important to John that his siblings were there for him—for love, support, and stability. And that he was there for them. His other life, his night life, was something they didn't talk about. His homosexuality was also something everyone accepted, but no one discussed, even though Michael was made one of the family. "All my family love Michael," Rechy says. "My sister Blanche calls him 'My Michael.' Before my brother Robert had a disastrous accident, he called him 'Mike' and always welcomed him with a tight hug. Before their deaths, Olga—whose affection was not easily won—would hug and kiss him, and Yvan would greet him with a familial hug. Rechy recalls, "Right before my sister Olga died, she called me, and I asked her whether she wanted to see me alone. She said, 'No, please bring Michael.' Whenever there are occasions of a celebratory dinner—awards, fund-raisers—I make sure that Michael sits next to Blanche. He, in turn, returns their love."

So unspoken was John's hustler-cruiser persona that he wasn't even aware that Olga had read all of his books until after her death. Olga called John one day to tell him she had breast cancer. The doctor wanted her to check into the hospital immediately, but she refused. Instead, she convinced everyone that the cancer was in remission. Shortly afterward, Rechy read in a magazine about a Tijuana faith healer who had been brought to the United States to stand trial for fraud. To his great surprise, Olga's name was listed as one of the people testifying on behalf of the healer. On the stand she bared her mutilated breast to the judge, exclaiming, "He gave us hope that we could recover from this." Olga died soon after that dramatic event. Rechy's niece told him that his sister had read all of his books, adding that Olga had once said, "If you ever doubt that I was a beautiful woman, read *The Miraculous Day of Amalia Gómez*. John based that character on me."

The death of Rechy's brother Yvan soon followed. In his last days the great athlete, whom their father always wanted John to be like, was in the hospital under heavy sedation. From time to time he woke up to watch sports on TV. Even in his weakened state Yvan roused himself to goad the team he favored. Rechy tells his favorite memory of his brother: "He has returned from the army, World War II, the front line. He smokes constantly; he's still very young. My father is shouting vile insults at me; I'm 13. My brother intercedes. 'Call him another name, and I'll shut your mouth!' he menaces my father. I love him for that time."

Rechy has always said that his oldest brother, Robert, was more of a father to him than his real father. In 1998 Robert was in a terrible car accident. He now has a type of brain disorder that keeps his mind tumbling through the past. "I hope he remembers that every Friday, his pay day—I was a kid—he would bring me a box of pastries, and I would hug him in gratitude," John says. "I hope he remembers teaching me, patiently, to drive, remembers buying me my first car—a bullet-like Studebaker. I hope he remembers only happy times." Robert is now in a home, confined to a wheelchair. When John visits him, it breaks his heart to see his handsome, proud brother in such a state. Once, John tried to remind him of something he invented, a "garnucho," where Robert would curl his thumb and index finger to snap them lightly on John's head in a gentle, loving mischief. While Robert sat in his wheelchair, John said, "Remember, Robert, the garnuchos?"

A smile appeared on Robert's lips, and he raised his hand, curling his thumb and index finger as he had decades ago.

"Only my sister Blanche—alone now, a proud, beautiful, elegant old lady—and I are alive from among our immediate family," Rechy says. "My sharp memory of her endures: She's 18; she's getting married to her handsome husband Gus. Still in her glorious white bride's dress at her reception, she removes her shoes and dances, her black hair courting the light as she swirls."

Although he is in a successful relationship, and his life more settled than ever, Rechy vigilantly maintains his body. He is still adamant that his lithe, hard torso be noticed and admired. "I'm proud of my endurability," he told one of his classes, "and so would you be. Don't turn into messes! And watch it—you're at a crucial age. A few steps into messdom and you're through."

Almost daily, when the weather allows, he goes to Griffith Park to sun himself in a brief bikini, testing himself, proving over and over that his days of being an object of desire are not necessarily behind him. He works out rigorously. "My body is still fabulous, for God's sake," Rechy said as he approached his seventh decade. "It's better than anyone else's in the park. Just a week ago a car drove by with these young Hispanic girls, screaming and pointing and whistling. They stopped the car and sent their little brother to take a photograph of me while I was lying there in my trunks."

Today Rechy is on the Internet at a site created as a tribute by one of his students. He has finished his 13th novel, titled *The Life and Adventures of Lyle Clemens*. Though not primarily about gay subjects, the novel features a prominent gay character as well as several minor ones. In this book Rechy extends his exploration of literary forms. "It's a modern novel set in Texas, Los Angeles, and Las Vegas," Rechy says, "and it is modeled after Fielding's 18th century novel *Tom Jones*. I hope it will help me to shed the appellation of 'gay writer,' which I resent. I am gay, and I am a writer. I want my work to be evaluated on the range of the best literature, where it belongs, uncategorized, unghettoized."

In 2002, Rechy continued a project he has been contemplating and working on for several decades. It is titled *Autobiography: A Novel*.

Though no longer single, Rechy still enjoys being in an overtly sexual environment. But sex with anonymous strangers is no longer necessary. Throughout his 60s, when he flung himself in the sexual arena, the only important thing to him was being admired. "I don't have any sexual contact in that park anymore," he says. "There are some cruisers there who resent it, and I can understand that. Because why put yourself in the atmosphere and then not participate? On the other hand, I'm not harming anyone. And this is something I get enjoyment from, and there's nothing secret about it."

With Michael, Rechy has developed new interests. Beyond hustling and cruising there are new worlds to discover and he is eager to explore them with his partner. His relationship with Michael has become the key component in his life. In 2001, when editors asked Rechy to contribute an autobiographical note to the writers' anthology *Contemporary Authors*, Rechy wrote about the relationship with the same passion he devoted to his art, giving both equal space in the piece.

In April 1999 the couple traveled to London. Rechy wrote about visiting the palaces and cathedrals with his partner, how together they marveled at the mysteries of Stonehenge. One highlight of the trip was an excursion to the moors where Emily Brontë once lived and wrote. There Rechy explored the terrain of another writer, the environment that had acted as Brontë's muse and had inspired the brooding intensity of her great work *Wuthering Heights*. Later, with Michael at his side, Rechy placed a bouquet of heather on Brontë's grave in the ancient church where her body rests.

In 2001 John and Michael traveled to Italy, where they stayed in five-star hotels, including one in Venice facing the Grand Canal. "First class all the way is the only way to travel through Europe," he told friends. Rechy was able to make use of the sights he encountered there in a personal essay:

> Venice. A room that faces the Grand Canal and a glistening Cathedral. Rome—Nero's palace buried in darkness, under the earth. The Coliseum (where, our private guide, Flamieta, tells us, Christians were not fed to the lions— that occurred only in Cecil B. DeMille's movies). The constant miracle of the Sistine paintings. The awesome splendor of that city spills before us as we stand looking down from the top of a hill on a vista of ruins that have achieved their own beautiful form, a vista carved out by history, a vista within which art seems grandly, recklessly squandered—so ubiquitous is it. Florence. We stare at Michelangelo's "unfinished blocks" of statuary. The figures are struggling to come out. He left them like that, to create that impression—and it does, extending to all art that struggles out of a metaphoric stone...
>
> A Mass at Maria Maggiore chapel in Rome. Michael is not a Catholic; I lapse every day. He suggests we take communion. We march up to the railing, and we take the host together.

Michael and John frequently spend "brief, beautiful vacations" at one of several luxurious hotels along the coast of California, where Rechy is fond of facing the ocean as he rereads Proust's *Remembrance of Things Past*.

Today Rechy is often referred to as an "outlaw," a label he does not shy from. But the characterization should be taken in context. Rechy's sixth book was, of course, titled *The Sexual Outlaw*, and in his sex life as a hustler and cruiser he has often transgressed outside the law. But Rechy has been an outsider ever since his childhood. It was then that he learned to use his individuality—falling outside of the norm—to his own advantage.

From his first published works Rechy deviated from accepted subject matter and traditional forms. Not only was he one of the first to explore the gay male hustling arena, he was also radical enough to record his vision of the war in heaven from the perspective of a woman claiming to be all the great, fallen, blamed women in history. He's given voice to a Mexican maid, a Bel Air matron, and Marilyn Monroe.

In spite of great success early in his career, he has refused to repeat himself in his art. With each new book he employs different narrative forms, experimenting with voice, structure, and subject matter. In his life beyond the sexual realm he has always made it a point to question conventional thinking.

Rechy has also consistently celebrated and defended other "outlaw" types—so-called stereotypes, including drag queens. In the army, he questioned the military's right to impose such stringent regulations on its soldiers.

When others brand him an outlaw, Rechy accepts the title as representing an attitude that has extended throughout virtually every aspect of his life. In the sexual arena, and in the literary world, John Rechy remains unique: a pioneer, a visionary, a proud outlaw.

At heart, Rechy has always been and always will be a hustler as much as he is a writer. Gavin Lambert remembers having dinner one night in 2001 with John and Michael. There was a wistful, nostalgic feeling about Rechy that evening. After leaving the restaurant, Rechy drove them through the neighborhoods—now radically different—where he once ruled as a hustler.

When asked by a journalist if he could be frozen in time at the age of 30, would he still be hustling, he replied without hesitation, "Yes! Oh, yes!" Even with a wonderful relationship, career recognition, and all the other fulfilling areas of his life, hustling remains a calling. "Look," he says, "I like good food. I like French food, and I like a lot of variations of food...so why limit myself to one kind of cuisine? So when you're talking about my array of experiences— if you take away any judgmental aspect to it, then the area of hustling was, for me, always very exciting. Yes."

"Would I like to be remembered as an object of desire? Sure," he says, "but I know I will be remembered primarily for my work. My body of work and my body."

Many years ago John Rechy, wearing tight jeans, a leather jacket, and no shirt, was thrown out of the Biltmore Hotel when a house detective spotted him stepping out of an elevator on his way to meet a gentleman who wanted to pay for his time. Thirty-five years later, Rechy stood in the same hotel to accept the PEN Lifetime Achievement award for his remarkable contribution to the world of letters. The hoody-looking boy sneaking into the hotel to make a score had finally caught up with the respected man he grew into. After years of searching for each other, the two could at last walk onstage together, shake hands, and take a bow as a single entity.

As a narcissist, as a street hustler, and as a great sex object of his day, Rechy succeeded where many of his contemporaries failed. While others drifted, aged, and became tragic, Rechy's narcissism, combined with his sensitivity and intellect, helped him survive. The writer enabled the character he created—the sexual outlaw—to stop time and achieve immortality. The many selves that make up John Rechy will endure between the pages of his novels, leaning seductively against a jukebox in a noisy bar, reaching tenderly for his mother's hand in a hushed room in El Paso.

But the John Rechy who will continue to fascinate is the man forever 30: the handsome sexual phantom, cruising parks and movie theaters, doing his numbers scene, muscles glistening in the sticky sunshine or catching moonlight in dark alleyways. He struts down the street, his sexuality trailing him like cologne, forever pumped, forever desirable, following and being followed—to nowhere and everywhere.

THE WORKS OF JOHN RECHY

City of Night (New York: Grove Press, 1963)

Numbers (New York: Grove Press, 1967)

This Day's Death (New York: Grove Press, 1969)

The Vampires (New York: Grove Press, 1971)

The Fourth Angel (New York: Viking Press, 1973)

The Sexual Outlaw (New York: Grove Press, 1977)

Rushes (New York: Grove Press, 1979)

Bodies and Souls (New York: Carroll & Graf, 1983)

Marilyn's Daughter (New York: Carroll & Graf, 1988)

The Miraculous Day of Amalia Gomez
(New York: Arcade Publishing, 1991)

Our Lady of Babylon (New York: Arcade Publishing, 1996)

The Coming of the Night (New York: Grove Press, 1999)

The Life and Adventures of Lyle Clemens
(New York: Grove Press, 2003)

Index of Names and Titles

In the following index, characters in Rechy's novels are indexed only when the actual person on whom he based those characters is discussed and such person's real name is unknown. Those entries are identified in this index with the notation "fictive name." In other instances, pseudonyms have been used for actual persons, and those entries are indicated with the notation "pseudonym." In some instances, only the first name of an actual person is known, and so it is listed under that name only. All other persons in this index are listed by their actual names.

ABOUT THE AUTHOR

Charles Casillo is the author of the novel *The Marilyn Diaries*. His articles, essays, and stories have appeared in a number of publications, including *The New York Times* and the *Los Angeles Times*. Casillo divides his time between Los Angeles and New York City and has seen the dark and shadowy terrain of John Rechy's books.